Taste *of* Home®
Boards,
Platters & More

TASTE OF HOME BOOKS • RDA ENTHUSIAST BRANDS, LLC • MILWAUKEE, WI

Visit us at **tasteofhome.com** for other *Taste of Home* books and products.

International Standard Book Number: 978-1-62145-830-2

Executive Editor: Mark Hagen
Senior Art Director: Raeann Thompson
Art Director: Courtney Lovetere
Designer: Carrie Peterson
Deputy Editor, Copy Desk: Dulcie Shoener
Copy Editor: Elizabeth Pollock Bruch

Cover Photography:
Photographer: Mark Derse
Set Stylist: Stacey Genaw
Food Stylist: Shannon Norris

Pictured on front cover:
Ultimate Charcuterie Board, p. 78

Pictured on back cover:
Pancake Board, p. 116; Halloween Treat Board, p. 178; S'mores Board, p. 106;
Taco Tuesday Platter, p. 146; Easter Candy Board, p. 166; Movie-Night Snack Board, p. 36

Printed in China
3 5 7 9 10 8 6 4 2

Glorious Grazing!

Today's parties are all about the board...the charcuterie board, that is! Whether hosting a big bash, happy hour, dinner party or holiday celebration, you're bound to impress with the cheese trays, snack platters and dessert plates found here!

Inside, you'll discover 56 easy-to-assemble boards as well as 219 recipes that go with them. From perfect antipasto and build-a-pizza platters to slumber-party sweets and Halloween treats, there's a board here for any occasion, any season of the year.

Best of all, simple step-by-step directions walk you through the basics of putting together every platter. You'll also find hints and tips from the pros at the *Taste of Home* Test Kitchen that will make your boards the talk of the party. In addition, smart suggestions and easy ideas help you customize each presentation to your own tastes and time lines. What could be easier?

It's time to surprise guests with beautiful veggie trays, brunch boards and even a Super Bowl snack stadium you've got to see to believe. Take a look inside the new **Boards, Platters & More,** and see why today's hosts find charcuterie a no-fuss solution to easy entertaining.

Contents

BOARD BASICS

SNACK BOARDS

PARTY BOARDS

MEAL BOARDS

HOLIDAY BOARDS

INDEX

BOARD BASICS:
WHAT IS CHARCUTERIE?

Charcuterie is a French word referring to a type of shop specializing in prepared meats. It also refers to the cured, preserved and dried meats sold in the shop, like salami, prosciutto and pancetta. A classic charcuterie board is a platter tailor-made for snacking, with a selection of cheeses, crackers, condiments and more alongside different meats.

WHAT TO PUT ON A...
CHARCUTERIE BOARD

THE BEST CHEESES
Variety in flavor, texture and color is key to a perfect board.

- Herbed Boursin—Soft and spreadable with a garlicky-herb flavor.
- Mimolette—Nutty with a unique crystalline texture.
- Smoked Gouda—Smoky with a slightly chewy exterior.
- Havarti—Creamy and mild.
- Blue Cheese—Crumbly in texture yet sharp and rich.
- Pimiento Cheese Spread—Slightly spicy and perfect for spreading.

THE BEST MEATS
Variety is as important for the meat selection as it is for the cheese.

- Prosciutto—Offers a saltiness that pairs well with most cheeses.
- Soppressata—Served in rounds, similar to salami but heartier.
- Calabrese—Has a bite and should be sliced thinner than soppressata.

- Mortadella—An Italian version of bologna with bits of white pork fat.
- Salami—This charcuterie staple is popular for its flavor and pricing.

THE BEST CRACKERS & CONDIMENTS
Look for specific textures and flavors to complement the cheese.

- Thyme- or Rosemary-Flavored Crackers—Offer an herbaceous base for any cheese.
- Rye Crackers—Along with a deep shade of brown, these crackers have a fantastic crunch.
- Baguette Slices—Chewy and soft, providing contrast to crispy crackers.
- Stone-Ground Mustard—Great to spread on crackers and top with a thin slice of meat.
- Tupelo Honey—Drizzle on salty meats for a sweet twist.

THE BEST FRUITS & VEGETABLES
If you're lacking in color on your board, fruits and vegetables are the answer.

- Sweety Drop Peppers—Miniature, tear shaped, red and sweet, these are a surprising addition to any board.
- Grapes—Red, green and purple grapes deliver three different pops of color.
- Dried Fruits—Pair well with most other items on the board and balance out their textures.

THE BEST NUTS & PICKLES
Nuts, pickles and olives add even more crunch and texture to your board.

- Olives—Set in a bowl for additional shape, texture and flavor.
- Walnuts or Pecans—A simple but flavor-packed upgrade from plain peanuts or cashews.
- Gherkins—Pickles bring some brine to the variety of flavors.
- Marcona Almonds—Slightly oily and salty, these nuts are perfect to pair with cheeses and meats or to enjoy separately.

HOW TO BUILD A...
BASIC CHARCUTERIE BOARD

Follow these steps when putting together a board or platter of your own.

EASY ASSEMBLY

Step 1: Pull the cheeses out of the refrigerator about an hour before assembling your board. Cheese is at its fullest flavor when it's at room temperature.

If you're using several different types of cheese, set the cheese on the board first. Always pre-cut a few slices or crumble a corner of a wedge to let guests know how each cheese is supposed to be consumed. Crumble a corner of blue cheese, for instance, slice a bit of mimolette and add a wheel of Boursin.

Step 2: Add small bowls to the board. (If you're using several bowls on your board, you might want to start with those instead of the cheeses.) Bowls of different sizes and colors will add visual interest.

If you want to use decorative elements to elevate your charcuterie board, place them next so you won't have to tuck them under foods later. For example, you might add a few clusters of food-safe greenery such as lemon leaves, fig leaves or grape leaves.

Step 3: Add the meats. Fold slices of meat in different ways to add visual interest, texture and height. For example, arrange slices of the soppressata in an S shape. Fold the calabrese slices in half and fan them out. Fold prosciutto and mortadella into quarters. Keep meats of similar colors apart from one another on the board.

Step 4: Distribute crackers and condiments around the board, thinking about which items pair best and placing them near each other. This helps your guests enjoy the best flavor combinations.

Pile the thyme-flavored crackers near the prosciutto, keep the honey near the blue cheese and set the mustard near the smoky Gouda.

Step 5: Fill in some of the gaps on the board with grapes and dried fruits.

Step 6: Fill in the very last open spaces of the board with the nuts and pickles.

Step 7: Add mini utensils to the board, including cheese knives and spoons for condiments. Set out extra cheese knives, appetizer plates and napkins.

Next, grab a plate and start noshing! Guests may feel shy about digging into your perfectly arranged charcuterie board. When you start eating, you're letting them know that everything is ready for them to pile on their plates and enjoy the wonderful board.

Do you have to make homemade recipes for a charcuterie board? Absolutely not! That's the beauty of a board! Even though this book includes more than 200 recipes perfect for platters, it also calls for store-bought items such as crackers, veggies, and even popcorn and candy. You'll be amazed at all of the impressive boards you can build with convenience items.

Can you make a charcuterie board ahead of time? Even though it's best to take cheese out of the refrigerator about an hour ahead of time, you should assemble a board as close to the serving time as possible.

How do I store the leftovers on a charcuterie board after the party? You can wrap a board tightly and store it in the fridge for next-day snacking, but it's best to remove groupings of like items, storing each appropriately. (Wrap the cheese and set it in the fridge, put crackers in a resealable bag and store in the pantry, etc.)

What else can you put on a charcuterie board? Variety is key when selecting ingredients for a board, and no food is off limits. Hummus, pretzels, pita wedges, potato chips and even sweets like truffles or chocolate-covered nuts work well on a traditional meat-and-cheese charcuterie board. Jazz things up with sliced donut peaches in late spring, figs in early summer or late fall, and pomegranates in winter.

Snack Boards

Need a few casual munchies? Look no further than these platters of snackable specialties.

THYME–SEA SALT
CRACKERS, 14

MARINATED
OLIVES, 15

ROSEMARY
WALNUTS, 15

Traditional Charcuterie Board

SOUTHERN PIMIENTO
CHEESE SPREAD, 14

HOW TO BUILD A...
TRADITIONAL CHARCUTERIE BOARD

ITEMS TO INCLUDE

- Blue cheese
- Havarti, sliced
- Smoked Gouda, sliced
- Mimolette, sliced
- Herbed Boursin, full round
- Southern Pimiento Cheese Spread
- Red sweety drop peppers
- Marinated Olives
- Prosciutto
- Soppressata
- Mortadella
- Thyme-Sea Salt Crackers
- Assorted crackers and baguette slices
- Stone ground mustard
- Tupelo honey
- Purple, green and red grapes
- Dried apricots
- Rosemary Walnuts
- Gherkin pickles
- Marcona almonds

EASY ASSEMBLY

Step 1: Scatter the cheeses around the board or platter.

Step 2: Fill small bowls with the Southern Pimento Cheese Spread, red peppers and Marinated Olives, and place them throughout the board.

Step 3: Fold the meat slices, fanning them out in groupings on the board.

Step 4: Distribute the crackers, baguette slices, mustard and honey around the board.

Step 5: Fill in some of the gaps on the board with grapes and dried apricots.

Step 6: Fill in remaining gaps with Rosemary Walnuts, pickles and almonds. Add utensils, including spoons and cheese knives.

SOUTHERN PIMIENTO CHEESE SPREAD

Pimiento cheese is the ultimate southern comfort food. We serve it as a dip for crackers, chips and celery or slather it on burgers and hot dogs.
—Eileen Balmer, South Bend, IN

PREP: 10 MIN. + CHILLING
MAKES: 1¼ CUPS

- 1½ cups shredded cheddar cheese
- 1 jar (4 oz.) diced pimientos, drained and finely chopped
- ⅓ cup mayonnaise
  Assorted crackers

Combine cheese, pimientos and mayonnaise. Refrigerate for at least 1 hour. Serve with crackers.
2 Tbsp.: 116 cal., 11g fat (4g sat. fat), 21mg chol., 144mg sod., 1g carb. (0 sugars, 0 fiber), 4g pro.

THYME-SEA SALT CRACKERS

These homemade crackers are decidedly light and crispy. They are irresistible on their own as a snack or pair well with a sharp white cheddar.
—Jessica Wirth, Charlotte, NC

PREP: 25 MIN. • **BAKE:** 10 MIN./BATCH
MAKES: ABOUT 7 DOZEN

- 2½ cups all-purpose flour
- ½ cup white whole wheat flour
- 1 tsp. salt
- ¾ cup water
- ¼ cup plus 1 Tbsp. olive oil, divided
- 1 to 2 Tbsp. minced fresh thyme
- ¾ tsp. sea or kosher salt

1. Preheat oven to 375°. In a large bowl, whisk flours and salt. Gradually add water and ¼ cup oil, tossing with a fork until dough holds together when pressed. Divide dough into 3 portions.
2. On a lightly floured surface, roll out each portion of dough to ⅛-in. thickness. Cut with a floured 1½-in. round cookie cutter. Place 1 in. apart on ungreased baking sheets. Prick each cracker with a fork; brush lightly with remaining oil. Mix thyme and sea salt; sprinkle over crackers.
3. Bake 9-11 minutes or until bottoms are lightly browned.
1 cracker: 23 cal., 1g fat (0 sat. fat), 0 chol., 45mg sod., 3g carb. (0 sugars, 0 fiber), 0 pro.

PLATTER POINTERS
These crackers are dairy-free and vegan-friendly. If any of your guests follow those diets, be sure to point out the snacks when presenting your charcuterie board.

ROSEMARY WALNUTS

My Aunt Mary started making this recipe years ago, and each time we visited her she would have a batch ready for us. The cayenne adds an unexpected zing to the savory combo of rosemary and walnuts. When you need a good housewarming or hostess gift, double the batch and save one for yourself.
—Renee D. Ciancio, New Bern, NC

MARINATED OLIVES

These olives are nice to have for get-togethers because they're simple to make and they'll add a little zest to your cheese platter or snack buffet.
—Marguerite Shaeffer, Sewell, NJ

PREP: 10 MIN. + MARINATING
MAKES: 4 CUPS

- 2 cups large pimiento-stuffed olives, drained
- 1 cup pitted kalamata olives, drained
- 1 cup pitted medium ripe olives, drained
- ¼ cup olive oil
- 2 Tbsp. lemon juice
- 1 Tbsp. minced fresh thyme or 1 tsp. dried thyme
- 2 tsp. minced fresh rosemary or ½ tsp. dried rosemary, crushed
- 2 tsp. grated lemon zest
- 4 garlic cloves, slivered
  Pepper to taste

1. Place olives in a bowl. Combine the remaining ingredients; pour over olives and stir. Cover olives and refrigerate for 1-2 days before serving, stirring several times each day.
2. Olives may be refrigerated for up to 2 weeks. Serve with a slotted spoon.
¼ cup: 98 cal., 10g fat (1g sat. fat), 0 chol., 572mg sod., 3g carb. (0 sugars, 0 fiber), 0 pro.

TAKES: 20 MIN. • **MAKES:** 2 CUPS

- 2 cups walnut halves
  Cooking spray
- 2 tsp. dried rosemary, crushed
- ½ tsp. kosher salt
- ¼ to ½ tsp. cayenne pepper

1. Place walnuts in a small bowl. Spritz with cooking spray. Add the seasonings; toss to coat. Place in a single layer on a baking sheet.
2. Bake at 350° for 10 minutes. Serve warm, or cool completely and store in an airtight container.
¼ cup: 166 cal., 17g fat (2g sat. fat), 0 chol., 118mg sod., 4g carb. (1g sugars, 2g fiber), 4g pro. **Diabetic exchanges:** 3 fat.

Cashew Cheese Platter

CASHEW CHEESE

Spread this vegan cheese on crackers or serve it with fresh vegetables.
—*Taste of Home* Test Kitchen

PREP: 1 HOUR + CHILLING
MAKES: ¾ CUP

- 1 **cup raw cashews**
- ⅓ **cup water**
- 2 **Tbsp. nutritional yeast**
- 2 **tsp. lemon juice**
- ½ **tsp. salt**
- ⅛ **tsp. garlic powder**
  Red grapes, cucumber sticks or slices, crackers

Place the cashews in a small bowl. Add enough warm water to cover completely. Soak the cashews for 1-2 hours; drain and discard water. Add soaked cashews, ⅓ cup water, nutritional yeast, lemon juice, salt and garlic powder to food processor. Cover and process until smooth, 1-2 minutes, scraping down sides occasionally. Transfer to serving dish. Cover and refrigerate at least 1 hour before serving. Serve with grapes, cucumbers and crackers.

1 Tbsp.: 56 cal., 4g fat (1g sat. fat), 0 chol., 101mg sod., 3g carb. (1g sugars, 0 fiber), 2g pro. **Diabetic exchanges:** 1 fat.

SWISS CHEESE FONDUE

This rich and fancy fondue is a great appetizer, particularly on chilly nights. Don't be surprised when the pot is scraped clean and the platter is empty!
—*Taste of Home* Test Kitchen

TAKES: 30 MIN. • **MAKES:** ABOUT 4 CUPS

- 1 garlic clove, halved
- 2 cups white wine, chicken broth or unsweetened apple juice, divided
- ¼ tsp. ground nutmeg
- 7 cups shredded Swiss cheese
- 2 Tbsp. cornstarch
  Cubed bread, sliced watermelon radishes, carrots and radishes

1. Rub garlic clove over the bottom and sides of a fondue pot; discard garlic and set fondue pot aside. In a large saucepan over medium-low heat, bring 1¾ cups wine and the nutmeg to a simmer. Gradually add the cheese, stirring well after each addition until the cheese is melted (cheese will separate from wine).

2. Combine cornstarch and remaining wine until smooth; gradually stir into cheese mixture. Cook and stir until thickened and mixture is blended and smooth. Transfer to prepared fondue pot and keep warm. Serve with bread cubes and vegetables.

¼ cup: 214 cal., 15g fat (9g sat. fat), 44mg chol., 90mg sod., 2g carb. (0 sugars, 0 fiber), 13g pro.

Fondue Platter

Tex-Mex Platter

CONTEST-WINNING
GRILLED CORN SALSA, 19

QUICK TACO DIP, 20

GUACAMOLE, 20

HOW TO BUILD A...
TEX-MEX PLATTER

Skip the same old nacho platter and kick things up a level with a colorful assortment of savory southwestern flavors.

ITEMS TO INCLUDE
- Contest-Winning Grilled Corn Salsa
- Quick Taco Dip
- Guacamole
- Assorted tortilla chips
- Assorted mini sweet peppers, halved and seeded

EASY ASSEMBLY
Step 1: Spoon the salsa, taco dip and guacamole into small bowls. Set bowls on the platter.

Step 2: Set groups of tortilla chips on the platter.

Step 3: Fill in gaps with the mini sweet peppers.

Step 4: Add serving spoons to bowls.

CONTEST-WINNING GRILLED CORN SALSA

Nothing beats the flavor of grilled vegetables, and this is a super way to use your garden bounty. I grill the veggies any time I'm grilling something else, then whip up the salsa and put it in the fridge to marinate. It's even better the next day.
—Teri Kman, Laporte, CO

PREP: 30 MIN.
GRILL: 10 MIN. PER BATCH + CHILLING
MAKES: 7½ CUPS

- 8 **medium ears sweet corn, husks removed**
- 2 **small yellow summer squash, cut into ½-in. slices**
- 1 **medium sweet red pepper, cut into 4 wedges**
- 1 **medium red onion, cut into ½-in. rings**
- 1 **medium tomato, seeded and chopped**

BASIL VINAIGRETTE
- ½ **cup olive oil**
- ⅓ **cup white balsamic or cider vinegar**
- 12 **fresh basil leaves, chopped**
- 1 **tsp. salt**
- 1 **tsp. garlic powder**
- 1 **tsp. dried oregano**

1. Fill a Dutch oven two-thirds full with water; bring to a boil. Add corn. Reduce heat; cover and simmer until crisp-tender, about 5 minutes. Remove corn; cool slightly.

2. On a lightly oiled grill rack, grill the corn, summer squash, red pepper and onion, covered, over medium heat until lightly browned, turning occasionally, 8-10 minutes.

3. Cut corn from cobs; cut the squash, red pepper and onion into bite-size pieces. Place grilled vegetables in a large bowl; add tomato.

4. In a small bowl, whisk the vinaigrette ingredients. Pour over vegetables; toss to coat. Cover and refrigerate until chilled. Serve with a slotted spoon.

¼ cup: 60 cal., 4g fat (1g sat. fat), 0 chol., 84mg sod., 6g carb. (2g sugars, 1g fiber), 1g pro. **Diabetic exchanges:** ½ starch, ½ fat.

QUICK TACO DIP

I've made this recipe more times than I can count! The colorful dip always looks very appealing on a party table, and the taste never disappoints.
—Rhonda Biancardi, Blaine, MN

TAKES: 10 MIN. • **MAKES:** 12 SERVINGS

- 1 pkg. (8 oz.) cream cheese, softened
- 1 cup sour cream
- 1 carton (8 oz.) French onion dip
- 1 envelope reduced-sodium taco seasoning
- 4 cups shredded lettuce
- 2 cups shredded cheddar cheese
- 1½ cups chopped tomatoes
  Sliced ripe olives, drained, optional
  Tortilla chips

In a bowl, beat the cream cheese, sour cream, onion dip and taco seasoning until blended. Spread onto a 12-in. round serving platter. Top with lettuce, cheese, tomatoes and, if desired, olives. Serve with tortilla chips.
1 serving: 232 cal., 20g fat (12g sat. fat), 42mg chol., 482mg sod., 6g carb. (4g sugars, 0 fiber), 7g pro.

GUACAMOLE

This is one of our favorite spicy snack food recipes, and it's quick and easy to prepare when friends drop by on short notice. It also makes a great side dish for a complete southwestern-style meal. Mild or sweet peppers can be substituted for the chiles for those who like their guacamole a little less spicy.
—Anne Tipps, Duncanville, TX

TAKES: 10 MIN. • **MAKES:** ABOUT 1½ CUPS

- 1 medium ripe avocado, halved, seeded and peeled
- 4½ tsp. lemon juice
- 1 small tomato, seeded and finely chopped
- ¼ cup finely chopped red onion

- 1 Tbsp. finely chopped green chiles
- 1 garlic clove, minced
- ¼ tsp. salt, optional
  Tortilla chips

In a large bowl, coarsely mash the avocado with the lemon juice. Stir in the tomato, onion, chiles, garlic and salt if desired. Cover; chill. Serve with tortilla chips.
2 Tbsp.: 29 cal., 3g fat (0 sat. fat), 0 chol., 5mg sod., 2g carb. (1g sugars, 1g fiber), 0 pro.

HOW TO KEEP THAT GUACAMOLE GREEN

It's easy to make your guac ahead of time and keep it nice and green. Just use a thin layer of water to banish browning. Here's how:

Step 1: In an airtight container, use a spoon to flatten the surface of the guacamole and remove any air pockets.

Step 2: Slowly pour in about ½ in. water to cover the surface, using the spoon to gently disperse the water.

Step 3: Refrigerate, covered, up to 2 days. To serve, carefully pour off water, stir guacamole and enjoy.

QUICK PICANTE SAUCE

Hot pepper sauce and a jalapeno pepper give this snappy sauce just the right amount of zip. It makes a great dip for tortilla chips or a tangy sauce for tacos and fajitas. This is always a big hit at parties and office gatherings. I even make it for my mother when she needs to take an appetizer to a party.
—Barbara Sellers, Shreveport, LA

TAKES: 5 MIN. • **MAKES:** 5 SERVINGS

- 1   can (14½ oz.) diced tomatoes, drained
- ½   cup coarsely chopped onion
- ½   cup minced fresh cilantro
- 1   jalapeno pepper, seeded and halved
- 3   Tbsp. lime juice
- 1   Tbsp. chili powder
- 1   garlic clove, halved
- ½   tsp. salt
- ¼   tsp. grated lime zest
- 5   drops hot pepper sauce
     Tortilla chips

In a blender, combine the first 10 ingredients; cover and process until smooth. Serve with tortilla chips.
Note: Wear disposable gloves when cutting hot peppers; the oils can burn skin. Avoid touching your face.
¼ cup: 32 cal., 0 fat (0 sat. fat), 0 chol., 415mg sod., 7g carb. (4g sugars, 2g fiber), 1g pro.

CUSTOMIZE YOUR BOARD

GINGERED MANGO SALSA
Zesty cilantro meets cool mint in this change-of-pace salsa. We love it with grilled chicken. You can substitute papaya for the mango, if you'd like.
—Barb Fore, McAllen, TX

PREP: 15 MIN. + STANDING
MAKES: 1¼ CUPS

- 1   cup chopped peeled mango
- ¼   cup chopped red onion
- ¼   cup minced fresh cilantro
- ¼   cup lime juice
- 2   Tbsp. minced fresh mint
- 1   Tbsp. minced fresh gingerroot
- ½   tsp. olive oil
- ¼   tsp. salt

In a bowl, combine all ingredients. Let stand for 30 minutes before serving.
¼ cup: 39 cal., 1g fat (0 sat. fat), 0 chol., 120mg sod., 9g carb. (7g sugars, 1g fiber), 0 pro.
Mango Black Bean Salsa: Omit the mint, gingerroot, olive oil and salt. Add 1 can (15 oz.) black beans (rinsed and drained), 1 can (11 oz.) Mexicorn (drained), 1 tsp. garlic salt and ¼ tsp. ground cumin. Serve as a condiment with meat or as an appetizer with tortilla chips. Yield: 3½ cups.

Game-Night Munchies Board

CRANBERRY CHERRY PUNCH, 24

MINI CORN DOGS, 25

HONEY MUSTARD SAUCE, 25

LAKE CHARLES DIP, 24

HOW TO BUILD A...
GAME-NIGHT MUNCHIES BOARD

Hand-held snacks and game night go hand in hand, so serve up this tasty assortment of bite-sized greats.

ITEMS TO INCLUDE

- Mini Corn Dogs with Honey Mustard Sauce
- Ketchup
- Lake Charles Dip
- Salsa
- Sweet potato waffle fries
- Fresh vegetables, sliced
- Crackers
- Cranberry Cherry Punch

EASY ASSEMBLY

Step 1: Set Mini Corn Dogs on a board or an individual serving platter. Add small bowls of Honey Mustard Sauce and ketchup.

Step 2: Add small serving bowls of Lake Charles Dip and salsa.

Step 3: Prepare waffle fries according to package directions. Set in serving bowl and add to the board or pile the fries directly onto the board.

Step 4: Fill in gaps with the vegetables and crackers.

Step 5: Serve with glasses of Cranberry Cherry Punch.

Platter Pointer: Placing the fries and fresh veggies into individual serving bowls helps keep warm and cold foods separate on the board.

CRANBERRY CHERRY PUNCH

This brightly colored beverage is just wonderful for holidays, and it looks festive in a glass punch bowl.
—Lori Daniels, Beverly, WV

PREP: 15 MIN. + FREEZING • **MAKES:** 3½ QT.

- ⅓ cup fresh or frozen cranberries
- 2 lemon slices, cut into 6 pieces
- 1 pkg. (3 oz.) cherry gelatin
- 1 cup boiling water
- 3 cups cold water
- 6 cups cranberry juice, chilled
- ¾ cup thawed lemonade concentrate
- 1 liter ginger ale, chilled

1. Place several cranberries and a piece of lemon in each compartment of an ice cube tray; fill with water and freeze.
2. In a punch bowl or large container, dissolve gelatin in boiling water. Stir in the cold water, cranberry juice and lemonade concentrate. Just before serving, stir in ginger ale. Serve over cranberry-lemon ice cubes.

¾ cup: 99 cal., 0 fat (0 sat. fat), 0 chol., 17mg sod., 25g carb. (24g sugars, 0 fiber), 1g pro. **Diabetic exchanges:** 1 starch, ½ fruit.

LAKE CHARLES DIP

Italian salad dressing mix gives this simply delicious dip its wonderful flavor. Serve it with fresh veggies or crackers for a fast and easy appetizer.
—Shannon Copley, Upper Arlington, OH

PREP: 15 MIN. + CHILLING
MAKES: 1½ CUPS

- 1 cup sour cream
- 2 Tbsp. reduced-fat mayonnaise
- 1 Tbsp. Italian salad dressing mix
- ⅓ cup finely chopped avocado
- 1 tsp. lemon juice
- ½ cup finely chopped seeded tomato
  Optional: Assorted crackers, cucumber slices, julienned sweet red pepper and carrot sticks

In a small bowl, combine sour cream, mayonnaise and dressing mix. Toss avocado with lemon juice; stir into the sour cream mixture. Stir in tomato. Cover and refrigerate at least 1 hour. Serve with crackers and assorted vegetables as desired.

¼ cup: 111 cal., 9g fat (5g sat. fat), 27mg chol., 216mg sod., 3g carb. (2g sugars, 1g fiber), 2g pro.

FRESH FINGERS

Place lemon wedges and a shallow dish of warm water at each place setting. When fingers get greasy or sticky from snacking, simply splash them in the water and rub with the lemon to freshen up quickly and keep game pieces clean. That's truly a win-win.

MINI CORN DOGS WITH HONEY MUSTARD SAUCE

Bring a county fair favorite into your home with these bite-sized corn dogs! Kids and the young at heart love them.
—Geralyn Harrington, Floral Park, NY

TAKES: 30 MIN. • **MAKES:** 2 DOZEN

1⅔ cups all-purpose flour
⅓ cup cornmeal
3 tsp. baking powder
1 tsp. salt
3 Tbsp. cold butter
1 Tbsp. shortening
1 large egg, room temperature
¾ cup 2% milk
24 miniature hot dogs
HONEY MUSTARD SAUCE
⅓ cup honey
⅓ cup prepared mustard
1 Tbsp. molasses

1. In a large bowl, combine the first 4 ingredients. Cut in the butter and shortening until mixture resembles coarse crumbs. Beat together egg and milk; stir into dry ingredients until a soft dough forms. Dough will be sticky.
2. Turn onto a generously floured surface; knead 6-8 times or until smooth, adding additional flour as needed. Roll out to ¼-in. thickness. Cut with a 2¼-in. biscuit cutter. Fold each dough circle over a miniature hot dog and press edges to seal. Place on greased baking sheets.
3. Bake at 450° until golden brown, 10-12 minutes. In a small bowl, combine sauce ingredients. Serve with corn dogs.
1 corn dog: 109 cal., 5g fat (2g sat. fat), 18mg chol., 306mg sod.,14g carb. (5g sugars, 0 fiber), 3g pro.

HOW TO HOST A GAME NIGHT

With these ideas, your next game night will be filled with fun and food—plus just a little friendly competition, of course.

PICK WHAT TO PLAY
After you and your crew decide on a night that works for everyone, here comes the hard part: agreeing on a game. Be sure to gear your selection toward your group. If you have little ones, opt for a classic like Candy Land. School-age kids love Sequence. And teens and adults can't seem to get enough of Catan.

SELECT YOUR SNACKS
You'll want your menu full of small, mess-free munchies that can be grabbed, dunked and devoured in between rounds.

SET THE TABLE
First, place the game and its pieces on the table to ensure there's enough space. You can even divvy up the tokens, deal the cards and set up the scorecards in advance. Next, set out your board and snacks.

PLAY CLEAN
And no, we don't mean playing by the rules! That's important, too, but so is keeping the table and game pieces tidy. Make some napkins and hand sanitizer readily available. (See the idea for fresh fingers on the opposite page.)

GAME ON
For optimal family bonding, make game night a tech-free zone. Place phones in a separate room and turn off the TV. Now it's time to snack—then attack!

Beet & Veggie Platter

ROASTED BEETROOT & GARLIC HUMMUS

This hummus is so tasty and healthy, and it's the prettiest pink snack I've ever seen. This is a great recipe to prepare in large batches and keep in the fridge for lunches and snacks throughout the week.
—Elizabeth Worndl, Toronto, ON

PREP: 25 MIN. • **BAKE:** 45 MIN.
MAKES: 4 CUPS

- 3 fresh medium beets (about 1 lb.)
- 1 whole garlic bulb
- ½ tsp. salt, divided
- ½ tsp. coarsely ground pepper, divided
- 1 tsp. plus ¼ cup olive oil, divided
- 1 can (15 oz.) garbanzo beans or chickpeas, rinsed and drained
- 3 to 4 Tbsp. lemon juice
- 2 Tbsp. tahini
- ½ tsp. ground cumin
- ½ tsp. cayenne pepper
- ¼ cup plain Greek yogurt, optional
  Minced fresh dill weed or parsley
  Asparagus, peppers, cherry tomatoes, carrots, cucumbers, and root vegetable chips

1. Preheat oven to 375°. Pierce beets with a fork; place in a microwave-safe bowl and cover loosely. Microwave beets on high for 4 minutes, stirring halfway through. Cool slightly. Wrap beets in individual foil packets.
2. Remove the papery outer skin from garlic bulb, but do not peel or separate the cloves. Cut bulb in half crosswise. Sprinkle halves with ¼ tsp. salt and ¼ tsp. pepper; drizzle with 1 tsp. oil. Wrap halves in individual foil packets. Roast beets and garlic until cloves are soft, about 45 minutes.
3. Remove from oven; unwrap. Rinse beets with cold water; peel when cool enough to handle. Squeeze garlic from skins. Place beets and garlic in a food processor. Add the garbanzo beans, lemon juice, tahini, cumin, cayenne pepper and remaining olive oil, salt and pepper. Process until smooth. If desired, pulse 2 Tbsp. Greek yogurt with beet mixture, dolloping remaining yogurt over finished hummus. Sprinkle with dill or parsley. Serve in a small bowl on a platter with assorted fresh vegetables and chips.

¼ cup: 87 cal., 5g fat (1g sat. fat), 0 chol., 131mg sod., 8g carb. (3g sugars, 2g fiber), 2g pro.

HOW TO PEEL BEETS

After preparing, baking and cooling the beets, peel off what's left of the stems. Then grab two clean paper towels and hold one in each hand. Pick up a beet with both hands. Hold the beet firmly and twist your hands in opposite directions. The skin should slide right off, and your hands will stay clean.

A Board for Every Taste

GARLIC BLUE
CHEESE DIP, 29

SMOKED
SALMON DIP, 31

MUSTARD
DIP, 29

BACON CHEDDAR
DIP, 31

YUMMY
CHOCOLATE DIP, 30

HOW TO BUILD...
A BOARD FOR EVERY TASTE

From savory to sweet, there's a taste sensation for everyone on this versatile board. Perfect for any occasion, it's a great way to use up your farmer's-market bounty. Assemble the board as noted below or add your own dippers.

ITEMS TO INCLUDE
- Garlic Blue Cheese Dip
- Smoked Salmon Dip
- Mustard Dip
- Bacon Cheddar Dip
- Yummy Chocolate Dip
- Crackers
- Radishes, halved
- Carrots, sliced
- Mini cucumbers, sliced
- Pretzel Crisps®
- Granny Smith apple, sliced
- Red Delicious apple, sliced

EASY ASSEMBLY
Step 1: Spoon each of the 5 dips into small serving bowls. Space the bowls evenly on a board or serving platter.

Step 2: Fill in gaps on the board with groupings of the crackers, radishes, carrots, cucumbers, pretzels and red and green apples.

Step 3: Add serving utensils to dips before serving.

GARLIC BLUE CHEESE DIP
This thick, creamy dip is my mom's recipe and an all-time family favorite. It also makes a tasty substitute for mayonnaise on chicken and turkey sandwiches.
—Lillian Nardi, Richmond, CA

TAKES: 10 MIN. • **MAKES:** ABOUT 1½ CUPS

- ½ cup milk
- 1 pkg. (8 oz.) cream cheese, cubed
- 1 cup (4 oz.) crumbled blue cheese
- 2 garlic cloves, peeled
  Assorted vegetables or crackers

In a blender, combine the milk, cream cheese, blue cheese and garlic; cover and process until blended. If desired, top with additional crumbled blue cheese just before serving. Serve with vegetables or crackers.
2 Tbsp.: 113 cal., 10g fat (6g sat. fat), 31mg chol., 218mg sod., 1g carb. (1g sugars, 0 fiber), 4g pro.

MUSTARD DIP
You can't go wrong with a fast-to-fix appetizer like this! It's wonderful with pretzels, but try it with fresh veggies and pita wedges, too.
—Elsie Hyer, Souderton, PA

PREP: 5 MIN. • **MAKES:** 1½ CUPS

- 1 can (14 oz.) sweetened condensed milk
- ¼ cup ground or prepared mustard
- 3 Tbsp. prepared horseradish
- 1 Tbsp. Worcestershire sauce
  Assorted pretzels

In a bowl, combine all ingredients until smooth (mustard will thicken as it stands). Serve with pretzels. Store in the refrigerator.
2 Tbsp.: 124 cal., 4g fat (2g sat. fat), 11mg chol., 68mg sod., 19g carb. (18g sugars, 1g fiber), 3g pro.

CUSTOMIZE YOUR BOARD

Consider working in one of these no-fuss dips.

Cucumber Onion Dip

In a small bowl, beat one 8-oz. pkg. softened cream cheese, ½ cup finely chopped seeded peeled cucumber, ¼ cup finely chopped onion, 2 Tbsp. mayonnaise, ⅛ tsp. salt and ⅛ tsp. pepper until blended. Refrigerate until serving.

Honey Peanut Apple Dip

In a large bowl, beat one 8-oz. pkg. cream cheese until smooth. Beat in 1 cup finely chopped peanuts, ⅔ cup honey and 1 tsp. vanilla extract until combined. Refrigerate leftovers.

Horseradish Crab Dip

In a large bowl, beat one 8-oz. pkg. cream cheese, 2-3 Tbsp. picante sauce and 1-2 Tbsp. prepared horseradish until blended. Stir in one 6-oz. can crabmeat, drained.

Peanut Butter Fruit Dip

In a bowl, combine 1 cup vanilla yogurt, ½ cup peanut butter and ⅛ tsp. ground cinnamon; mix well. Fold in ½ cup whipped topping. Refrigerate the dip until serving.

Ranch Jalapeno Dip

In a blender or food processor, prepare 1 envelope ranch salad dressing mix according to package directions. Add 2 pickled seeded jalapeno peppers, 1 seeded jalapeno pepper and 2 Tbsp. minced fresh cilantro; cover and process 2-3 minutes or until combined. Cover and refrigerate at least 1 hour.

YUMMY CHOCOLATE DIP

Turn fresh fruit into an irresistible and tantalizing snack or dessert with this dreamy, creamy chocolate dip. Four ingredients and 10 minutes are all it takes! You could also serve with graham cracker sticks for an easy after-school snack.
—Stacey Shew, Cologne, MN

TAKES: 10 MIN. • **MAKES:** 2 CUPS

- ¾ cup semisweet chocolate chips
- 1 carton (8 oz.) whipped topping, divided
- ½ tsp. ground cinnamon
- ½ tsp. rum extract or vanilla extract
  Assorted fresh fruit and shortbread cookies

1. In a microwave, melt chocolate chips; stir until smooth. Stir in ½ cup whipped topping, cinnamon and extract; cool for 5 minutes.

2. Fold in remaining whipped topping. Serve with fruit and cookies. Refrigerate leftovers.
Note: This recipe was tested in a 1,100-watt microwave.
¼ cup: 155 cal., 9g fat (8g sat. fat), 0 chol., 2mg sod., 16g carb. (12g sugars, 1g fiber), 1g pro.

Chocolate Caramel Dip: Beat 8 oz. softened cream cheese with 1 cup each caramel and chocolate ice cream topping. Fold in the whipped topping. Serve with fruit and cookies.

Spiced Fruit Dip: Beat 8 oz. softened cream cheese with 1 cup confectioners' sugar and 2 tsp. pumpkin pie spice. Fold in the whipped topping. Serve with fruit and cookies.

BACON CHEDDAR DIP

Give this recipe a try if you're looking for a deliciously different dip to serve with crackers, potato chips or vegetables. Ranch salad dressing adds a little zest.
—Kathy Westendorf, Westgate, IA

PREP: 5 MIN. + CHILLING
MAKES: 2½ CUPS

- 2 cups sour cream
- 1 cup finely shredded cheddar cheese
- 1 envelope ranch salad dressing mix
- 4 bacon strips, cooked and crumbled
  Minced chives, optional
  Crackers and/or assorted fresh vegetables

In a large bowl, combine the sour cream, cheddar cheese, salad dressing mix and bacon. Cover and refrigerate for at least 1 hour. If desired, top with minced chives and additional crumbled bacon just before serving. Serve with crackers and/or vegetables.
¼ cup: 156 cal., 14g fat (8g sat. fat), 24mg chol., 345mg sod., 4g carb. (2g sugars, 0 fiber), 5g pro.

SMOKED SALMON DIP

Salmon is practically a way of life here in the Pacific Northwest. My husband can make a meal of this dip. It's great for snack time and holidays parties alike.
—Doreen McDaniels, Seattle, WA

TAKES: 30 MIN. • **MAKES:** ABOUT 3 CUPS

- 1 can (6 oz.) pitted ripe olives, drained
- 8 green onions, cut into 2-in. pieces
- 1 can (14¾ oz.) pink salmon, drained, flaked and bones removed
- ⅔ cup mayonnaise
- 8 drops liquid smoke, optional
  Assorted crackers and vegetables

Place olives and onions in a blender or food processor; cover and process for about 15 seconds. Add salmon, mayonnaise and liquid smoke if desired; process until dip reaches desired consistency. Chill. If desired, top with additional chopped green onions just before serving. Serve with crackers and vegetables.
2 Tbsp.: 86 cal., 8g fat (1g sat. fat), 8mg chol., 285mg sod., 2g carb. (0 sugars, 1g fiber), 3g pro.

ADD YOU OWN DIPPERS
Consider adding the following when assembling this board.

- Pineapple slices
- Sweet red pepper
- Asparagus
- Strawberries
- Sliced kiwi
- Celery sticks
- Broccoli florets
- Slices of pound cake
- Cubes of angel food cake

- Cookies
- Baguette slices
- Mini bagels
- Pita wedges
- Slices of cocktail rye
- Cooked shrimp
- Tortilla chips
- Banana chips
- Dried apricots

Build Your Own
Bruschetta Board

MAMMA'S
CAPONATA, 33

MAMMA'S CAPONATA

This is fabulous as an appetizer, but you can easily turn it into a meal. Instead of having it on bread, serve it over bowls of warm pasta.
—Georgette Stubin, Canton, MI

PREP: 30 MIN. • **COOK:** 40 MIN.
MAKES: 6 CUPS

- 1 **large eggplant, peeled and chopped**
- ¼ **cup plus 2 Tbsp. olive oil, divided**
- 2 **medium onions, chopped**
- 2 **celery ribs, chopped**
- 2 **cans (14½ oz. each) diced tomatoes, undrained**
- ⅓ **cup chopped ripe olives**
- ¼ **cup red wine vinegar**
- 2 **Tbsp. sugar**
- 2 **Tbsp. capers, drained**
- ½ **tsp. salt**
- ½ **tsp. pepper**
  French bread baguettes, sliced and toasted

1. In a Dutch oven, saute eggplant in ¼ cup oil until tender. Remove from pan and set aside. In the same pan, saute onions and celery in remaining 2 Tbsp. oil until tender. Stir in tomatoes and eggplant. Bring to a boil. Reduce the heat; simmer, uncovered, for 15 minutes.
2. Add the olives, vinegar, sugar, capers, salt and pepper. Return to a boil. Reduce heat; simmer, uncovered, for 20 minutes or until thickened. Serve warm or at room temperature with baguettes.
¼ cup: 57 cal., 4g fat (1g sat. fat), 0 chol., 134mg sod., 6g carb. (4g sugars, 2g fiber), 1g pro. **Diabetic exchanges:** 1 vegetable, ½ fat.

CUSTOMIZE YOUR BOARD

CHEESY BRUSCHETTA SPREAD

Every bite of this cheesy dip delivers tons of flavor. I have been asked over and over again for the recipe. It's so easy to make and a great appetizer for any time of year.
—Maggie McDermott, Central Square, NY

PREP: 15 MIN. • **COOK:** 1½ HOURS
MAKES: ABOUT 4 CUPS

- 1 **pkg. (8 oz.) cream cheese, softened**
- ½ **cup prepared pesto**
- ¼ **tsp. salt**
- ⅛ **tsp. pepper**
- 2 **cups grape tomatoes**
- 1 **carton (8 oz.) fresh mozzarella cheese pearls, drained**

  Minced fresh basil, optional
  French bread slices (½ in. thick), toasted

In a small bowl, mix cream cheese, pesto, salt and pepper until combined. Transfer to a greased 3-qt. slow cooker. Top with tomatoes and mozzarella cheese. Cook, covered, on low until heated though and cheese begins to melt, 1½-2 hours. If desired, sprinkle with the basil. Serve with toasted bread.
2 Tbsp.: 61 cal., 5g fat (3g sat. fat), 13mg chol., 96mg sod., 1g carb. (1g sugars, 0 fiber), 2g pro.

MUSHROOM OLIVE BRUSCHETTA

After experimenting with different ingredients and flavor combinations, I came up with this variation on traditional tomato-based bruschetta. I've also used this recipe as a stuffing for chicken breast, and sometimes will add a little feta cheese. You can make it ahead of time and keep it in the refrigerator, but be sure to bring it to room temperature before serving—that makes it taste best!
—Colleen Blasetti, Palm Coast, FL

PREP: 40 MIN. • **BAKE:** 10 MIN.
MAKES: 2 DOZEN

- 1¾ cups sliced baby portobello mushrooms
- ¼ cup chopped onion
- 1 anchovy fillet
- 1 Tbsp. olive oil
- ½ tsp. minced garlic
- ½ cup finely chopped tomatoes
- ¼ cup chopped pitted green olives
- ¼ cup chopped ripe olives
- 1 Tbsp. capers, drained
- ¼ tsp. dried thyme
- ¼ tsp. dried basil
- ¼ tsp. dried oregano
- ⅛ tsp. pepper
- 24 slices French bread baguette (½ in. thick)
- 2 Tbsp. butter, melted
- ¼ cup grated Parmesan cheese

1. In a large skillet, saute mushrooms, onion and anchovy in oil until the vegetables are tender. Add the garlic; cook 1 minute longer. Remove from heat. Stir in tomatoes, olives, capers, thyme, basil, oregano and pepper.
2. Place bread slices on an ungreased baking sheet. Brush with butter; sprinkle with the Parmesan cheese. Bake at 375° until lightly browned, 8-9 minutes. With a slotted spoon, top each slice with 1 Tbsp. of the mushroom mixture.

1 appetizer: 44 cal., 2g fat (1g sat. fat), 3mg chol., 127mg sod., 5g carb. (0 sugars, 0 fiber), 2g pro.

RUSTIC TUSCAN PEPPER BRUSCHETTA

If you love sweet red, yellow and orange peppers, pair them with fresh mint for a cold kitchen appetizer. Marinate for up to one hour before assembling.
—Noelle Myers, Grand Forks, ND

TAKES: 30 MIN. • **MAKES:** 10 SERVINGS

- 2 Tbsp. olive oil
- 2 Tbsp. balsamic vinegar
- 1 Tbsp. honey
- 1 Tbsp. minced fresh mint
- 1 each medium sweet yellow, orange and red pepper, cut into thin 1-in. strips
- 6 oz. fresh goat cheese
- ⅔ cup whipped cream cheese
- 48 assorted crackers

1. In a large bowl, whisk oil, vinegar, honey and mint. Add peppers; toss to coat. Let stand 15 minutes.
2. Meanwhile, in a small bowl, beat goat cheese and cream cheese. Spread 1 rounded tsp. on each cracker. Drain peppers well. Arrange peppers on cheese-topped crackers.

1 appetizer: 34 cal., 2g fat (1g sat. fat), 5mg chol., 60mg sod., 3g carb. (1g sugars, 0 fiber), 1g pro.

PLATTER POINTER
Bruschetta can be messy, so be sure to offer napkins alongside your bruschetta board.

CRUSTY FRENCH BREAD

I love to treat guests to these crusty loaves. Don't hesitate to try this recipe even if you are not an accomplished bread baker. It's so easy because there's no kneading.
—Christy Freeman, Central Point, OR

PREP: 30 MIN. + RISING
BAKE: 20 MIN. + COOLING
MAKES: 2 LOAVES (10 PIECES EACH)

   1   pkg. (¼ oz.) active dry yeast
1½   cups warm water (110° to 115°), divided
   1   Tbsp. sugar
   2   tsp. salt
   1   Tbsp. shortening, melted
   4   to 5 cups all-purpose flour
       Cornmeal

1. In a large bowl, dissolve yeast in ½ cup water. Add the sugar, salt, shortening, remaining 1 cup water and 3½ cups flour. Beat until smooth. Stir in enough remaining flour to form a soft dough. Do not knead. Cover and let rise in a warm place until doubled, about 1 hour.
2. Turn onto a floured surface. Divide in half; let rest for 10 minutes. Roll each half into a 10x8-in. rectangle. Roll up from a long side; pinch to seal. Place seam side down on 2 greased baking sheets that have been sprinkled with cornmeal. Sprinkle the tops with cornmeal. Cover and let rise until doubled, about 45 minutes.
3. With a sharp knife, make 5 diagonal cuts across the top of each loaf. Bake loaves at 400° until lightly browned, 20-30 minutes. Remove from pans to wire rack to cool.
1 piece: 100 cal., 1g fat (0 sat. fat), 0 chol., 237mg sod., 20g carb. (1g sugars, 1g fiber), 3g pro.

STRAWBERRY RICOTTA BRUSCHETTA

Here's a sweet spin on bruschetta. A creamy ricotta cheese spread is the ideal complement to the sweet, minty strawberry topping.
—Laura Stricklin, Jackson, MS

TAKES: 25 MIN. • **MAKES:** 2 DOZEN

24   slices French bread baguette (½ in. thick)
   3   Tbsp. butter, melted
   3   cups fresh strawberries, chopped
   3   Tbsp. minced fresh mint
   3   Tbsp. honey
½   cup ricotta cheese
   2   Tbsp. seedless strawberry jam
1½   tsp. grated lemon zest

1. Brush the bread slices with butter; place on an ungreased baking sheet. Bake at 375° until lightly browned, 8-10 minutes.
2. Meanwhile, in a small bowl, mix the strawberries, mint and honey. In another bowl, combine the ricotta, jam and lemon zest. Spread ricotta mixture over toast; top with the strawberry mixture.
1 piece: 89 cal., 3g fat (1g sat. fat), 6mg chol., 88mg sod., 14g carb. (4g sugars, 1g fiber), 2g pro. **Diabetic exchanges:** 1 starch, ½ fat.

PARMESAN RANCH
POPCORN, 37

Movie-Night
Snack Board

HOW TO BUILD A...
MOVIE-NIGHT SNACK BOARD

Dim the lights, grab a blanket and settle in with family, friends and your favorite flick. Top off your cozy night with this assortment of concession-stand favorites.

ITEMS TO INCLUDE

- Parmesan Ranch Popcorn
- Good & Plenty
- M&Ms
- Milk Duds
- Cheddar popcorn
- Snow Caps
- Raisinets
- Caramel popcorn
- Red Vines
- Peanut butter cups
- Gummy bears
- Sour Patch Kids
- Kit Kats
- Mini pretzels
- Skittles

EASY ASSEMBLY

Step 1: Set the Parmesan Ranch Popcorn in the center of a rimmed tray or platter.

Step 2: Fill small bowls with Good & Plenty, M&Ms, Milk Duds, cheddar popcorn, Snow Caps or whatever snacks you feel work best served in bowls. Scatter bowls on and around tray.

Step 3: Fill in any gaps with the remaining items.

Platter Pointer: Try unwrapping distinctly shaped candies and setting them on the tray. Smaller items that might get lost, such as the Raisinets, are best kept in their small movie-theater-like boxes or served in bowls.

PARMESAN RANCH POPCORN

Make ho-hum popcorn worthy of a carnival with a savory seasoning blend.
—*Taste of Home* Test Kitchen

PREP: 10 MIN. • **MAKES:** 3½ QT.

- ¼ cup grated Parmesan cheese
- 2 Tbsp. ranch salad dressing mix
- 1 tsp. dried parsley flakes
- ¼ tsp. onion powder
- ⅓ cup butter, melted
- 3½ qt. popped popcorn

Mix first 4 ingredients. Drizzle butter over popcorn; toss with cheese mixture. Store in airtight containers.
1 cup: 112 cal., 10g fat (4g sat. fat), 13mg chol., 243mg sod., 6g carb. (0 sugars, 1g fiber), 1g pro.

CUSTOMIZE YOUR BOARD

Use these recipes to create your own Movie-Night Snack Board.

MOVIE-NIGHT MUNCHIE MIX

Why not enjoy concession-style snacks at home? I took some of my favorites and combined them to make a sweet and savory mix.
—Dawn Moore, Warren, PA

PREP: 15 MIN. + COOLING • **MAKES:** 4½ QT.

- 3 cups Corn Chex
- 3 cups Rice Chex
- 5 Tbsp. butter, cubed
- 3 Tbsp. white cheddar popcorn seasoning
- 1 pkg. (3.3 oz.) butter-flavored microwave popcorn, popped
- 2 cups caramel-filled chocolate candies
- 1 cup red licorice bites

1. In a large microwave-safe bowl, combine Corn Chex and Rice Chex. Place butter in a small microwave-safe bowl. Microwave on high until just melted, 20-25 seconds. Whisk in the popcorn seasoning until smooth. Pour over cereal; toss to coat.
2. Microwave, uncovered, on high for 2-3 minutes, stirring after each minute. Immediately spread onto waxed paper; cool completely. Stir in popcorn and candies. Store in an airtight container.
1 cup: 192 cal., 8g fat (5g sat. fat), 10mg chol., 336mg sod., 27g carb. (15g sugars, 1g fiber), 2g pro.

PEANUT CARAMEL CORN

A sweet, crunchy, lighter alternative to traditional caramel corn, this can't-stop-eating-it treat is hard to beat.
—Lois Ward, Puslinch, ON

PREP: 20 MIN. • **BAKE:** 45 MIN.
MAKES: 2 QT.

- 8 cups air-popped popcorn
- ½ cup salted peanuts
- ½ cup packed brown sugar
- 3 Tbsp. light corn syrup
- 4½ tsp. molasses
- 1 Tbsp. butter
- ¼ tsp. salt
- ½ tsp. vanilla extract
- ⅛ tsp. baking soda

1. Place popcorn and peanuts in a large bowl coated with cooking spray; set aside.
2. In a large heavy saucepan, combine brown sugar, corn syrup, molasses, butter and salt. Bring to a boil over medium heat, stirring constantly. Boil for 2-3 minutes without stirring.
3. Remove from the heat; stir in vanilla and baking soda (mixture will foam). Quickly pour over the popcorn and mix well.
4. Transfer to a 15x10x1-in. baking pan coated with cooking spray. Bake at 250° for 45 minutes, stirring every 15 minutes. Remove from pan and place on waxed paper to cool. Store in an airtight container.
1 cup: 181 cal., 6g fat (2g sat. fat), 4mg chol., 155mg sod., 30g carb. (18g sugars, 2g fiber), 3g pro. **Diabetic exchanges:** 2 starch, 1 fat.

MOVIE-THEATER PRETZEL RODS

My kids and all of their friends clamor for these large, chewy pretzel rods. They are fantastic fresh from the oven.
—Lisa Shaw, Burnettsville, IN

PREP: 70 MIN. + RISING • **BAKE:** 10 MIN.
MAKES: 32 PRETZEL RODS

    1   pkg. (¼ oz.) active dry yeast
 1½   cups warm water (110° to 115°)
    2   Tbsp. sugar
    2   Tbsp. butter, melted
 1½   tsp. salt
    4   to 4½ cups all-purpose flour
    8   cups water
   ⅓   cup baking soda
    1   large egg yolk
    1   Tbsp. cold water
        Optional: Coarse salt and warm
        cheese sauce

1. In a large bowl, dissolve yeast in warm water. Add the sugar, butter, salt and 2 cups flour. Beat until smooth. Stir in enough remaining flour to form a soft dough (dough will be sticky).
2. Turn dough onto a floured surface; knead until smooth and elastic, about 6-8 minutes. Place in a greased bowl, turning once to grease top. Cover and let rise in a warm place until doubled, about 1 hour.
3. In a large saucepan, bring 8 cups water and baking soda to a boil. Punch dough down; divide into 32 portions. Roll each into a 5-in. log. Add to boiling water, a few at a time, for 30 seconds. Remove with a slotted spoon; drain on paper towels.
4. Place on greased baking sheets. Lightly beat egg yolk and cold water; brush over pretzels. If desired, sprinkle with coarse salt. Bake at 425° until golden brown, 9-11 minutes. Remove from pans to wire racks. Serve warm with cheese sauce if desired.
1 pretzel: 69 cal., 1g fat (1g sat. fat), 8mg chol., 156mg sod., 13g carb. (1g sugars, 0 fiber), 2g pro.

LICORICE CARAMELS

Fans of black licorice won't be able to stop eating these gooey caramels. I appreciate how easy they are.
—Donna Higbee, Riverton, UT

PREP: 20 MIN. • **COOK:** 20 MIN. + STANDING
MAKES: ABOUT 12 DOZEN

    1   tsp. plus 1 cup butter, divided
    2   cups sugar
 1½   cups light corn syrup
    1   can (14 oz.) sweetened condensed
        milk
   ½   tsp. salt
    2   tsp. anise extract
   ¼   tsp. black food coloring

1. Line an 8-in. square dish with foil; grease foil with 1 tsp. butter.
2. In a large heavy saucepan, combine the sugar, corn syrup, milk, salt and remaining 1 cup butter; cook and stir over medium heat until a candy thermometer reads 244° (firm-ball stage).
3. Remove from the heat; stir in extract and food coloring. Immediately pour into prepared pan (do not scrape saucepan). Let stand until firm.
4. Using foil, lift candy out of pan; remove foil. Using a buttered knife, cut into ¼-in. strips. Cut each strip in half lengthwise; cut crosswise into 3 pieces. Wrap individually in waxed paper; twist ends.
1 piece: 92 cal., 3g fat (2g sat. fat), 10mg chol., 65mg sod., 16g carb., 0 fiber, 1g pro.

PLATTER POINTER
A board with this many treats could get overwhelming, so pick a few items that have simple, easily recognizable shapes such peanut butter cups, M&Ms and Milk Duds. This is a reason why you should set the popcorn in the middle of the tray—it needs to be the star of the show!

After-School Snack Board

HAM PICKLE
PINWHEELS, 41

HOW TO BUILD AN...
AFTER-SCHOOL SNACK BOARD

Surprise the kids with this eye-fetching selection of lighter bites, including berries, veggies and fruit.

ITEMS TO INCLUDE
- Ham Pickle Pinwheels
- Yogurt-covered raisins
- Animal crackers
- Blueberries
- Banana chips
- Goldfish crackers
- Cheddar cheese, sliced
- Mozzarella cheese, sliced
- Teddy grahams
- Grapes
- Mini pretzels
- Celery sticks
- Baby carrots
- Graham crackers
- Clementines

EASY ASSEMBLY

Step 1: Line the Ham Pickle Pinwheels across the board.

Step 2: Set yogurt-covered raisins, animal crackers, blueberries, banana chips and goldfish crackers in small serving bowls. Arrange bowls above and below the pinwheels.

Step 3: Using small cookie cutters, cut cheese slices into shapes. Arrange cheese in groupings on board.

Step 4: Fill in gaps on board with groupings of remaining ingredients.

HAM PICKLE PINWHEELS

My mom introduced me to these compact appetizers a number of years ago, and I've been making them for parties ever since. They are easy to make and are always well received by guests.
—Gloria Jarrett, Loveland, OH

PREP: 15 MIN. + CHILLING
MAKES: 3½ DOZEN

- 1 pkg. (8 oz.) cream cheese, cubed
- ¼ lb. sliced Genoa salami
- 1 Tbsp. prepared horseradish
- 7 slices deli ham
- 14 to 21 okra pickles or dill pickle spears

1. In a food processor, combine cream cheese, salami and horseradish; cover and process until blended. Spread over ham slices.

2. Remove stems and ends of okra pickles. Place 2 or 3 okra pickles or 1 dill pickle down the center of each ham slice. Roll up tightly and cover. Refrigerate for at least 2 hours. Cut into 1-in. pieces.

1 piece: 34 cal., 3g fat (1g sat. fat), 9mg chol., 105mg sod., 1g carb. (0 sugars, 0 fiber), 2g pro.

PLATTER POINTER
When assembling any board, try to balance colors and shapes. For instance, avoid piling 2 or 3 orange foods too close to one another, and try to put some space between round items such as grapes, berries and raisins.

CUSTOMIZE YOUR BOARD

Use these recipes to create your own After-School Snack Board.

CRUNCHY GRANOLA

This crisp, lightly sweet mixture is great just eaten out of hand or as an ice cream topping. We love it!
—Lorna Jacobsen, Arrowwood, AB

PREP: 15 MIN. • **BAKE:** 30 MIN. + COOLING
MAKES: 8 CUPS

- ⅔ **cup honey**
- ½ **cup canola oil**
- ⅓ **cup packed brown sugar**
- 2 **tsp. vanilla extract**
- 4 **cups old-fashioned oats**
- 1 **cup sliced almonds**
- 1 **cup sweetened shredded coconut**
- ½ **cup sesame seeds**
- ½ **cup salted sunflower kernels**
- 2 **cups raisins**

1. Preheat oven to 300°. In a small saucepan, combine honey, oil and brown sugar; cook and stir over medium heat until sugar is dissolved. Remove from the heat; stir in vanilla.
2. In a large bowl, combine oats, almonds, coconut, sesame seeds and sunflower kernels. Add the honey mixture, stirring until evenly coated. Spread onto 2 greased 15x10x1-in. baking pans.
3. Bake 20 minutes, stirring frequently. Stir in the raisins. Bake until lightly toasted, about 10 minutes longer. Cool in pans on wire racks, stirring occasionally. Store granola in an airtight container.

½ cup: 366 cal., 18g fat (3g sat. fat), 0 chol., 51mg sod., 50g carb. (30g sugars, 5g fiber), 6g pro.

BACON RANCH DIP

I used reduced-fat items to lighten up this Parmesan and bacon dip. Not only it is a snap to mix up the night before a party, but the proportions also can easily be adjusted for smaller or larger groups. I get requests for the recipe whenever I serve it.
—Pam Garwood, Lakeville, MN

PREP: 5 MIN. + CHILLING • **MAKES:** 1½ CUPS

- ½ cup reduced-fat mayonnaise
- ½ cup reduced-fat ranch salad dressing
- ½ cup fat-free sour cream
- ½ cup shredded Parmesan cheese
- ¼ cup crumbled cooked bacon
  Assorted fresh vegetables

In a small bowl, combine the first 5 ingredients. Cover and refrigerate at least 1 hour before serving. Serve with vegetables.

¼ cup: 172 cal., 11g fat (3g sat. fat), 18mg chol., 542mg sod., 13g carb. (0 sugars, 0 fiber), 7g pro. **Diabetic exchanges:** 2 fat, 1 starch.

LIME-HONEY FRUIT SALAD

Nothing is more refreshing to me than a seasonal fruit salad enhanced with this simple lime-honey dressing.
—Victoria Shevlin, Cape Coral, FL

PREP: 20 MIN. + CHILLING
MAKES: 12 SERVINGS

- 1 tsp. cornstarch
- ¼ cup lime juice
- ¼ cup honey
- ½ tsp. poppy seeds
- 3 medium gala or Red Delicious apples, cubed
- 2 medium pears, cubed
- 2 cups seedless red grapes
- 2 cups green grapes

1. In a small microwave-safe bowl, combine cornstarch and lime juice until smooth. Microwave, uncovered, on high for 20 seconds; stir. Cook 15 seconds longer; stir. Stir in the honey and poppy seeds.

2. In a large bowl, combine the apples, pears and grapes. Pour dressing over the fruit; toss to coat. Cover and refrigerate overnight.

Note: This recipe was tested in a 1,100-watt microwave.

¾ cup: 96 cal., 0 fat (0 sat. fat), 0 chol., 2mg sod., 25g carb. (21g sugars, 2g fiber), 1g pro. **Diabetic exchanges:** 1½ fruit.

HOMEMADE PEANUT BUTTER

We eat a lot of peanut butter, so I decided to make my own. I checked the price of peanut butter up here against the cost of making my own and found mine to be much cheaper, with the added value of knowing what goes into it! Not to mention it's a lot tastier.
—Marge Austin, North Pole, AK

TAKES: 15 MIN. • **MAKES:** ABOUT 1 CUP

- 2 cups unsalted dry roasted peanuts
- ½ tsp. salt
- 1 Tbsp. honey

Process peanuts and salt in a food processor until desired consistency, about 5 minutes, scraping down side as needed. Add honey; process just until blended. Store in an airtight container in refrigerator.

1 Tbsp.: 111 cal., 9g fat (1g sat. fat), 0 chol., 75mg sod., 5g carb. (2g sugars, 2g fiber), 4g pro. **Diabetic exchanges:** 2 fat.

Hot Cocoa Platter

MINT TWIST MERINGUES, 47

HOMEMADE MARSHMALLOW POPS, 49

CHEWY GINGER COOKIES, 47

HOT CHOCOLATE
BOMBS, 48

HOLIDAY
HOT CHOCOLATE
MIX, 46

CHOCOLATE-DIPPED
BEVERAGE SPOONS, 46

HOW TO BUILD A...
HOT COCOA PLATTER

There are so many options for what to include on your hot chocolate board! Here's how we built our board, but feel free to get creative.

ITEMS TO INCLUDE

- Hot Chocolate Bombs
- Holiday Hot Chocolate Mix
- Hot milk
- Flavored liqueurs
- Homemade Marshmallow Pops
- Small candies and chocolates
- Chewy Ginger Cookies
- Mint Twist Meringues
- Small cookies and biscotti
- Chocolate-Dipped Beverage Spoons
- Peppermint sticks
- Stir sticks

EASY ASSEMBLY

Step 1: Place Hot Chocolate Bombs and Holiday Hot Chocolate Mix on the board. (Leave room on the buffet to put a carafe of hot milk and flavored liqueurs near the bombs and mix so people don't need to reach across the entire board when creating their beverages.)

Step 2: Set Homemade Marshmallow Pops on a small plate or platter. Add to the board.

Step 3: Add small bowls and groupings of candies and chocolates, such as butter mints, wrapped caramels and chocolate chips.

Step 4: Working around the bowls, arrange cookies and biscotti in groups.

Step 5: Fill in gaps with Chocolate-Dipped Beverage Spoons, peppermint sticks and stir sticks.

Step 6: Find a spot or two for additional spoons or small tongs guests can use to scoop up marshmallows and other toppings on the board.

CHOCOLATE-DIPPED BEVERAGE SPOONS

These make cute gifts during the holidays. To set the chocolate quickly, simply chill the dipped spoons in the freezer.
—Marcy Boswell, Menifee, CA

PREP: 45 MIN. + CHILLING
MAKES: 2 DOZEN

- 1 cup milk chocolate chips
- 3½ tsp. shortening, divided
- 1 cup white baking chips
- 24 spoons
  Optional: Coarse sugar or chocolate sprinkles

In a microwave-safe bowl, melt milk chocolate chips with 2 tsp. shortening; stir until smooth. Repeat with the white baking chips and remaining shortening. Dip the spoons into either mixture, tapping handles on bowl edges to remove excess. Place spoons on a waxed paper-lined baking sheet. Pipe or drizzle milk chocolate over white-dipped spoons and white mixture over milk chocolate-dipped spoons. Use a toothpick or skewer to swirl chocolate. If desired, decorate with coarse sugar or sprinkles. Chill for 5 minutes or until set. Use as stirring spoons for cocoa or coffee.
1 spoon: 81 cal., 5g fat (3g sat. fat), 3mg chol., 12mg sod., 8g carb. (8g sugars, 0 fiber), 1g pro.

HOLIDAY HOT CHOCOLATE MIX

This is the recipe I make for holiday gifts. I put the mix in decorative jars and tie pretty ribbons around the jars to create festive gifts.
—Debbie Klejeski, Sturgeon Lake, MN

TAKES: 10 MIN. • **MAKES:** 3 QT. MIX

- 1 pkg. (25.6 oz.) nonfat dry milk powder, about 10 cups
- 1 jar (6 oz.) nondairy coffee creamer, about 1¾ cups
- 3¾ cups instant chocolate drink mix
- ½ cup confectioners' sugar

Place all ingredients in a very large bowl or kettle. Stir until well blended. Store in an airtight container or pack into small gift containers. To serve, add ¼ cup chocolate mix to ⅔ cup hot water.
¼ cup: 316 cal., 2g fat (1g sat. fat), 8mg chol., 305mg sod., 57g carb. (53g sugars, 2g fiber), 17g pro.

MILK MATTERS

For the creamiest hot chocolate, we recommend using whole milk, which has a high fat content. In a saucepan over medium heat, warm the milk until steaming (about 140°). Don't let it boil or the milk will scald. To keep the milk warm for hours, use an insulated coffee carafe.

CHEWY GINGER COOKIES

These moist, delicious ginger cookies have an old-fashioned appeal that'll take you back to Grandma's kitchen. I'm never surprised when these treats quickly disappear from my cookie jar.
—Bernice Smith, Sturgeon Lake, MN

PREP: 15 MIN. • **BAKE:** 10 MIN./BATCH
MAKES: ABOUT 4 DOZEN

- ¾ cup shortening
- 1¼ cups sugar, divided
- 1 large egg, room temperature
- ¼ cup molasses
- 1 tsp. vanilla extract
- 2 cups all-purpose flour
- 1 tsp. ground cinnamon
- 1 tsp. ground ginger
- 1 tsp. baking soda
- ½ tsp. salt
- ½ tsp. ground cloves

1. Preheat oven to 375°. In a large bowl, cream shortening and 1 cup sugar until light and fluffy. Beat in the egg, molasses and vanilla. Combine dry ingredients; add to creamed mixture and mix well.
2. Roll into 1-in. balls; roll in remaining sugar. Place 1½ in. apart on ungreased baking sheets.
3. Bake for 10 minutes or until lightly browned. Remove to wire racks. Store in an airtight container.
1 cookie: 73 cal., 3g fat (1g sat. fat), 4mg chol., 53mg sod., 11g carb. (6g sugars, 0 fiber), 1g pro.

MINT TWIST MERINGUES

Meringues flavored with peppermint are a yuletide tradition, but I also use extracts like almond and vanilla to make these crispy delights year-round.
—Cheryl Perry, Hertford, NC

PREP: 30 MIN. • **BAKE:** 40 MIN. + STANDING
MAKES: 2 DOZEN

- 2 large egg whites
- ½ tsp. cream of tartar
- ¼ tsp. peppermint extract
- ½ cup sugar
- ¼ cup crushed red mint candies

1. Place egg whites in a small bowl; let egg whites stand at room temperature 30 minutes.
2. Preheat oven to 250°. Add cream of tartar and extract to egg whites; beat on medium speed until foamy. Gradually add sugar, 1 Tbsp. at a time, beating on high after each addition until sugar is dissolved. Continue beating until stiff glossy peaks form.
3. Cut a small hole in the tip of a pastry bag or in a corner of a food-safe plastic bag; insert a plain piping tip. Transfer meringue to bag. Pipe 1½-in.-diameter cookies 2 in. apart onto parchment paper-lined baking sheets. Sprinkle with crushed candies.
4. Bake 40-45 minutes or until firm to the touch. Turn oven off; leave meringues in oven 1 hour. Remove from pans to a wire rack. Store in an airtight container.
1 cookie: 17 cal., 0 fat (0 sat. fat), 0 chol., 5mg sod., 4g carb. (3g sugars, 0 fiber), 0 pro.

SNACK: HOT COCOA PLATTER   47

HOT CHOCOLATE BOMBS

These hot chocolate filled spheres are all the rage! Make them ahead of time as a holiday gift or to have on hand when you have a hot chocolate craving.
—Rashanda Cobbins, Milwaukee, WI

PREP: 45 MIN. + CHILLING + DECORATING
MAKES: 6 CHOCOLATE BOMBS

- 22 oz. semisweet chocolate, such as Baker's Chocolate, finely chopped
- ½ cup baking cocoa
- ½ cup nonfat dry milk powder
- ¼ cup confectioners' sugar
- 6 Tbsp. vanilla marshmallow bits (not miniature marshmallows) Optional: Sprinkles, colored sanding sugar, melted candy melts

1. Place chocolate in a microwave-safe bowl. Microwave, uncovered, on high for 1 minute; stir. Microwave, stirring every 30 seconds, until chocolate is melted and smooth, 1-2 minutes longer. The chocolate should not exceed 90°.

2. Using silicone half-round molds for making 6 chocolate bombs (2½-in. diameter), brush 1 Tbsp. melted chocolate evenly inside each of 12 openings all the way to the edges, rewarming the melted chocolate as needed. Refrigerate the molds until chocolate is set, 3-5 minutes. Brush on a thin second layer of chocolate. Refrigerate again 8-10 minutes or until set. Place remaining melted chocolate into a piping bag fitted with a small round decorating tip; set aside.

3. Remove chocolate shells from molds. In a medium bowl, whisk together baking cocoa, milk powder and confectioners' sugar. Place 3 Tbsp. cocoa mixture into half the chocolate shells. Top with 1 Tbsp. of the marshmallow bits.

4. Pipe a small amount of melted chocolate around edges of shells. Carefully top each filled shell with an empty shell, pressing lightly to seal, using additional melted chocolate if necessary. If desired, decorate with optional ingredients. Refrigerate until set. Store in a tightly sealed container.

To prepare hot chocolate: Place a hot chocolate bomb in a mug; add 1 cup warm milk and stir to dissolve.

1 chocolate bomb: 619 cal., 34g fat (20g sat. fat), 1mg chol., 31mg sod., 36g carb. (29g sugars, 4g fiber), 10g pro.

Salted Caramel Hot Chocolate Bombs: Fill spheres with hot cocoa mix, 1 Tbsp. caramel chips and a pinch of flake sea salt. Drizzle outside with melted dark chocolate and melted caramel chips; sprinkle with flake sea salt.

Peppermint Hot Chocolate Bombs: Fill spheres with hot cocoa mix, 1 Tbsp. white baking chips and 1 Tbsp. finely crushed peppermint candies. Drizzle outside with melted white chocolate tinted pink and red; top with additional crushed peppermint candies.

TEST KITCHEN TIP
When making the bombs, you can replace the baking cocoa, milk powder and confectioners' sugar with prepared hot cocoa mix.

MAKING HOT CHOCOLATE BOMBS

Step 1: Using a food-safe paintbrush, coat molds evenly with melted chocolate; chill.

Step 2: Fill half the chocolate shells with hot cocoa mixture.

Step 3: Pipe a small amount of melted chocolate around edges of shells.

Step 4: Carefully top filled shells with unfilled shells to form spheres, pressing lightly to seal. Use more melted chocolate if needed.

HOMEMADE MARSHMALLOW POPS

Homemade marshmallows are fun to eat on a stick or to stir into your favorite hot chocolate. Their melt-in-your-mouth texture appeals to both the young and the young at heart.
—Jennifer Andrzejewski, Carmel Valley, CA

PREP: 55 MIN. + STANDING
MAKES: 15 MARSHMALLOWS

- ½ cup cold water
- 3 envelopes unflavored gelatin
- 2 cups sugar
- 1 cup light corn syrup
- ½ cup water
- ¼ tsp. salt
- 1 tsp. almond extract
- ½ cup confectioners' sugar, divided
  Lollipop sticks

1. In a large bowl, combine cold water and gelatin; set aside.
2. Meanwhile, in a large heavy saucepan over medium heat, combine the sugar, corn syrup, water and salt. Bring to a boil, stirring occasionally. Cover and cook for 2 minutes to dissolve sugar crystals; uncover and cook on medium-high heat, without stirring, until a candy thermometer reads 240° (soft-ball stage).
3. Remove mixture from the heat and gradually add to the gelatin bowl. Beat on medium speed for 14 minutes. Add almond extract; beat 1 minute longer. Sprinkle 2 Tbsp. confectioners' sugar into a greased 13x9-in. pan.
4. With greased hands, spread the marshmallow mixture into prepared pan. Top with 2 Tbsp. confectioners' sugar. Cover; cool at room temperature for 6 hours or overnight.
5. Cut 15 snowflakes with a greased 2½-in. snowflake-shaped cookie cutter; toss snowflake marshmallows in remaining confectioners' sugar. Gently press a lollipop stick into each snowflake. Store in an airtight container in a cool, dry place.

1 marshmallow pop: 82 cal., 0 fat (0 sat. fat), 0 chol., 24mg sod., 21g carb. (16g sugars, 0 fiber), 1g pro.

Easy Dessert Board

ORANGE CARAMEL
SAUCE, 51

HOW TO BUILD AN...
EASY DESSERT BOARD

It's time to dunk, dip, sprinkle and spoil yourself. Create this simply snackable board next time you want to sweeten up movie night, a sleepover or simply a cozy night at home.

ITEMS TO INCLUDE
- Orange Caramel Sauce
- Chocolate sprinkles
- Chocolate-covered pretzel sticks
- Hard candy sticks
- Hazelnut spread
- Strawberries
- Pizzelles
- Gingersnaps
- Meringue cookies
- Shortbread cookies
- Wrapped truffles

EASY ASSEMBLY

Step 1: Set bowls of the Orange Caramel Sauce, chocolate sprinkles, pretzel sticks and candy sticks onto the platter. Add the hazelnut spread.

Step 2: Add a grouping of strawberries.

Step 3: Add groupings of the pizzelles, gingersnaps and cookies.

Step 4: Fill in any gaps with the wrapped truffles.

ORANGE CARAMEL SAUCE
We added a touch of orange extract to a creamy caramel sauce to make a rich homemade topping you won't find in stores. Try it drizzled over ice cream or as a dip for strawberries or sliced apples.
—*Taste of Home* Test Kitchen

PREP: 10 MIN.
COOK: 10 MIN. + CHILLING
MAKES: 1⅓ CUPS

1 cup packed brown sugar
1 cup heavy whipping cream
½ cup sweetened condensed milk
½ tsp. orange extract
Ice cream or dessert of choice

1. In a large saucepan, cook and stir brown sugar and cream over medium heat until sugar is dissolved. Bring to a boil; cook until mixture is reduced by half, about 5 minutes. Remove from the heat. Stir in milk and orange extract. Cover and refrigerate.

2. Just before serving, warm over low heat. Serve with ice cream or dessert of choice.

2 Tbsp.: 215 cal., 10g fat (6g sat. fat), 38mg chol., 37mg sod., 30g carb. (30g sugars, 0 fiber), 2g pro.

TEST KITCHEN TIP
Heavy whipping cream is a rich cream that ranges from 36% to 40% butterfat and that doubles in volume when whipped. Sweetened condensed milk, on the other hand, is made with cow's milk from which water has been removed and to which sugar has been added. It's a thick, sweet canned product used in candy, sweet sauces and dessert recipes.

Party Boards

These incredible presentations are sure to be the guest of honor at celebrations all year long.

Birthday Board

BIRTHDAY CAKE
FUDGE, 56

THICK SUGAR
COOKIES, 55

YELLOW
CUPCAKES, 56

HOW TO BUILD A...
BIRTHDAY BOARD

ITEMS TO INCLUDE
- Thick Sugar Cookies
- Icing writers
- Gummy bears
- Gumballs
- M&M's Minis
- Jelly beans
- Lollipops
- Yellow Cupcakes (half with chocolate frosting, half with vanilla)
- Oreos (regular, golden and mini)
- Fudge-striped cookies
- Circus Animal Cookies
- Birthday Cake Fudge
- Kit Kat bars, unwrapped
- Caramel corn
- Hershey's Kisses
- Swedish Fish candies

EASY ASSEMBLY
Step 1: Prepare Thick Sugar Cookies as directed but use a 4- or 6-inch cookie cutter to create 1 larger cookie. Use icing writers to decorate the large cookie with "Happy Birthday."

Step 2: Fan remaining Thick Sugar Cookies in the middle of the board in a circle. Set large cookie on top.

Step 3: Fill small bowls with the gummy bears, gumballs, M&M's and jelly beans. Stand the lollipops in a tall glass. Set all on board.

Step 4: Arrange Yellow Cupcakes on the board in 2 groupings. Add Oreos in like groupings. Set fudge-striped and animal cookies next to the Oreos on opposite sides.

Step 5: Stack Birthday Cake Fudge squares and Kit Kats on opposite sides of the board. Fill in gaps with groupings of the remaining items.

THICK SUGAR COOKIES
Thicker than the norm, this sugar cookie is like the type you'd find at a bakery. My children often request these for their birthdays, and they are always happy to help decorate.
—Heather Biedler, Martinsburg, WV

PREP: 25 MIN. + CHILLING
BAKE: 10 MIN./BATCH + COOLING
MAKES: ABOUT 3 DOZEN

- 1 **cup butter, softened**
- 1 **cup sugar**
- 2 **large eggs, room temperature**
- 3 **large egg yolks, room temperature**
- 1½ **tsp. vanilla extract**
- ¾ **tsp. almond extract**
- 3½ **cups all-purpose flour**
- 1½ **tsp. baking powder**
- ¼ **tsp. salt**

FROSTING
- 4 **cups confectioners' sugar**
- ½ **cup butter, softened**
- ½ **cup shortening**
- 1 **tsp. vanilla extract**
- ½ **tsp. almond extract**
- 2 **to 3 Tbsp. 2% milk**
  Assorted colored nonpareils, optional

1. In a large bowl, cream the butter and sugar until light and fluffy, 5-7 minutes. Beat in eggs, egg yolks and extracts. In another bowl, whisk flour, baking powder and salt; gradually beat into creamed mixture. Shape into a disk; wrap and refrigerate 1 hour or until firm enough to roll.
2. Preheat oven to 375°. On a lightly floured surface, roll dough to ½-in. thickness. Cut with a floured 2-in. cookie cutter. Place 1 in. apart on ungreased baking sheets.
3. Bake until edges begin to brown, 10-12 minutes. Cool cookies on baking sheets for 5 minutes. Remove cookies to wire racks to cool completely.
4. For the frosting, in a large bowl, beat the confectioners' sugar, butter, shortening, extracts and enough milk to reach desired consistency. Spread over cookies. If desired, sprinkle with the nonpareils.

1 frosted cookie : 219 cal., 11g fat (6g sat. fat), 49mg chol., 92mg sod., 28g carb. (18g sugars, 0 fiber), 2g pro.

BIRTHDAY CAKE FUDGE

This decadent treat is the perfect thing to make your birthday special. Or prepare it ahead and package it as a surprise gift for a friend.
—Rashanda Cobbins, Milwaukee, WI

PREP: 10 MIN. + CHILLING
MAKES: 64 PIECES

- 1 can (14 oz.) sweetened condensed milk
- 1½ cups white baking chips
- 3 Tbsp. butter
- ⅛ tsp. salt
- 1½ cups Funfetti cake mix, unprepared
- 3 Tbsp. sprinkles

1. Line an 8-in. square pan with foil or parchment; grease lightly. In a large heavy saucepan, cook and stir condensed milk, baking chips, butter and salt over low heat until smooth. Remove from heat; stir in cake mix until dissolved. Spread into prepared pan; top with sprinkles. Refrigerate, covered, until firm, about 2 hours.
2. Using foil, lift the fudge out of the pan. Remove foil; cut fudge into 1-in. squares. Store in an airtight container in the refrigerator.
1 piece: 59 cal., 2g fat (2g sat. fat), 4mg chol., 47mg sod., 9g carb. (7g sugars, 0 fiber), 1g pro.

PLATTER POINTER
Immediately before serving, sprinkle nonpareils over the entire birthday board for even more colorful confetti-like fun.

YELLOW CUPCAKES

On any given day, someone needs a gorgeous homemade cupcake. This buttery cake base works with any frosting and decorates beautifully.
—*Taste of Home* Test Kitchen

PREP: 20 MIN. • **BAKE:** 15 MIN. + COOLING
MAKES: 2 DOZEN

- ⅔ cup butter, softened
- 1¾ cups sugar
- 2 large eggs, room temperature
- 1½ tsp. vanilla extract
- 2½ cups all-purpose flour
- 2½ tsp. baking powder
- ½ tsp. salt
- 1¼ cups 2% milk
  Frosting of your choice

1. Preheat oven to 350°. Line 24 muffin cups with paper liners.
2. In a large bowl, cream butter and sugar until light and fluffy, 5-7 minutes. Add the eggs, 1 at a time, beating well after each addition. Beat in vanilla. In another bowl, whisk flour, baking powder and salt; add to the creamed mixture alternately with milk, beating well after each addition.
3. Fill prepared cups three-fourths full. Bake 15-20 minutes or until a toothpick inserted in center comes out clean. Cool in pans for 10 minutes before removing cupcakes to wire racks to cool completely. Spread with frosting.
1 cupcake: 163 cal., 6g fat (4g sat. fat), 32mg chol., 138mg sod., 25g carb. (15g sugars, 0 fiber), 2g pro.

CUSTOMIZE YOUR BOARD

BIRTHDAY CAKE MARTINI
Celebrate your birthday with this sweet and festive martini. If it's too strong for your taste, add more half-and-half.
—*Taste of Home* Test Kitchen

TAKES: 5 MIN. • **MAKES:** 1 SERVING

RAINBOW S'MOREO COOKIES
Homemade Oreo-style cookies are pretty great on their own, but they're even better when you add graham cracker crumbs to the dough, stuff them with marshmallow creme and roll them in sprinkles. You can change the color of the sprinkles to match various holidays.
—Colleen Delawder, Herndon, VA

PREP: 15 MIN. + CHILLING
BAKE: 10 MIN./BATCH + COOLING
MAKES: ABOUT 2 DOZEN

- ½ cup unsalted butter, softened
- 1 cup sugar
- 1 large egg, room temperature
- 1 tsp. vanilla extract
- ½ cup baking cocoa
- ¾ cup graham cracker crumbs
- ¾ cup all-purpose flour
- 1 tsp. baking powder
- ¼ tsp. kosher salt
- 1 jar (7 oz.) marshmallow creme
  Rainbow sprinkles

1. Preheat oven to 350°. Cream the butter and sugar until light and fluffy, 5-7 minutes. Beat in egg and vanilla. Beat in cocoa. In another bowl, whisk cracker crumbs, flour, baking powder and salt; gradually beat into creamed mixture. Refrigerate dough until firm, at least 30 minutes.
2. Shape dough into 1-in. balls. Place 2 in. apart on parchment-lined baking sheets. Flatten with bottom of a glass dipped in sugar. Bake 6-8 minutes or until set. Cool on pans for 3 minutes. Remove cookies to wire racks to cool completely.
3. Spread marshmallow creme on bottoms of half of the cookies; cover with remaining cookies. Roll edges in sprinkles. Serve immediately. Or, freeze the cookies in covered containers, separating layers with waxed paper. Thaw cookies briefly before serving.
1 sandwich cookie: 131 cal., 5g fat (3g sat. fat), 18mg chol., 64mg sod., 20g carb. (14g sugars, 1g fiber), 1g pro.

Nonpareils
- 2 tsp. honey
  Ice cubes
- 2 oz. cake-flavored vodka
- 1 oz. white chocolate liqueur
- 1 oz. amaretto
- 2 oz. half-and-half cream

1. Sprinkle nonpareils on a plate. Moisten rim of a martini glass with honey; hold glass upside down and dip rim into nonpareils.
2. Fill a mixing glass or tumbler three-fourths full of ice. Add vodka, white chocolate liqueur, amaretto and cream; stir until condensation forms on outside of glass. Strain vodka mixture into the prepared glass; serve immediately.
1 martini: 592 cal., 6g fat (4g sat. fat), 30mg chol., 39mg sod., 59g carb. (25g sugars, 0 fiber), 2g pro.

PERUVIAN CHICHA MORADA, 60

SPICED MANGO–ALMOND TART, 59

SEAFOOD BITES, 60

Festive & Fruity Board

HOW TO BUILD A...
FESTIVE & FRUITY BOARD

Colors, textures, sweet treats and savory staples combine to make this board a standout.

ITEMS TO INCLUDE
- Spiced Mango-Almond Tart
- Peruvian Chicha Morada
- Seafood Bites
- Olives
- Marcona almonds
- Prosciutto, thinly sliced
- Thin, crisp breadsticks
- Blue cheese
- Gouda
- Artisanal crackers
- Deli ham, thinly sliced
- Dry-cured salami
- Red and green grapes
- Fresh figs, halved

EASY ASSEMBLY

Step 1: Slice the Spiced Mango-Almond Tart and arrange on the board.

Step 2: Set glasses of Peruvian Chicha Morada on or near the board.

Step 3: Group a few of the Seafood Bites on the board.

Step 4: Add small bowls of olives and marcona almonds.

Step 5: Cut prosciutto slices in half. Wrap a prosciutto piece around each breadstick. Pile wrapped breadsticks onto the board.

Step 6: Add blue cheese, Gouda, artisanal crackers, ham and salami.

Step 7: Fill in gaps with grapes and figs. Add serving pieces as desired.

SPICED MANGO-ALMOND TART

There are many tarts in the world, but this one is extra gorgeous. Present it with a sprinkle of confectioners' sugar, some whipped cream and a few mint leaves.
—Lisa Speer, Palm Beach, FL

PREP: 35 MIN. + FREEZING • **BAKE:** 25 MIN.
MAKES: 2 TARTS (8 SERVINGS EACH)

- 1 pkg. frozen puff pastry, thawed (17.3 oz., 2 sheets)
- ⅔ cup almond paste, divided
- 2 large mangoes, peeled and thinly sliced,l
- 2 Tbsp. lemon juice
- 3 Tbsp. packed brown sugar
- 1½ tsp. ground cinnamon
- ½ tsp. ground ginger
  Dash ground cloves

1. Preheat oven to 375°. Working with 1 puff pastry sheet at a time, unfold pastry onto a large sheet of parchment paper dusted lightly with flour. Roll pastry into a 10-in.-square. Transfer pastry and parchment paper to a baking sheet. Using a sharp knife, score a ½-in. border around edges of pastry.
2. On a separate sheet of parchment paper, roll ⅓ cup almond paste to ⅛-in. thickness. Peel off almond paste in pieces and arrange on puff pastry, keeping within edges of cut border.
3. In a large bowl, toss mango slices with lemon juice; arrange half the slices over the almond paste. In a small bowl, mix brown sugar and spices; sprinkle half the mixture over the mango slices on the tart. Place tart in freezer to chill for 10 minutes. Repeat with remaining ingredients.
4. Bake 25-35 minutes or until crust is golden brown. If baking 2 tarts at a time, switch position of pans halfway through baking. Serve warm.

1 piece: 232 cal., 11g fat (2g sat. fat), 0 chol., 103mg sod., 32g carb. (12g sugars, 4g fiber), 3g pro.

PERUVIAN CHICHA MORADA

Chicha morada is a nonalcoholic Peruvian beverage made by boiling purple corn called maiz morado *with water, pineapple rinds, cinnamon, cloves, sugar and lime. This fruity drink can be traced all the way back to the precolonial era in Peru.*
—Andrea Potischman, Menlo Park, CA

PREP: 20 MIN. + CHILLING • **COOK:** 50 MIN.
MAKES: 8 SERVINGS

- 1 fresh pineapple
- 1 pkg. (15 oz.) dried purple corn on the cob
- 12 cups water
- ¾ cup sugar
- 3 cinnamon sticks (3 in.)
- 10 whole cloves
- ⅓ cup lime juice
- 1 medium green apple, chopped

1. Peel pineapple, removing any eyes from the fruit. Reserve half the peel. Remove and discard the core. Chop pineapple and reserve for garnish.
2. Rinse corn cobs and place them in a Dutch oven. Add the water, reserved pineapple peel, sugar, cinnamon and cloves. Bring to a boil; reduce heat. Simmer, uncovered, 50 minutes. Strain. Refrigerate until chilled, at least 1 hour. Stir in lime juice.
3. Serve over ice with apple and reserved chopped pineapple.
¾ cup: 99 cal., 0 fat (0 sat. fat), 0 chol., 1mg sod., 26g carb. (24g sugars, 1g fiber), 0 pro.

SEAFOOD BITES

Chinese mustard, five-spice powder and wasabi give these appetizers a spicy Asian flavor. I first made them with leftover Dungeness crab, but a good-quality canned crabmeat works well too.
—Margee Berry, White Salmon, WA

TAKES: 30 MIN. • **MAKES:** 40 APPETIZERS

- 40 wonton wrappers
- 1 pkg. (8 oz.) cream cheese, softened
- ¼ cup sweet-and-sour sauce
- 1 large egg
- ⅓ cup chopped green onions
- ½ tsp. Chinese-style mustard
- ¼ tsp. prepared wasabi or horseradish
  Dash Chinese five-spice powder
- 1 cup lump crabmeat, drained
- 2 Tbsp. black sesame seeds

1. Preheat oven to 350°. Press each wonton wrapper into a greased miniature muffin cup. Bake until wonton wrappers are golden brown, 6-7 minutes.
2. In a small bowl, beat the cream cheese, sweet-and-sour sauce and egg. Stir in the green onions, mustard, wasabi and five-spice powder. Fold in crab. Spoon 1 Tbsp. of the crab mixture into each cup. Sprinkle with sesame seeds. Bake until heated through, 10-12 minutes longer. Top with additional chopped green onions if desired.
1 wonton cup: 52 cal., 2g fat (1g sat. fat), 14mg chol., 96mg sod., 6g carb. (1g sugars, 0 fiber), 2g pro.

ITALIAN OLIVES

A friend shared this recipe with me more than 25 years ago. I still get raves when I serve these olives as part of a board or an antipasto platter.
—Jean Johnson, Reno, NV

PREP: 10 MIN. + CHILLING • **MAKES:** 4 CUPS

- 2 **cans (6 oz. each) pitted ripe olives, drained**
- 1 **jar (5¾ oz.) pimiento-stuffed olives, drained**
- 2 **Tbsp. finely chopped celery**
- 2 **Tbsp. finely chopped onion**
- 2 **Tbsp. capers, rinsed and drained**
- ¼ **cup olive oil**
- 2 **Tbsp. red wine vinegar**
- 2 **garlic cloves, minced**
- 1 **tsp. dried basil**
- 1 **tsp. dried oregano**
- 1 **tsp. crushed red pepper flakes**
- ¼ **tsp. salt**

1. In a large bowl, combine the first 5 ingredients. In a small bowl, whisk the oil, vinegar, garlic, basil, oregano, pepper flakes and salt; pour over olive mixture. Toss to coat.

2. Cover and refrigerate for at least 3 hours before serving. Store in the refrigerator for up to 3 days.

⅛ cup: 30 cal., 3g fat (0 sat. fat), 0 chol., 167mg sod., 1g carb. (0 sugars, 0 fiber), 0 pro.

PLATTER POINTER
If adding Prosciutto-Wrapped Asparagus to your board, place it on the platter after setting down the tart. (You'll need room for the spears and the dipping sauce.) Place the prosciutto-wrapped breadsticks on the opposite side of the board for the best overall appearance.

CUSTOMIZE YOUR BOARD

PROSCIUTTO-WRAPPED ASPARAGUS WITH RASPBERRY SAUCE

Grilling the prosciutto with the asparagus gives this appetizer a salty crunch that's perfect for dipping into a sweet glaze. When a dish is this delicious and easy to prepare, you owe it to yourself to try it!
—Noelle Myers, Grand Forks, ND

TAKES: 30 MIN. • **MAKES:** 16 APPETIZERS

- ⅓ **lb. thinly sliced prosciutto or deli ham**
- 16 **fresh asparagus spears, trimmed**
- ½ **cup seedless raspberry jam**
- 2 **Tbsp. balsamic vinegar**

1. Cut prosciutto slices in half. Wrap a prosciutto piece around each asparagus spear; secure ends with wooden toothpicks soaked in water.

2. Grill asparagus, covered, on an oiled rack over medium heat 6-8 minutes or until prosciutto is crisp, turning once. Discard toothpicks.

3. In a small microwave-safe bowl, microwave jam and vinegar on high for 15-20 seconds or until jam is melted. Serve with asparagus.

1 asparagus spear with 1½ tsp. sauce: 50 cal., 1g fat (0 sat. fat), 8mg chol., 184mg sod., 7g carb. (7g sugars, 0 fiber), 3g pro. **Diabetic exchanges:** ½ starch.

BEER DIP, 66

QUICK TORTILLA
PINWHEELS, 64

GRIDIRON
CAKE, 64

CHUNKY
SALSA, 66

TOUCHDOWN
COOKIES, 65

Snack
Stadium

SPINACH & TURKEY PINWHEELS, 66

VEGGIE DILL DIP, 65

HOW TO BUILD A...
SNACK STADIUM

ITEMS TO INCLUDE

- Gridiron Cake
- Spinach & Turkey Pinwheels
- Quick Tortilla Pinwheels
- Beer Dip
- Chunky Salsa
- Wrapped chocolates
- Touchdown Cookies
- Veggie Dill Dip
- Carrot sticks
- Celery sticks
- Corn chips
- Goldfish crackers
- Pretzels
- Bugles
- Mixed popcorn
- Snack mix
- Tortilla chips

EASY ASSEMBLY

Step 1: Set Gridiron Cake in the middle of what will be the overall display.

Step 2: Divide the Spinach & Turkey Pinwheels and Quick Tortilla Pinwheels among 4 mini loaf foil pans. Set 2 pans along each short end of cake.

Step 3: Spoon the Beer Dip and Chunky Salsa into two 2-lb. loaf foil pans. Set each pan on a long side of the cake.

Step 4: Fill two additional 2-lb. loaf foil pans with chocolates and Touchdown Cookies. Set 1 pan behind the Beer Dip and 1 behind the Chunky Salsa.

Step 5: Spoon Veggie Dill Dip into two 5-in. foil tart pans. Set each pan of dip onto plastic drinking cups on opposite corners of the stadium. Fill 2 additional plastic drinking cups with carrots and celery; set on remaining corners.

Step 6: Wrap 12 soda-can-carton ends with paper. Fill with remaining items; add to stadium around cake and pans.

QUICK TORTILLA PINWHEELS

Prepare these easy, cheesy pinwheels several days in advance if desired. Serve with your choice of mild or hot salsa or picante sauce.
—Barbara Keith, Faucett, MO

PREP: 15 MIN. + CHILLING
MAKES: ABOUT 5 DOZEN

- 1 cup sour cream
- 1 pkg. (8 oz.) cream cheese, softened
- ¾ cup sliced green onions
- ½ cup finely shredded cheddar cheese
- 1 Tbsp. lime juice
- 1 Tbsp. minced seeded jalapeno pepper
- 8 to 10 flour tortillas (8 in.), room temperature
  Salsa or picante sauce

Combine the first 6 ingredients in a bowl. Spread on 1 side of tortillas and roll up tightly. Wrap and refrigerate for at least 1 hour. Slice into 1-in. pieces. Serve with salsa or picante sauce.
Note: Wear disposable gloves when cutting hot peppers; the oils can burn skin. Avoid touching your face.
1 pinwheel: 47 cal., 3g fat (2g sat. fat), 6mg chol., 51mg sod., 4g carb. (0 sugars, 0 fiber), 1g pro.

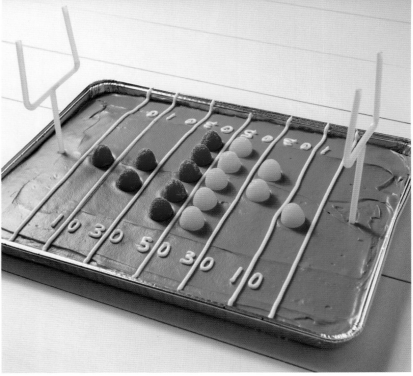

GRIDIRON CAKE

Celebrate any big game with this creative and easy-to-make snack cake with yummy cream cheese frosting.
—Sarah Farmer, Waukesha, WI

PREP: 45 MIN. • **BAKE:** 25 MIN. + COOLING
MAKES: 20 SERVINGS

CAKE
- ⅔ cup butter, softened
- 1¾ cups sugar
- 1 Tbsp. vanilla extract
- 2 large eggs, room temperature
- 2½ cups all-purpose flour
- 2½ tsp. baking powder
- ½ tsp. salt
- 1¼ cups 2% milk

FROSTING
- 1 pkg. (8 oz.) cream cheese, softened
- ½ cup butter, softened
- 3¾ cups confectioners' sugar
- 1 Tbsp. 2% milk
- 1 tsp. vanilla extract
  Green paste food coloring

DECORATION
- 2 goals posts made from yellow bendable straws
  Large gumdrops in 2 colors

1. Preheat oven to 350°. Grease a half sheet (17x12x1-in.) foil cake pan.
2. In a bowl, cream butter and sugar until light and fluffy, 5-7 minutes. Add vanilla and eggs, 1 at a time, beating well after each addition. In another bowl, whisk flour, baking powder and salt; beat into creamed mixture alternately with milk. Transfer to prepared pan.
3. Bake until a toothpick inserted in center of the cake comes out clean, 25-30 minutes. Place cake in pan on a wire rack; cool completely.
4. For frosting, beat cream cheese and butter. Add confectioners' sugar, milk and vanilla. Reserve ¼ cup frosting for field markings. Tint remaining frosting green; spread over top of cake. Use the white frosting to pipe white yard lines and numbers. Decorate the field with the goal posts made of straws. Add gumdrops for football players.
1 piece: 365 cal., 16g fat (9g sat. fat), 60mg chol., 255mg sod., 54g carb. (41g sugars, 0 fiber), 4g pro.

TOUCHDOWN COOKIES

With some simple touches, you can transform regular sugar cookies into a special sweet treat for the football fans at your party.

—Sister Judith LaBrozzi, Canton, OH

PREP: 25 MIN. + CHILLING
BAKE: 10 MIN./BATCH + COOLING
MAKES: 4½ DOZEN

- 1 cup butter, softened
- 1 cup sugar
- 2 large eggs, room temperature
- 1 tsp. vanilla extract
- 3 cups all-purpose flour
- 2 tsp. cream of tartar
- 1 tsp. baking soda

GLAZE
- 4 cups confectioners' sugar
- 8 to 10 Tbsp. hot water
   Black paste food coloring
- 6 to 8 tsp. baking cocoa

1. In a large bowl, cream the butter and sugar until light and fluffy, 5-7 minutes. Add the eggs, 1 at a time, beating well after each addition. Beat in the vanilla. Combine the flour, cream of tartar and baking soda; gradually add to creamed mixture and mix well. Cover; refrigerate 3 hours or until easy to handle.

2. On a lightly floured surface, roll out dough to ⅛-in. thickness. Cut with a football-shaped cookie cutter and a small person-shaped (gingerbread) cookie cutter. Place cutouts 2 in. apart on ungreased baking sheets.

3. Bake at 350° for 8-10 minutes or until cookies are lightly browned. Remove to wire racks to cool.

4. In a bowl, combine the confectioners' sugar and enough hot water to achieve spreading consistency; beat until smooth. Divide glaze into thirds. Leave a third white; set aside. Stir black food coloring into another third; set aside. Add cocoa to the last third; stir until smooth. Spread brown glaze over football cookies. Pipe white glaze for the football laces. Spread or pipe white glaze over people cookies to make shirts. Pipe black stripes over white shirts for referee stripes.

1 cookie: 108 cal., 4g fat (2g sat. fat), 16mg chol., 53mg sod., 18g carb. (12g sugars, 0 fiber), 1g pro.

VEGGIE DILL DIP

I like to keep this good-for-you dip and a variety of cut-up veggies on hand for an easy snack.

—Hazel Baber, Yuma, AZ

PREP: 10 MIN. + CHILLING
MAKES: 2½ CUPS

- 2 cups 1% cottage cheese
- 3 Tbsp. fat-free milk
- ¾ cup fat-free mayonnaise
- 1 Tbsp. dried minced onion
- 1 Tbsp. dried parsley flakes
- 1 tsp. dill weed
- 1 tsp. seasoned salt
- ¼ tsp. garlic powder

In a blender, blend cottage cheese and milk until smooth. Transfer to a bowl. Stir in the remaining ingredients; mix well. Cover and chill overnight. Serve with raw vegetables.

2 Tbsp.: 37 cal., 0 fat (0 sat. fat), 2mg chol., 303mg sod., 3g carb. (2g sugars, 0 fiber), 5g pro.

SODA-CARTON SEATS

To create box seats around your snack stadium, draw a wide triangle on the long side of a soda carton. Cut the box to form a diagonal stand shape. Repeat with opposite side of carton.

BEER DIP

Ranch dressing mix flavors this fast-to-fix pretzel dip packed with shredded cheese. Once you start eating it, you can't stop!
—Michelle Long, New Castle, CO

TAKES: 5 MIN. • **MAKES:** 3½ CUPS

- 2 pkg. (8 oz. each) cream cheese, softened
- ⅓ cup beer or nonalcoholic beer
- 1 envelope ranch salad dressing mix
- 2 cups shredded cheddar cheese
   Pretzels

In a large bowl, beat cream cheese, beer and dressing mix until smooth. Stir in shredded cheddar cheese. Serve with pretzels.
2 Tbsp.: 89 cal., 8g fat (5g sat. fat), 26mg chol., 177mg sod., 1g carb. (0 sugars, 0 fiber), 3g pro.

SPINACH & TURKEY PINWHEELS

Need an awesome snack for game day? My kids love these four-ingredient turkey pinwheels. Go ahead and make them the day before; they won't get soggy!
—Amy Van Hemert, Ottumwa, IA

TAKES: 15 MIN. • **MAKES:** 8 SERVINGS

- 1 carton (8 oz.) spreadable garden vegetable cream cheese
- 8 flour tortillas (8 in.)
- 4 cups fresh baby spinach
- 1 lb. sliced deli turkey

Spread cream cheese over tortillas. Layer with spinach and turkey. Roll up tightly. If not serving immediately, cover and refrigerate. To serve, cut each roll crosswise into 6 slices.
6 pinwheels: 307 cal., 13g fat (6g sat. fat), 52mg chol., 866mg sod., 31g carb. (1g sugars, 2g fiber), 17g pro.

CHUNKY SALSA

This fresh-tasting salsa is wonderfully chunky. If you like it hotter, add more habanero peppers; if you prefer a mild salsa, add fewer (or use jalapenos).
—Dana Hayes, Canton, OH

PREP: 45 MIN. • **PROCESS:** 15 MIN.
MAKES: 7 PINTS

- 5 lbs. tomatoes
- 5 cups chopped onions (about 3 large)
- 5 cups chopped green peppers (about 4 large)
- 2½ cups chopped sweet red peppers (about 2 large)
- 2 habanero peppers, seeded and finely chopped
- 1 cup white vinegar
- 1 can (6 oz.) tomato paste
- 3 tsp. salt

1. Fill a Dutch oven two-thirds full of water; bring to a boil. Prepare a container of ice water. Score an "X" on the bottom of each tomato. Using a slotted spoon, place the tomatoes, 1 at a time, into the boiling water for 30-60 seconds. Remove tomatoes and immediately plunge into ice water. Slip off and discard peels; chop tomatoes.
2. In a stockpot, combine the remaining ingredients. Stir in tomatoes. Bring to a boil over medium-high heat. Reduce heat; simmer, uncovered, until desired thickness is reached, 15-20 minutes.
3. Carefully ladle hot mixture into hot 1-pint jars, leaving ½-in. headspace. Remove air bubbles; wipe rims and adjust lids. Process for 15 minutes in a boiling-water canner.
Note: Wear disposable gloves when cutting hot peppers; the oils can burn skin. Avoid touching your face.
¼ cup: 18 cal., 0 fat (0 sat. fat), 0 chol., 131mg sod., 4g carb. (2g sugars, 1g fiber), 1g pro.

CUSTOMIZE YOUR BOARD

Use these recipes to create your own Snack Stadium.

ITALIAN OYSTER CRACKERS

My friends and family love these crackers, which are easily made in the slow cooker. I often serve them right from the slow cooker so everyone can eat them warm.
—Angela Lively, Conroe, TX

PREP: 10 MIN. • **COOK:** 1 HOUR
MAKES: 8 SERVINGS

- 2   **pkg. (9 oz. each) oyster crackers**
- ¼   **cup canola oil**
- 3   **garlic cloves, minced**
- 1   **envelope Italian salad dressing mix**
- 1   **tsp. dill weed**
- ¼   **cup butter, melted**
- ½   **cup grated Parmesan cheese**

1. Combine the crackers, oil, garlic, Italian salad dressing mix and dill weed in a 6-qt. slow cooker. Cook, covered, on low 1 hour.
2. Drizzle melted butter over crackers; sprinkle with cheese. Stir to coat.
3. Transfer mixture to a baking sheet; let stand until cool. Store in airtight container.
¾ cup: 407 cal., 20g fat (6g sat. fat), 20mg chol., 1057mg sod., 49g carb. (2g sugars, 2g fiber), 8g pro.

FOOTBALL CAKE POPS

My son loves football! For his eighth birthday, I made cake pops with a rich chocolate cake center and a tasty peanut butter coating. These are sure to be winners at parties, bake sales and sports-watching events.
—Jenny Dubinsky, Inwood, WV

PREP: 2 HOURS + CHILLING.
BAKE: 35 MIN. + COOLING
MAKES: 4 DOZEN

- 1   **pkg. chocolate cake mix (regular size)**
- 1   **cup cream cheese frosting**
- 1   **cup dark chocolate chips**
- 1   **cup peanut butter chips**
- 1   **Tbsp. shortening**
- 48   **4-in. lollipop sticks**
- ¼   **cup white decorating icing**

1. Bake cake according to package directions; cool completely. In a large bowl, break cake into fine crumbles. Add the frosting and stir until fully incorporated, adding more frosting if needed, until mixture maintains its shape when squeezed together with palm of hand. Roll 1 Tbsp. into a ball; mold into a football shape. Place on a parchment-lined baking sheet. Repeat with remaining mixture. Refrigerate the cake pops until firm, about 30 minutes.
2. Meanwhile, place chocolate chips, peanut butter chips and shortening in a microwave-safe bowl. Microwave for 30 seconds and stir. Repeat, stirring every 30 seconds until melted and smooth, adding more shortening if needed. Do not overheat.
3. Dip a lollipop stick into the chocolate mixture; insert stick halfway through a football shape, taking care not to break through the other side. Return to the baking sheet until set; repeat to form remaining cake pops. Coat each cake pop with chocolate mixture, allowing excess to drip off. Reheat and stir the chocolate mixture as needed. Return cake pops to baking sheets, ensuring they do not touch one another. Allow chocolate coating to set until firm to the touch. To decorate, use icing to draw laces onto cake pops.
1 cake pop: 132 cal., 7g fat (3g sat. fat), 12mg chol., 96mg sod., 17g carb. (12g sugars, 1g fiber), 2g pro.

HOMEMADE TORTILLA CHIPS

I make these homemade tortilla chips to serve with roasted tomatillo salsa. They have a little heat from the chipotle. If you prefer things on the mild side, just sprinkle with salt after frying.
—David Ross, Spokane Valley, WA

TAKES: 25 MIN. • **MAKES:** 4 SERVINGS

- ¾ tsp. salt
- ½ tsp. ground chipotle pepper
- 10 corn tortillas (6 in.)
  Canola or corn oil for deep-fat frying

1. In a small bowl, mix salt and chipotle powder. Cut each tortilla into 4 wedges. In an electric skillet, heat 1 in. of oil to 350°. Fry tortilla wedges, several at a time, 2-3 minutes on each side or until golden brown. Drain on paper towels.
2. Transfer chips to a large bowl; sprinkle with salt mixture and gently toss to coat.

10 chips: 183 cal., 8g fat (1g sat. fat), 0 chol., 479mg sod., 27g carb. (1g sugars, 4g fiber), 3g pro.

TEST KITCHEN TIP
Try adding a squeeze of lime to your chips right before serving for extra flair.

FOOTBALL FEST EMPANADAS

Classic empanadas from South America are pastries stuffed with beef or chicken and then fried. Chicken goes well with black beans, corn and jalapenos in this baked version with a southwestern spin.
—Jane Whittaker, Pensacola, FL

PREP: 30 MIN. • **BAKE:** 10 MIN./BATCH
MAKES: 2 DOZEN

- 1 jar (16 oz.) black bean and corn salsa
- ½ cup frozen corn, thawed
- 2 jalapeno peppers, seeded and minced
- 3 Tbsp. minced fresh cilantro, divided
- 2 tsp. lime juice
- 1 pkg. (9 oz.) ready-to-use Southwestern chicken strips, chopped
- 2 pkg. (14.1 oz. each) refrigerated pie pastry
- 4 oz. quesadilla cheese, shredded or ¾ cup shredded Monterey Jack cheese
- 1 large egg, lightly beaten

1. In a large bowl, combine the salsa, corn, jalapenos, 2 Tbsp. cilantro and lime juice. In another bowl, combine the chicken, remaining cilantro and ½ cup salsa mixture; set aside. Reserve remaining salsa for serving.
2. Unroll a pastry sheet onto a lightly floured surface. Using a floured 4-in. round cookie cutter placed halfway on edge of pastry, cut out 48 football shapes (4x3 in. each). Repeat with the remaining dough, chilling and rerolling scraps as needed.
3. Transfer half the pastry cutouts to greased baking sheets. Place 1 Tbsp. chicken mixture in the center of each; top each with 1½ tsp. cheese. Brush edges of pastry with beaten egg. Top with remaining cutouts; press edges with a fork to seal. Cut slits in the tops to resemble football laces. Brush tops with beaten egg.
4. Bake at 450° for 8-12 minutes or until golden brown. Serve warm with reserved salsa mixture. Refrigerate any leftovers.

1 empanada with 1 Tbsp. salsa:
197 cal., 11g fat (5g sat. fat), 27mg chol., 291mg sod., 20g carb. (2g sugars, 1g fiber), 6g pro.

Antipasto Platter

ANTIPASTO

We entertain often, and antipasto is one of our favorite crowd-pleasers. Guests love having their choice of so many delicious nibbles, including pepperoni and cubes of provolone.

—Teri Lindquist, Gurnee, IL

PREP: 10 MIN. + CHILLING
MAKES: 16 SERVINGS (4 QT.)

1 jar (24 oz.) pepperoncini, drained
1 can (15 oz.) garbanzo beans or chickpeas, rinsed and drained
2 cups halved fresh mushrooms
2 cups halved cherry tomatoes
½ lb. provolone cheese, cubed
1 can (6 oz.) pitted ripe olives, drained
1 pkg. (3½ oz.) sliced pepperoni
1 bottle (8 oz.) Italian vinaigrette
   Lettuce leaves

1. In a large bowl, combine the pepperoncini, beans, mushrooms, tomatoes, cheese, olives and pepperoni. Pour vinaigrette over mixture; toss to coat.
2. Refrigerate at least 30 minutes or overnight. Arrange on a lettuce-lined platter. Serve with toothpicks.

1 cup: 178 cal., 13g fat (4g sat. fat), 15mg chol., 852mg sod., 8g carb. (2g sugars, 2g fiber), 6g pro.

SLEEPING BAG
BLONDIES, 72

Slumber
Party Board

HOW TO BUILD A...
SLUMBER PARTY BOARD

ITEMS TO INCLUDE
- Sleeping Bag Blondies
- Waffle cone
- Blue, pink and purple rock candy sticks
- Pink and purple lollipops

Purple Items
- Grape Gummy Watermelons
- Sour Punch Ropes Grape
- Grape Gummy Life Savers
- Mike & Ike Grape Candy
- Saltwater taffy
- Purple Chocolate Sixlets
- Purple foil-wrapped chocolate coins

Pink Items
- Gumballs
- Strawberry Sugared Gummy Bears
- Pink and white mints
- Cream puffs dipped in pink frosting
- Cotton candy

- Yogurt-covered pretzels, raspberry
- Twizlers Pull 'n' Peel, Cherry
- Starburst All Pink Strawberry
- Jelly beans
- Melty Mints

Blue Items
- Light blue M&Ms
- Blue foil-wrapped chocolates
- Gumballs
- Cotton candy
- Jelly beans
- Sour Punch Ropes Blue Raspberry
- Hershey's Kisses
- Saltwater taffy
- Berry Blue Gummy Bears
- Gummy Sharks
- Blue and white mints
- Blueberry Sugared Gummy Bears
- Wrapped hard candy

EASY ASSEMBLY
Step 1: Line Sleeping Bag Blondies across the board.

Step 2: Lay waffle cone on board; fill with rock candy sticks and lollipops.

Step 3: Fill top left corner of board with purple items, working down and around the brownies and around the sugar cone,

Step 4: Fill top right corner of board with pink items, working down and around the brownies and around the sugar cone,

Step 5: Working around brownies, fill remainder of the board with blue items.

Platter Pointer: Using the cotton candy, create "nests" to hold smaller items on the board.

SLEEPING BAG BLONDIES

Here's the only golden brownie recipe you'll ever need. These tasty pecan bars can be dressed up for slumber parties, camping trips and Girl Scout events.
—Sharon Bickett, Chester, SC

PREP: 20 MIN. • **BAKE:** 35 MIN. + COOLING
MAKES: 16 BLONDIE BROWNIES

- 1 cup butter, softened
- 1 cup sugar
- 1 cup packed brown sugar
- 2 large eggs, room temperature
- 2 tsp. vanilla extract
- 2 cups self-rising flour
- 2 cups chopped pecans, optional
- 1½ cups white frosting
  Brown, yellow, blue, pink and red gel food coloring
- 8 large marshmallows
- 16 miniature vanilla wafers

1. Preheat oven to 325°. Line a 13x9-in. baking pan with foil, letting the ends extend up sides; grease foil. In a large bowl, cream butter and sugars until light and fluffy, 5-7 minutes. Beat in eggs and vanilla. Gradually beat in flour. If desired, stir in pecans.
2. Spread mixture into prepared pan. Bake until a toothpick inserted in the center comes out clean, 35-40 minutes. Cool on a wire rack.
3. Lifting with foil, remove brownie from pan. Trim ½ in. off edges. Cut remaining brownie lengthwise in half; cut each half crosswise into 8 bars to make 16 sleeping bags.
4. Divide into 3 portions; tint with desired colors for the hair, face and sleeping bags. Transfer to small piping bags, reserving a small amount of each frosting to attach wafers. Cut small hole in a corner of each piping bag. Pipe each of the sleeping bag colors over brownies, smoothing frosting with an offset spatula. If desired, make quilted sleeping bag patterns by gently pressing edge of offset spatula into the frosting.

5. For pillows, cut marshmallows in half; place on end of brownies, cut side down. Pipe faces onto wafers using frosting or, if desired, draw faces with edible marker. Attach vanilla wafers to pillows; pipe hair around face. If desired, decorate with sprinkles.
Note: As a substitute for each cup of self-rising flour, place 1½ tsp. baking powder and ½ tsp. salt in a measuring cup. Add all-purpose flour to measure 1 cup.
1 brownie: 392 cal., 16g fat (9g sat. fat), 54mg chol., 352mg sod., 59g carb. (43g sugars, 0 fiber), 3g pro.

CUTE CREATIONS
Take the Sleeping Bag Blondies to another level when you gently score the frosting for quilt patterns. Add assorted sprinkles for fun, or give the tiny tots little toys with the addition of mini bear-shaped crackers and Gummy Bears.

In a blender, combine the milk, ice cream and strawberries; cover and process until smooth. Drizzle the inside of a chilled glass with fudge topping. Add ice cream mixture. Garnish with whipped cream and a cherry. Serve immediately.

1 serving: 302 cal., 6g fat (4g sat. fat), 29mg chol., 173mg sod., 56g carb. (42g sugars, 3g fiber), 11g pro.

SWEET-TOOTH POPCORN

I like to be creative with this recipe and add different things to make it festive for different occasions. Everyone says the sweet and salty taste is addictive.
—Daynna Puckett, Heavener, OK

PREP: 25 MIN. + STANDING • **MAKES:** 4 QT.

- 1 **pkg. (3.3 oz.) butter-flavored microwave popcorn**
- 1 **lb. white candy coating, chopped**
- 1 **cup peanut M&M's**
- 1 **cup Reese's pieces**
- 1 **cup salted cashews**
- 1 **cup pecan halves**

1. Microwave popcorn according to package directions. Place in a large bowl. In a microwave, melt candy coating; stir until smooth. Pour over popcorn and stir until coated. Combine the M&M's, Reese's pieces, cashews and pecans; stir into popcorn mixture.
2. Immediately spread onto waxed paper; let stand until set. Break into pieces. Store in an airtight container.
1 cup: 400 cal., 26g fat (12g sat. fat), 1mg chol., 145mg sod., 40g carb. (32g sugars, 2g fiber), 5g pro.

CUSTOMIZE YOUR BOARD

PARTY ANIMAL SNACK MIX

A colorful and fun snack mix doesn't get any easier than this. Mix and match with your sweet and salty favorites.
—*Taste of Home* Test Kitchen

TAKES: 5 MIN.

- **Air-popped popcorn**
- **Pastel miniature marshmallows**
- **Chocolate-covered raisins**
- **Salted peanuts**
- **Frosted and plain animal crackers**

Combine all ingredients. Store in an airtight container.
Note: Total yield and nutritional values for this recipe will change depending on the amounts of ingredients used.

SLUMBER PARTY SHAKE

I don't crave sweets that often, but one thing I can't resist is a creamy milkshake. This slimmed-down version tastes just like one straight off a Steak 'n Shake menu. One taste and you'll be slurping it down!
—*Taste of Home* Test Kitchen

TAKES: 10 MIN. • **MAKES:** 1 SERVING

- ⅔ **cup fat-free milk**
- ⅔ **cup reduced-fat strawberry ice cream**
- ⅔ **cup frozen unsweetened sliced strawberries**
- 1 **Tbsp. fat-free hot fudge ice cream topping**
- 2 **Tbsp. whipped cream in a can**
- 1 **maraschino cherry**

Sundae
Funday
Buffet

CHOCOLATE CHIP
STRAWBERRY
ICE CREAM, 75

HOW TO BUILD A...
SUNDAE FUNDAY BUFFET

I scream, you scream, we all scream for ice cream! Invite the gang to build their own sundae or "scooper"-duper cone with this icy idea. We piled cones and toppings on a three-tiered serving piece—but feel free to use whatever platters, bowls and boards you happen to have on hand.

ITEMS TO INCLUDE
- Sugar cones
- Cake cones
- Waffle cones
- Peanuts
- Milk chocolate English toffee pieces
- Star-shaped sprinkles
- Mini marshmallows
- Jimmies
- Shredded coconut
- Maraschino cherries
- Fudge sauce
- Chocolate Chip Strawberry Ice Cream

EASY ASSEMBLY

Step 1: Pile ice cream cones onto a tray (or stand them in glasses).

Step 2: Spoon peanuts, toffee pieces, sprinkles, marshmallows, jimmies and coconut into small bowls. Set bowls on tray with jar of cherries.

Step 3: Set out the fudge sauce and a container of Chocolate Chip Strawberry Ice Cream.

Step 4: Add spoons, bowls, ice cream scoops and serving utensils.

Platter Pointer: You can add a few store-bought ice cream flavors to give your guests additional choices at the buffet. Don't forget whipped cream, sliced bananas, strawberries or other toppings you think guests might enjoy.

CHOCOLATE CHIP STRAWBERRY ICE CREAM

My husband and I have a favorite DQ Blizzard Treat that we order every time, so I came up with my own version of it. Be sure to chill the mixture completely before adding it to the ice cream maker.
—Sandy Martin, Elizabethtown, PA

PREP: 25 MIN. + COOLING
PROCESS: 15 MIN. + FREEZING
MAKES: 1½ QT.

- 1⅔ cups sugar
- 5 Tbsp. cornstarch, divided
- 4 cups 2% milk
- 2 large egg yolks
- 1⅓ cups heavy whipping cream
- ⅔ cup half-and-half cream
- 3 tsp. vanilla extract
- ¼ cup light corn syrup
- 3 cups fresh strawberries, hulled
- 1 dark chocolate candy bar (8 oz.), finely chopped
  Optional: Whipped cream and maraschino cherries

1. In a large heavy saucepan, whisk sugar and 4 Tbsp. cornstarch until blended; whisk in milk until smooth. Bring to a boil, stirring constantly; cook and stir 1-2 minutes or until thickened. Reduce heat to low. In a small bowl, whisk a small amount of hot mixture into egg yolks; return all to the pan, whisking constantly. Cook over low heat, stirring constantly, until mixture thickens and a thermometer reads 160°, 2-3 minutes. Immediately remove from heat.

2. Quickly transfer to a large bowl; place bowl in a pan of ice water. Stir gently and occasionally for 2 minutes. Stir in cream, half-and-half and vanilla. Press plastic wrap onto surface of custard. Refrigerate several hours or overnight.

3. Fill cylinder of ice cream maker two-thirds full; freeze according to manufacturer's directions.

4. Meanwhile, place remaining 1 Tbsp. cornstarch in a large skillet. Whisk in the corn syrup until smooth; add the strawberries. Bring mixture to a boil over medium heat; cook and stir until thickened, about 2 minutes. Mash strawberries; cool.

5. During last 5 minutes of processing, add strawberry mixture and chocolate to the ice cream maker. Transfer ice cream to freezer containers, allowing enough headspace for expansion. Freeze at least 4 hours or until firm. If desired, serve with whipped cream and maraschino cherries.
½ cup: 397 cal., 19g fat (12g sat. fat), 76mg chol., 59mg sod., 56g carb. (50g sugars, 2g fiber), 6g pro.

CUSTOMIZE YOUR BOARD

Use these recipes to create your own Sundae Funday Buffet.

EASY RHUBARB SAUCE

Celebrate spring with the sweet-tart taste of rhubarb in this simple sauce. I enjoy it on toast, English muffins and pancakes, but it's equally decadent drizzled on pound cake or ice cream.
—Jackie Hutshing, Sonoma, CA

TAKES: 20 MIN. • **MAKES:** 1¼ CUPS

- ⅓ cup sugar
- ¼ cup water
- 2¼ cups sliced fresh or frozen rhubarb
- 1 tsp. grated lemon zest
- ⅛ tsp. ground nutmeg
  Pound cake or vanilla ice cream

1. In a small saucepan, bring sugar and water to a boil. Add rhubarb; cook and stir 5-10 minutes or until the rhubarb is tender and the mixture is slightly thickened. Remove from heat; stir in the lemon zest and nutmeg.
2. Serve the sauce either warm or chilled over pound cake or ice cream. Refrigerate any leftovers.
Note: If using frozen rhubarb, measure rhubarb while still frozen, then thaw completely. Drain in a colander but do not press liquid out.
¼ cup: 64 cal., 0 fat (0 sat. fat), 0 chol., 2mg sod., 16g carb. (14g sugars, 1g fiber), 1g pro.

EASY STRAWBERRY CHEESECAKE ICE CREAM

When I got my ice cream maker, a friend shared her dreamy freezy cheesecake recipe with me.
—Joan Hallford, North Richland Hills, TX

PREP: 15 MIN.
PROCESS: 25 MIN. + FREEZING
MAKES: 1½ QT.

- 1 cup half-and-half cream
- 1 Tbsp. vanilla extract
- 2 tsp. grated lemon zest
- 2 tsp. lemon juice
- 1 cup sugar
- 1 pkg. (8 oz.) cream cheese, cubed and softened
- 1 cup heavy whipping cream
- 1½ cups fresh strawberries
  Crushed graham crackers, optional

1. Place the first 6 ingredients in a blender; cover and blend until smooth. Add whipping cream; cover and blend until combined. Transfer mixture to a large bowl.
2. Add strawberries to blender; cover and blend until pureed. Stir into the cream mixture.
3. Fill cylinder of ice cream maker no more than two-thirds full; freeze mixture according to manufacturer's directions. (Refrigerate any remaining mixture until ready to freeze.)
4. Transfer the ice cream to freezer containers, allowing headspace for expansion. Freeze 4-6 hours or until firm. If desired, serve with crushed graham crackers and additional fresh strawberries, sliced.
½ cup: 234 cal., 16g fat (10g sat. fat), 58mg chol., 87mg sod., 20g carb. (20g sugars, 0 fiber), 2g pro.

RICH HOT FUDGE SAUCE

I've been making this scrumptious topping since the early 1980s. It always turns out smooth and yummy, and it satisfies any chocoholic's cravings.
—Carol Hunihan, Ann Arbor, MI

TAKES: 30 MIN. • **MAKES:** 3½ CUPS

- ¾ cup butter, cubed
- 1 cup heavy whipping cream
- 1⅓ cups packed brown sugar
- ¼ cup sugar
- 1 cup baking cocoa
- ½ cup plus 2 Tbsp. light corn syrup
  Pinch salt
- 2 oz. unsweetened chocolate, chopped
- 1 Tbsp. vanilla extract
- 1 to 2 tsp. rum extract

1. Place butter and cream in a heavy saucepan; cook and stir over medium-low heat until butter is melted. Add sugars; cook and stir until dissolved, 3-4 minutes.
2. Add cocoa, corn syrup and salt; cook and stir until blended, about 3 minutes. Stir in chopped chocolate until melted. Reduce heat to low; cook and stir until mixture reaches the desired thickness, 10-15 minutes.
3. Remove from heat; stir in extracts. Serve warm. Refrigerate leftovers.
2 Tbsp.: 166 cal., 9g fat (6g sat. fat), 25mg chol., 103mg sod., 21g carb. (18g sugars, 1g fiber), 1g pro.

CREAMY LAYERED BLUEBERRY ICE POPS

These delicious ice pops can be made with other berries, too, such as raspberries or blackberries. The rosemary sprig and lemon zest add layers of flavor.
—Gloria Bradley, Naperville, IL

PREP: 25 MIN. + FREEZING
COOK: 10 MIN. + COOLING
MAKES: 10 POPS

- ⅓ cup agave nectar
- ¼ cup water
- 1 fresh rosemary sprig
- 1 lemon zest strip (2 in.)
- 1 Tbsp. lemon juice
- 2 cups fresh or frozen blueberries
- 2 Tbsp. sugar
- 2¼ cups frozen whipped topping, thawed
- 10 freezer pop molds or 10 paper cups (3 oz. each) and wooden pop sticks

1. For lemon syrup, place the first 4 ingredients in a small saucepan; bring to a boil, stirring occasionally. Remove from heat; let stand, covered, 10 minutes. Remove rosemary and the lemon zest. Stir in the lemon juice; cool syrup completely.
2. Place the blueberries and sugar in another saucepan; cook and stir over medium heat 5-7 minutes or until the berries pop. Cool completely.
3. Add whipped topping to the lemon syrup; whisk to blend. Transfer half the mixture to a pastry bag. Pipe into molds. Add a layer of blueberries. Pipe the remaining whipped topping mixture over berries. Close molds with holders. If using paper cups, top with foil and insert sticks through foil.
4. Freeze until firm, about 4 hours. To serve, dip freezer pop molds briefly in warm water before removing pops.
1 pop: 104 cal., 3g fat (3g sat. fat), 0 chol., 0 sod., 19g carb. (18g sugars, 1g fiber), 0 pro.
Diabetic exchanges: 1 starch, ½ fat.

> **TEST KITCHEN TIP**
> The flavor of lime would be great in this recipe, too. Just substitute equal parts lime zest and juice for the lemon.

Ultimate Charcuterie Board

SPARKLING RED
WINE SANGRIA, 80

ANTIPASTO
KABOBS, 81

MARINATED
MOZZARELLA & TOMATO
APPETIZERS, 80

THE BEST
HUMMUS, 81

HOW TO BUILD AN...
ULTIMATE CHARCUTERIE BOARD

Cheese, nuts, meats, dip, crackers, fruit, veggies...this board has it all!

ITEMS TO INCLUDE
- Marinated Mozzarella & Tomato Appetizers
- The Best Hummus
- Pistachios
- Marcona almonds
- Pickled red onions
- Cornichons
- Blue cheese
- Goat cheese
- Antipasto Kabobs
- Thin breadsticks
- Prosciutto-wrapped mozzarella
- Cheddar cheese, sliced
- Green grapes
- Purple grapes
- Watermelon radish, thinly sliced
- Radishes, halved

- Carrots, peeled
- Cucumbers, cut into wedges
- Mini sweet bell peppers, sliced
- Assorted crackers
- Dried apricots
- Cashews
- Sparkling Red Wine Sangria

EASY ASSEMBLY

Step 1: Put Marinated Mozzarella & Tomato Appetizers, The Best Hummus, pistachios and almonds in small bowls. Drain pickled red onions and cornichons and combine in another small bowl. Scatter all bowls around a large board or platter.

Step 2: Set blue cheese and goat cheese on the board.

Step 3: Add groupings of Antipasto Kabobs, breadsticks and prosciutto-wrapped mozzarella to the board.

Step 4: Add cheddar and bunches of grapes to the board.

Step 5: Fill in gaps with vegetables, crackers, apricots and cashews.

Step 6: Add serving utensils.

Step 7: Serve with Sparkling Red Wine Sangria.

SPARKLING RED WINE SANGRIA

Sangria is a Spanish drink of wine mixed with fruit juice, sherry or brandy, cut fruit and spices. It's best to mix up the sangria and let it sit for an hour or more before serving, which allows the flavors of the fruit and wine to blend together.
—*Taste of Home* Test Kitchen

TAKES: 5 MIN. • **MAKES:** 6 SERVINGS

- 1 bottle (750 ml) dry red wine
- 1 cup sugar
- ½ cup orange liqueur
- ½ cup brandy
- 3 cups lemon-lime soda
- 1 cup sliced fresh strawberries
- 1 cup fresh blueberries
- 1 cup fresh raspberries
- 1 large navel orange, sliced

In a pitcher, stir together the wine, sugar, orange liqueur and brandy until the sugar dissolves. Stir in soda, berries and orange slices. Chill until ready to serve.

1 cup: 448 cal., 0 fat (0 sat. fat), 0 chol., 18mg sod., 69g carb. (61g sugars, 3g fiber), 1g pro.

MARINATED MOZZARELLA & TOMATO APPETIZERS

This party hit was inspired by a dish I ate at a restaurant. The combination of flavors is simply sensational. It's best served chilled and should marinate for a few days—the longer the better.
—Mary Ann Lee, Clifton Park, NY

PREP: 15 MIN. + MARINATING
BAKE: 5 MIN. • **MAKES:** 16 SERVINGS

- ½ cup Italian salad dressing
- 2 Tbsp. minced fresh basil
- 2 Tbsp. minced fresh chives
- ½ tsp. coarsely ground pepper
- 2 cartons (8 oz. each) miniature fresh mozzarella cheese balls, drained
- 2 cups cherry tomatoes
- 12 slices French bread baguette (½ in. thick), cut into quarters
- 2 tsp. olive oil
- ⅛ tsp. salt

1. Preheat oven to 450°. Combine salad dressing, basil, chives and pepper. Add the cheese and tomatoes; toss to coat. Refrigerate, covered, at least 3 hours to let flavors blend.
2. Meanwhile, toss baguette pieces with oil and salt; arrange on a baking sheet. Bake until toasted, 4-5 minutes. Cool completely. Just before serving, add toasted bread to cheese mixture; toss to combine. If desired, thread tomatoes, cheese and bread onto skewers for serving.

¼ cup: 119 cal., 8g fat (4g sat. fat), 22mg chol., 171mg sod., 5g carb. (2g sugars, 0 fiber), 6g pro.

ANTIPASTO KABOBS

My husband and I met at a cooking class. We have loved creating menus and entertaining ever since. These make-ahead skewers are a favorite.
—Denise Hazen, Cincinnati, OH

PREP: 35 MIN. + MARINATING
MAKES: 40 KABOBS

- 1 pkg. (9 oz.) refrigerated cheese tortellini
- 40 pimiento-stuffed olives
- 40 large pitted ripe olives
- ¾ cup Italian salad dressing
- 40 thin slices pepperoni
- 20 thin slices hard salami, halved

1. Cook tortellini according to package directions. Drain; rinse in cold water. In a large bowl, combine tortellini, olives and salad dressing. Toss to coat; cover and refrigerate 4 hours or overnight.
2. Drain the mixture, discarding the marinade. For each appetizer, thread a stuffed olive, a folded pepperoni slice, a tortellini, a folded salami piece and a ripe olive onto a skewer.
1 kabob: 66 cal., 5g fat (1g sat. fat), 9mg chol., 315mg sod., 4g carb. (0 sugars, 0 fiber), 2g pro.

THE BEST HUMMUS

Hummus is my go-to appetizer whenever I need something easy and impressive. Over the years I've picked up a number of tricks that make this the best hummus you'll ever have.
—James Schend, Pleasant Prairie, WI

PREP: 25 MIN. + CHILLING • **COOK:** 20 MIN.
MAKES: 1½ CUPS

- 1 can (15 oz.) garbanzo beans or chickpeas, rinsed and drained
- ½ tsp. baking soda
- ¼ cup fresh lemon juice
- 1 Tbsp. minced garlic
- ½ tsp. kosher salt
- ½ tsp. ground cumin
- ½ cup tahini
- 2 Tbsp. extra virgin olive oil
- ¼ cup cold water
  Optional: Roasted garbanzo beans, toasted sesame seeds, ground sumac

1. Place garbanzo beans in a large saucepan; add water to cover by 1 in. Gently rub beans together to loosen outer skins. Pour off the water and any skins that are floating. Repeat 2-3 times until no skins float to the surface; drain. Return to saucepan; add baking soda and enough water to cover by 1 in. Bring to a boil; reduce heat. Simmer, uncovered, until beans are very tender and just starting to fall apart, 20-25 minutes.
2. Meanwhile, in a blender, process the lemon juice, garlic and salt until almost a paste. Let stand 10 minutes. Strain, discarding solids. Stir in cumin.
3. In a small bowl, stir together tahini and olive oil.
4. Drain beans; add to blender. Add cold water. Cover and process until completely smooth. Add the lemon mixture; process. With the blender running, slowly add tahini mixture, scraping sides as needed. Adjust seasoning with additional salt and cumin if desired.
5. Transfer to a serving bowl; cover and refrigerate at least 30 minutes. If desired, top with additional olive oil and assorted toppings.
¼ cup: 250 cal., 19g fat (3g sat. fat), 0 chol., 361mg sod., 15g carb. (2g sugars, 5g fiber), 7g pro.

PLATTER POINTER
Hummus is a great addition to boards because it works well with a wide assortment of veggies as well as pita bread, toasted pita chips, crackers, breadsticks and nuts.

Fruit & Cheese Board

CREAM CHEESE FRUIT DIP, 83

HOW TO BUILD A...
FRUIT & CHEESE BOARD

ITEMS TO INCLUDE
- Cream Cheese Fruit Dip
- Honey
- Brie cheese
- Medium mango, halved and scored
- Large kiwifruit, peeled, halved and thinly sliced
- Seedless watermelon, sliced
- Seedless red grapes
- Fresh or dried figs, halved
- Small navel oranges, thinly sliced
- Dried banana chips
- Unblanched almonds
- Blueberries
- Blackberries
- Strawberries, halved

EASY ASSEMBLY

Step 1: Spoon dip into a small serving bowl. Set bowl on board or platter with jar of honey and Brie.

Step 2: Add mango halves to board.

Step 3: Pile kiwi slices on the board in a circle as shown at left.

Step 4: Shingle watermelon slices in a grouping on the board.

Step 5: Fill in gaps on board with remaining items.

CREAM CHEESE FRUIT DIP
This no-fuss fruit dip goes well with strawberries, grapes and kiwi. You can also serve on a platter during Christmas with red and green apple slices. .
—Sheryl Renner, El Paso, TX

TAKES: 5 MIN. • **MAKES:** 1 CUP

- 1   pkg. (8 oz.) cream cheese, softened
- ¾   cup packed brown sugar
- 1   tsp. vanilla extract
    Assorted fresh fruit

In a small mixing bowl, beat cream cheese, brown sugar and vanilla until smooth. Serve with fresh fruit for dipping. Refrigerate leftovers.
2 Tbsp.: 178 cal., 10g fat (6g sat. fat), 31mg chol., 92mg sod., 21g carb. (21g sugars, 0 fiber), 2g pro.

PLATTER POINTERS

How do I store leftovers from this fruit charcuterie board?
Fresh fruit and cheese can be thrown into airtight containers or zip-top bags and stored in the refrigerator. Keep in mind that your charcuterie board's fixings will hold better if they've been sitting out for less than an hour. If it's been longer than that, you may want to toss them. You can always put out less food on your board initially, then add to it if you're worried about food waste.

What other types of fruit and cheese can I add to this charcuterie board?
Have fun playing around with your favorite types of cheese and fruit. For cheese, try goat or gouda. As for fruit, consider apricots, pears, apples or even star fruit.

FIRESIDE GLOGG, 87

HOT BUTTERED RUM, 86

SAUSAGE WONTON STARS, 86

LEMONY BACON–ARTICHOKE DIP, 85

SMOKED GOUDA & ROAST BEEF PINWHEELS, 87

Finger Food
Platter

HOW TO BUILD A...
FINGER FOOD PLATTER

Serve a warm-appetizer buffet on an extra-large board for snack grazing at its best! Hearty, comforting and bursting with savory goodness, these bites go together perfectly. Best of all, serving everything on a very large platter makes cleanup a snap!

ITEMS TO INCLUDE
- Lemony-Bacon Artichoke Dip
- Smoked Gouda & Roast Beef Pinwheels
- Sausage Wonton Stars
- Carrots
- Cucumbers, cut into wedges
- Hot Buttered Rum
- Fireside Glogg

EASY ASSEMBLY

Step 1: Set artichoke dip on a heat-resistant platter.

Step 2: Set pinwheels and wonton stars on platter.

Step 3: Add vegetables to platter.

Step 4: Serve with Hot Buttered Rum and Fireside Glogg.

Platter Pointer: If serving the dip straight from the oven, be sure your platter can handle the heat of the baking dish or set a towel or hot pad beneath the dish.

LEMONY BACON-ARTICHOKE DIP

Move over, spinach artichoke dip—bacon adds much more flavor. You might want to double this fabulous recipe because there are never any leftovers.
—Heidi Jobe, Carrollton, GA

PREP: 20 MIN. • **BAKE:** 25 MIN.
MAKES: 12 SERVINGS (3 CUPS)

5	thick-sliced bacon strips, chopped
1	can (14 oz.) water-packed quartered artichoke hearts, drained and chopped
2	garlic cloves, minced
2	pkg. (8 oz. each) reduced-fat cream cheese
⅓	cup sour cream
½	tsp. onion salt
¼	tsp. salt
⅛	tsp. pepper
2	Tbsp. lemon juice
½	cup grated Parmesan cheese Pita bread wedges, toasted

1. Preheat oven to 400°. In a large skillet, cook the bacon over medium heat until crisp, stirring occasionally. Remove with a slotted spoon; drain on paper towels. Discard drippings, reserving 2 tsp. in pan. Add artichoke hearts and garlic to drippings; cook and stir 1 minute.

2. In a large bowl, beat cream cheese, sour cream, onion salt, salt and pepper until smooth. Beat in the lemon juice. Fold in artichoke mixture and half of the bacon.

3. Transfer to a greased 2-qt. baking dish. Sprinkle with remaining bacon; top with Parmesan cheese. Bake, uncovered, until golden brown, 25-30 minutes. Serve with toasted pita wedges.

¼ cup: 166 cal., 13g fat (8g sat. fat), 39mg chol., 535mg sod., 4g carb. (2g sugars, 0 fiber), 8g pro.

HOT BUTTERED RUM

I received this recipe from a friend more than 30 years ago, and I think of her every winter when I stir up a batch of this delightful mix. It keeps well in the freezer.
—Joyce Moynihan, Lakeville, MN

TAKES: 15 MIN.
MAKES: 7 SERVINGS (3½ CUPS MIX)

- 1   cup butter, softened
- ½   cup confectioners' sugar
- ½   cup packed brown sugar
- 2   cups vanilla ice cream, softened
- 1   tsp. ground cinnamon
- 1   tsp. ground nutmeg

EACH SERVING

- ½   cup boiling water
- 1   to 3 Tbsp. rum

1. In a large bowl, cream butter and sugars until light and fluffy. Beat in the ice cream, cinnamon and nutmeg. Cover and store in the freezer.
2. For each serving, place ½ cup butter mixture in a mug; add boiling water and stir to dissolve. Stir in rum.
1 cup: 428 cal., 30g fat (19g sat. fat), 85mg chol., 221mg sod., 33g carb. (30g sugars, 0 fiber), 2g pro.

SAUSAGE WONTON STARS

These fancy-looking appetizers are ideal when entertaining large groups. The cute crunchy cups are stuffed with a cheesy pork sausage filling that kids of all ages enjoy. We keep a few in the freezer so we can easily reheat them for movie nights and late-night snacking.
—Mary Thomas, North Lewisburg, OH

TAKES: 30 MIN. • **MAKES:** 4 DOZEN

- 1   pkg. (12 oz.) wonton wrappers
- 1   lb. bulk pork sausage
- 2   cups shredded Colby cheese
- ½   medium green pepper, chopped
- ½   medium sweet red pepper, chopped
- 2   bunches green onions, sliced
- ½   cup ranch salad dressing

1. Preheat oven to 350°. Lightly press wonton wrappers onto the bottoms and up the sides of greased miniature muffin cups. Bake until edges are browned, about 5 minutes.
2. In a large skillet, cook sausage over medium heat until no longer pink, breaking into crumbles; drain. Stir in cheese, peppers, onions and salad dressing. Spoon a rounded Tbsp. into each wonton cup. Bake until heated through, 6-7 minutes.
1 appetizer: 69 cal., 5g fat (2g sat. fat), 10mg chol., 143mg sod., 4g carb. (0 sugars, 0 fiber), 3g pro.

SMOKED GOUDA & ROAST BEEF PINWHEELS

Our local deli makes terrific roast beef sandwiches. This pinwheel appetizer re-creates the taste. My family says the pinwheels have so many flavors for such a little treat.
—Pamela Shank, Parkersburg, WV

PREP: 20 MIN. • **BAKE:** 15 MIN./BATCH
MAKES: 4 DOZEN

- ¾ lb. sliced deli roast beef, finely chopped
- 1 pkg. (10 oz.) frozen chopped spinach, thawed and squeezed dry
- 1 pkg. (6½ oz.) garlic-herb spreadable cheese
- 1 cup shredded smoked Gouda cheese
- ¼ cup finely chopped red onion
- 2 tubes (8 oz. each) refrigerated crescent rolls

1. Preheat oven to 375°. In a small bowl, mix the first 5 ingredients until blended. On a lightly floured surface, unroll 1 tube of crescent dough into 1 long rectangle; press perforations to seal.
2. Spread half the roast beef mixture over dough. Roll up jelly-roll style, starting with a long side; pinch seam to seal. Using a serrated knife, cut roll crosswise into twenty-four ½-in. slices. Place on parchment-lined baking sheets, cut side down. Repeat with remaining crescent dough and roast beef mixture.
3. Bake until golden brown, roughly 12-14 minutes. Serve warm.

1 appetizer: 71 cal., 5g fat (2g sat. fat), 11mg chol., 160mg sod., 4g carb. (1g sugars, 0 fiber), 3g pro.

FIRESIDE GLOGG

An aromatic blend of spices flavor this superb wine-based beverage. It is served warmed, and its sweet fruity taste will warm you to your toes. This traditional Scandinavian recipe is served during the holidays.
—Sue Brown, West Bend, WI

PREP: 25 MIN. • **COOK:** 40 MIN.
MAKES: 8 SERVINGS (¾ CUP EACH)

- 4 cups port wine or apple cider, divided
- 3 cups fresh or frozen cranberries, thawed
- ¼ cup packed brown sugar
- 4 orange peel strips (3 in.)
- 3 cinnamon sticks (3 in.)
- 5 slices fresh peeled gingerroot
- 5 cardamom pods
- 5 whole cloves
- 4 cups apple cider or juice
- ½ cup blanched almonds
- ½ cup raisins

1. In a large saucepan, combine 3 cups wine, cranberries, brown sugar, orange peel, cinnamon, ginger, cardamom and cloves. Cook over medium heat until berries pop, about 15 minutes. Mash slightly and cook 10 minutes longer.
2. Strain and discard pulp, orange peel and spices. Return mixture to pan; stir in cider, almonds, raisins and remaining 1 cup wine. Bring to a boil. Reduce heat; simmer, uncovered, for 15 minutes. Serve warm.

¾ cup: 229 cal., 5g fat (0 sat. fat), 0 chol., 22mg sod., 39g carb. (29g sugars, 3g fiber), 2g pro.

Cozy
Night In

PARMESAN-COATED BRIE

This is such a wonderful appetizer! Your guests will be impressed. A golden exterior gives way to warm, melty cheese, making this perfect for a board that includes sliced French bread and crackers.
—Karen Grant, Tulare, CA

TAKES: 10 MIN. • **MAKES:** 8 SERVINGS

- 1 large egg
- 1 Tbsp. water
- ½ cup seasoned bread crumbs
- ¼ cup grated Parmesan cheese
- 1 round (8 oz.) Brie cheese or Brie cheese with herbs
- ¼ cup canola oil
   Assorted crackers and/or fresh fruit

1. In a shallow bowl, combine the egg and water. In another bowl, combine bread crumbs and Parmesan cheese. Dip the Brie in egg mixture, turning to coat all sides; coat with crumb mixture. Repeat.
2. In a small skillet, cook the Brie in oil over medium heat until golden brown, about 2 minutes on each side. Serve with crackers and/or fresh fruit.
2 Tbsp.: 202 cal., 16g fat (6g sat. fat), 57mg chol., 333mg sod., 5g carb. (0 sugars, 0 fiber), 9g pro.

IT'S WINE O'CLOCK

Invite friends for a casual yet comfy evening with this satisfying brie, fruit and cracker board. Pair the tasty appetizer with a sparkling rose wine or another light, fruity red such as Beaujolais.

CUSTOMIZE YOUR BOARD

PECANS DIABLO

Spices showcase pecans in a new light. This recipe is a zesty snack for any party, but the heat of the pecans well suits the cool, crisp evenings that come with fall and winter.
—Taste of Home Test Kitchen

TAKES: 25 MIN. • **MAKES:** 5 CUPS

- ¼ cup butter, melted
- ¾ tsp. dried rosemary, crushed
- ¼ to ½ tsp. cayenne pepper
- ¼ tsp. dried basil
- 5 cups pecan halves
- 2 tsp. kosher salt

1. In a large bowl, combine the butter, rosemary, cayenne and basil. Add pecans and toss to coat. Spread in a single layer in a 15x10x1-in. baking pan. Sprinkle with salt.
2. Bake, uncovered, at 325° until the pecans are crisp, 17-20 minutes, stirring occasionally. Cool completely. Store in an airtight container.
⅓ cup: 276 cal., 29g fat (4g sat. fat), 8mg chol., 272mg sod., 5g carb. (1g sugars, 3g fiber), 3g pro.

Easily Impressive Spread

REFRESHING
BERRY WINE, 92

SHRIMP
COCKTAIL, 93

CRAB WONTON
CUPS, 91

SIDECAR, 93

CHEESE-STUFFED
CHERRY TOMATOES, 94

PINEAPPLE
CHEESE BALL, 92

MARINATED SAUSAGE
KABOBS, 94

HOW TO BUILD AN...
EASILY IMPRESSIVE SPREAD

When you want to wow the crowd, give them this incredible spread. Whether you create one board or several, as we did, it's sure to impress.

ITEMS TO INCLUDE
- Pineapple Cheese Ball
- Cheese-Stuffed Cherry Tomatoes
- Marinated Sausage Kabobs
- Assorted sliced vegetables
- Crab Wonton Cups
- Shrimp Cocktail
- Lemon wedges
- Sidecar
- Refreshing Berry Wine

EASY ASSEMBLY

Step 1: Set the Pineapple Cheese Ball on a board.

Step 2: Gently place Cheese-Stuffed Cherry Tomatoes in a serving bowl. Set bowl on the board.

Step 3: Stack a grouping of Marinated Sausage Kabobs on the board.

Step 4: Fill in gaps on board with sliced vegetables.

Step 5: Fill one level of a tiered serving platter with Crab Wonton Cups.

Step 6: Prepare Shrimp Cocktail according to directions. Fill shot glasses or small cups with 1-2 Tbsp. sauce. Top each with 1 shrimp. Place on top tier of serving platter. Garnish tier with lemon wedges.

Step 7: Serve with Sidecar drinks and Refreshing Berry Wine

CRAB WONTON CUPS

Making appetizers with wonton wrappers couldn't be quicker or easier. I just press them into miniature muffin cups, bake, add a creamy seafood mixture and pop them in the oven one more time for a batch of hot and crispy finger food.
—Connie McDowell, Greenwood, DE

TAKES: 30 MIN. • **MAKES:** 32 APPETIZERS

- 32 **wonton wrappers**
  Cooking spray
- 1 **pkg. (8 oz.) cream cheese, softened**
- ½ **cup heavy whipping cream**
- 1 **large egg**
- 1 **Tbsp. Dijon mustard**
- 1 **tsp. Worcestershire sauce**
- 5 **drops hot pepper sauce**
- 1 **cup lump crabmeat, drained**
- ¼ **cup thinly sliced green onions**
- ¼ **cup finely chopped sweet red pepper**
- 1 **cup grated Parmesan cheese**
  Minced chives, optional

1. Preheat oven to 350°. Press wonton wrappers into miniature muffin cups coated with cooking spray. Spritz wrappers with cooking spray. Bake until lightly browned, 8-9 minutes.
2. Meanwhile, in a small bowl, beat cream cheese, cream, egg, mustard, Worcestershire sauce and hot pepper sauce until smooth. Stir in crab, green onions and red pepper. Gently spoon mixture into wonton cups. Sprinkle with Parmesan cheese.
3. Bake until filling is heated through, 10-12 minutes. Serve warm. Garnish cups with minced chives if desired. Refrigerate leftovers.
1 wonton cup: 77 cal., 5g fat (3g sat. fat), 26mg chol., 153mg sod., 5g carb. (0 sugars, 0 fiber), 3g pro.

REFRESHING BERRY WINE

This is an easy way to dress up wine for a party. Other fruit, such as watermelon balls or sliced peaches, can be used in place of the strawberry slices.
—Laura Wilhelm, West Hollywood, CA

PREP: 35 MIN. + CHILLING
MAKES: 8 SERVINGS

1¼ cups frozen unsweetened raspberries
1 cup white grape juice
1 bottle (750 ml) dry rosé wine
2 cups sliced fresh strawberries
Ice cubes
Fresh mint or rosemary sprigs

In a saucepan, combine raspberries and grape juice. Bring to a boil; reduce heat. Cook and stir over medium heat until liquid is almost evaporated, about 30 minutes. Remove from the heat. Press through a fine-mesh strainer into a bowl; discard seeds. Transfer puree to a pitcher. Stir in wine and strawberries. Refrigerate, covered, until chilled. Serve with ice; garnish with mint or rosemary sprigs.

¾ cup: 122 cal., 0 fat (0 sat. fat), 0 chol., 3mg sod., 14g carb. (7g sugars, 1g fiber), 0 pro.

PINEAPPLE CHEESE BALL

Pineapple lends a fruity tang to this tasty appetizer. Instead of one large cheese ball, you could make two smaller ones—one to set on a board and one to enjoy the day after the party!
—Anne Halfhill, Sunbury, OH

PREP: 20 MIN. + CHILLING
MAKES: 1 CHEESE BALL (3 CUPS)

2 pkg. (8 oz. each) cream cheese, softened
1 can (8 oz.) unsweetened crushed pineapple, drained
¼ cup finely chopped green pepper
2 Tbsp. finely chopped onion
2 tsp. seasoned salt
1½ cups finely chopped walnuts
Optional: Assorted crackers and fresh vegetables

In a small bowl, beat cream cheese, pineapple, green pepper, onion and seasoned salt until blended. Cover and refrigerate 30 minutes. Shape into a ball (mixture will be soft); coat in walnuts. Cover and refrigerate overnight. Serve with crackers and vegetables if desired.

2 Tbsp: 87 calories, 8g fat (2g saturated fat), 10mg cholesterol, 155mg sodium, 3g carbohydrate (1g sugars, 1g fiber), 3g protein.

SOFTEN CREAM CHEESE QUICKLY

In a hurry? To soften cream cheese fast, cut an unwrapped block into 1-in. cubes. This creates more exposed surface area, allowing room-temperature air to soften the cold cream cheese more quickly. Another easy trick is to place the sealed foil package in a bowl of warm water for about 20 minutes. Or simply pop a block of unwrapped cream cheese in the microwave for 15 seconds. Check for softness intermittently and reheat in 10-second increments until the cream cheese reaches the desired consistency.

SIDECAR

Welcome guests with this tart citrus delight. They'll adore the sunny drink.
—*Taste of Home* Test Kitchen

TAKES: 5 MIN. • **MAKES:** 1 SERVING

> Ice cubes
> 1 oz. brandy
> ⅔ oz. (4 tsp.) Triple Sec
> 1½ to 3 tsp. lemon juice
> GARNISH
> Lemon twist

1. Fill a shaker three-fourths full of ice. Add the brandy, Triple Sec and lemon juice. Cover and shake for 15-20 seconds or until condensation forms on outside of shaker. Strain into a chilled cocktail glass. Garnish with lemon twist.

1 sidecar: 137 cal., 0 fat (0 sat. fat), 0 chol., 2mg sod., 10g carb. (8g sugars, 0 fiber), 0 pro.

GREAT GARNISH
To make a thin citrus spiral to garnish a cocktail, the best tool to use is a channel knife, which cuts a thin rope from the peel. Roll the cut peel into a twist or gently wrap the peel around a straw to create a twist shape. Use a paring knife to make a wider twist.

SHRIMP COCKTAIL

During the '60s, shrimp cocktail was one of the most popular party foods around. And it's still a crowd favorite. It's the one appetizer that I serve for every special occasion as well as for "munchie" meals.
—Peggy Allen, Pasadena, CA

PREP: 30 MIN. + CHILLING
MAKES: ABOUT 6 DOZEN (1¼ CUPS SAUCE)

> 3 qt. water
> 1 small onion, sliced
> ½ medium lemon, sliced
> 2 sprigs fresh parsley
> 1 Tbsp. salt
> 5 whole peppercorns
> 1 bay leaf
> ¼ tsp. dried thyme
> 3 lbs. uncooked large shrimp, peeled and deveined (tails on)
> SAUCE
> 1 cup chili sauce
> 2 Tbsp. lemon juice
> 2 Tbsp. prepared horseradish
> 4 tsp. Worcestershire sauce
> ½ tsp. salt
> Dash cayenne pepper
> Lemon wedges, optional

1. In a Dutch oven, combine the first 8 ingredients; bring to a boil. Add shrimp. Reduce heat and simmer, uncovered, until shrimp turn pink, 4-5 minutes.
2. Drain shrimp; immediately rinse in cold water. Refrigerate until cold, 2-3 hours. In a small bowl, combine the sauce ingredients. Refrigerate sauce until serving.
3. Arrange shrimp on a serving platter; serve with sauce. If desired, serve with lemon wedges.
1 oz. cooked shrimp with about 2 tsp. sauce: 59 cal., 1g fat (0 sat. fat), 66mg chol., 555mg sod., 4g carb. (2g sugars, 0 fiber), 9g pro.

CHEESE-STUFFED CHERRY TOMATOES

We grow plenty of tomatoes, so my husband and I often hand-pick enough cherry tomatoes for these easy-to-fix appetizers. This is one of our favorite recipes, and it's impossible to eat just one.
—Mary Lou Robison, Greensboro, NC

PREP: 15 MIN. + CHILLING
MAKES: 1 DOZEN

- 1 pint cherry tomatoes
- 1 pkg. (4 oz.) crumbled feta cheese
- ½ cup finely chopped red onion
- ½ cup olive oil
- ¼ cup red wine vinegar
- 1 Tbsp. dried oregano
     Salt and pepper to taste

1. Cut a thin slice off the top of each tomato. Scoop out and discard pulp. Invert tomatoes onto paper towels to drain. Combine cheese and onion; spoon into tomatoes.
2. In a small bowl, whisk the oil, vinegar, oregano, salt and pepper. Spoon over tomatoes. Cover and refrigerate 30 minutes or until ready to serve.
1 stuffed tomato: 111 cal., 11g fat (2g sat. fat), 5mg chol., 93mg sod., 2g carb. (1g sugars, 1g fiber), 2g pro.

MARINATED SAUSAGE KABOBS

These flavorful and colorful appetizers are so fun they'll be the talk of the party. And they're easy: Simply assemble them the day before and forget about them! You'll love the marinade flavor.
—Joanne Boone, Danville, OH

PREP: 20 MIN. + MARINATING
MAKES: 3 DOZEN

- ¼ cup olive oil
- 1 Tbsp. white vinegar
- ½ tsp. minced garlic
- ½ tsp. dried basil
- ½ tsp. dried oregano
- 8 oz. cheddar cheese, cut into ¾-in. cubes
- 1 can (6 oz.) pitted ripe olives, drained
- 8 oz. hard salami, cut into ¾-in. cubes
- 1 medium sweet red pepper, cut into ¾-in. pieces
- 1 medium green pepper, cut into ¾-in. pieces

1. In a large shallow dish, combine the first 5 ingredients; add remaining ingredients. Stir to coat; refrigerate at least 4 hours. Drain, discarding the marinade.
2. Thread cheese, olives, salami and peppers onto skewers or toothpicks.
1 kabob: 69 cal., 6g fat (2g sat. fat), 12mg chol., 165mg sod., 1g carb. (0 sugars, 0 fiber), 3g pro.

Simply Spreadable Seafood Platter

CRAB AU GRATIN SPREAD

When it's party time, I love to serve this warm, comforting appetizer. It has a rich taste and is easy to whip up with convenient canned crab.
—Suzanne Zick, Maiden, NC

TAKES: 30 MIN. • **MAKES:** ABOUT 2 CUPS

- 2 Tbsp. plus 1 tsp. butter, divided
- 3 Tbsp. all-purpose flour
- ½ tsp. salt
- ⅛ tsp. paprika
- ½ cup half-and-half cream
- ½ cup whole milk
- ¼ cup white wine or chicken broth
- 1 can (6 oz.) crabmeat, drained, flaked and cartilage removed or ⅔ cup chopped imitation crabmeat
- 1 can (4 oz.) mushroom stems and pieces, drained and chopped
- 1½ tsp. minced chives
- ½ cup shredded cheddar cheese
- 1 Tbsp. dry bread crumbs
  Fresh vegetables and assorted crackers

1. In a large saucepan, melt 2 Tbsp. butter. Stir in flour, salt and paprika until smooth. Gradually add cream, milk and wine. Bring to a boil; cook and stir 1-2 minutes or until thickened. Stir in crab, mushrooms and chives; heat through. Stir in cheddar cheese just until melted.
2. Transfer to a greased shallow 1-qt. baking dish. Melt remaining butter; toss with bread crumbs. Sprinkle over crab mixture. Bake, uncovered, at 400° for 10-15 minutes or until bubbly. Let stand 5 minutes. Serve on a platter with vegetables and crackers. If desired, sprinkle with additional minced chives.

2 Tbsp.: 64 cal., 4g fat (2g sat. fat), 22mg chol., 185mg sod., 2g carb. (1g sugars, 0 fiber), 4g pro.

Pretzel Dip Platter

MUSTARD PRETZEL DIP

This flavorful dip is addictive, so be careful! It's also delicious served with pita chips, crackers and fresh veggies.
—Iola Egle, Bella Vista, AR

PREP: 10 MIN. + CHILLING
MAKES: 3½ CUPS

- 1 cup sour cream
- 1 cup mayonnaise
- 1 cup prepared mustard
- ½ cup sugar
- ¼ cup dried minced onion
- 1 envelope (1 oz.) ranch salad dressing mix
- 1 Tbsp. prepared horseradish
  Sourdough pretzel nuggets

In a large bowl, combine the first 7 ingredients. Cover and refrigerate for at least 30 minutes. Serve with pretzels. Refrigerate leftovers.

2 Tbsp.: 95 cal., 8g fat (2g sat. fat), 2mg chol., 342mg sod., 6g carb. (4g sugars, 0 fiber), 1g pro.

CUSTOMIZE YOUR BOARD

SOFT BEER PRETZEL NUGGETS

What goes together better than beer and pretzels? Not much that I can think of. That's why I put them together into one recipe. I'm always looking for new ways to combine fun flavors. I love the way this recipe turned out!
—Alyssa Wilhite, Whitehouse, TX

PREP: 1 HOUR + RISING
BAKE: 10 MIN./BATCH
MAKES: 8 DOZEN

- 1 bottle (12 oz.) amber beer or nonalcoholic beer
- 1 pkg. (¼ oz.) active dry yeast
- 2 Tbsp. unsalted butter, melted
- 2 Tbsp. sugar
- 1½ tsp. salt
- 4 to 4½ cups all-purpose flour
- 10 cups water
- ⅔ cup baking soda

TOPPING
- 1 large egg yolk
- 1 Tbsp. water
  Coarse salt, optional

1. In a small saucepan, heat beer to 110°-115°; remove from heat. Stir in yeast until dissolved. In a large bowl, combine butter, sugar, salt, yeast mixture and 3 cups flour; beat on medium speed until smooth. Stir in enough remaining flour to form a soft dough (dough will be sticky).
2. Turn dough onto a floured surface; knead until it is smooth and elastic, 6-8 minutes. Place in a greased bowl, turning once to grease the top. Cover and let rise in a warm place until doubled, about 1 hour.
3. Preheat oven to 425°. Punch dough down. Turn dough onto a lightly floured surface; divide and shape into 8 balls. Roll each into a 12-in. rope. Cut each rope into 1-in. pieces.
4. In a Dutch oven, bring 10 cups water and baking soda to a boil. Drop the nuggets, 12 at a time, into the boiling water. Cook for 30 seconds. Remove with a slotted spoon; drain well on paper towels.
5. Place on greased baking sheets. In a small bowl, whisk egg yolk and 1 Tbsp. water; brush over pretzels. Sprinkle with coarse salt if desired. Bake until golden brown, 10-12 minutes. Remove from pans to a wire rack to cool.

Freeze option: Freeze cooled pretzel nuggets in airtight containers. To use, thaw at room temperature or, if desired, microwave on high 20-30 seconds or until heated through.

6 pretzel nuggets: 144 cal., 2g fat (1g sat. fat), 8mg chol., 302mg sod., 26g carb. (2g sugars, 1g fiber), 4g pro.

HOMEMADE SOFT PRETZELS

Now that I'm home full time, I like to make all kinds of breads for meals, family gatherings and just for fun with my daughters. Both girls love to help when it comes to making bread, especially kneading the dough. This is one of their favorite recipes.
—Karen Stewart-Linkhart, Xenia, OH

PREP: 50 MIN. + CHILLING
BAKE: 15 MIN.
MAKES: 32 PRETZELS

- 2 pkg. (¼ oz. each) active dry yeast
- 2 cups warm water (110° to 115°)
- ½ cup sugar
- 2 tsp. salt
- ¼ cup butter, softened
- 1 large egg, room temperature
- 6½ to 7½ cups all-purpose flour
- 1 large egg yolk
- 2 Tbsp. water
  Coarse salt, optional

1. In a large bowl, dissolve yeast in warm water. Add sugar, salt, butter and egg. Stir in 3 cups flour; mix until smooth. Add enough additional flour to make a stiff dough. Cover the bowl tightly with foil; refrigerate 2-24 hours.
2. Punch dough down and divide in half. On a lightly floured surface, cut each half into 16 equal pieces. Roll each piece into a 20-in. rope. Shape into the traditional pretzel shape and place on a greased baking sheet.
3. In a small bowl, combine egg yolk and water; brush over the pretzels. Sprinkle with salt if desired. Cover and let rise in a warm place until doubled, about 25 minutes. Bake at 400° for 15 minutes or until brown.

1 pretzel: 122 cal., 2g fat (1g sat. fat), 17mg chol., 165mg sod., 23g carb. (3g sugars, 1g fiber), 3g pro.

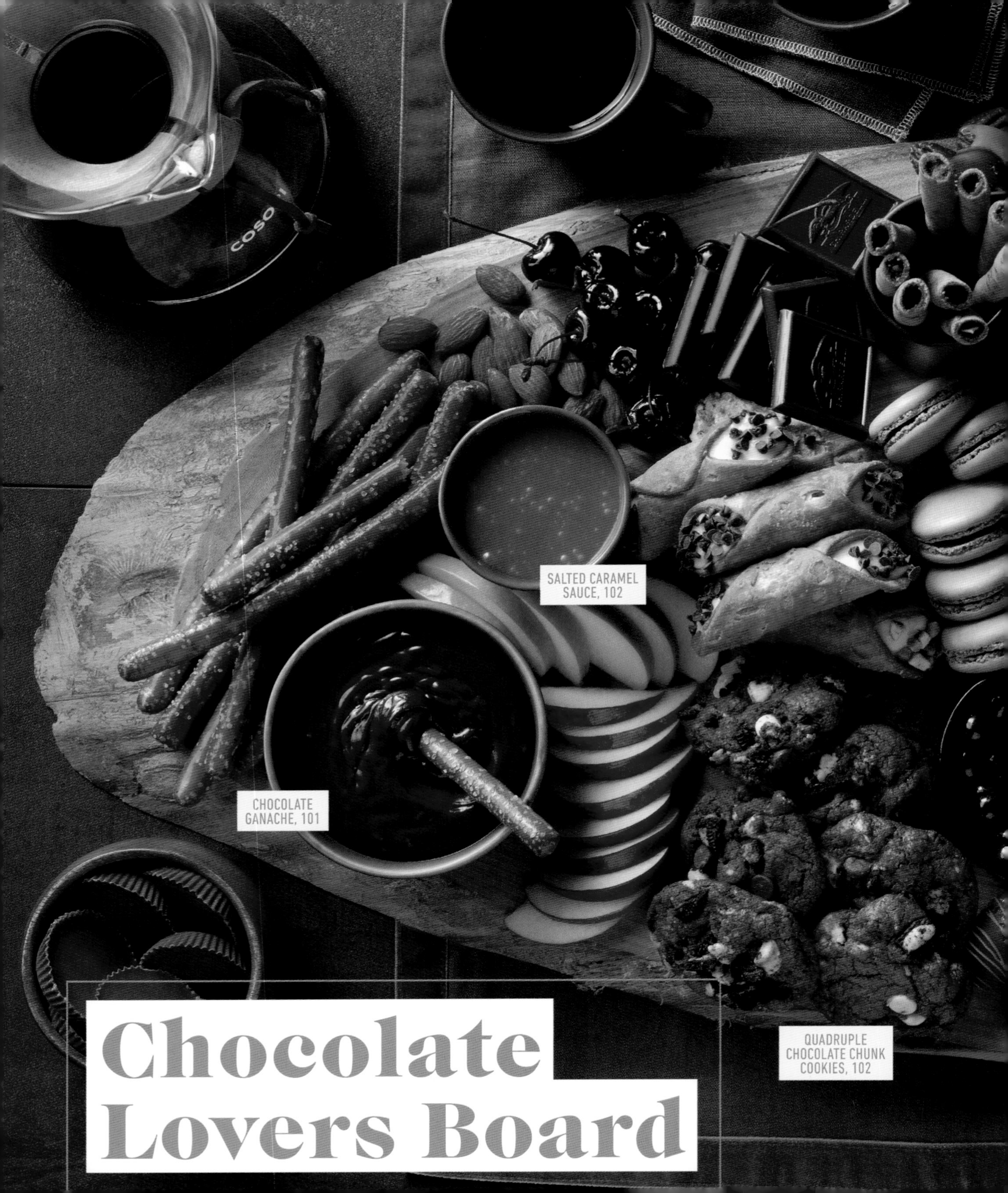
SALTED CARAMEL SAUCE, 102
CHOCOLATE GANACHE, 101
QUADRUPLE CHOCOLATE CHUNK COOKIES, 102
COSO

Chocolate Lovers Board

TURTLE CANDIES, 100

CHOCOLATE TRUFFLES, 100

CHOCOLATE CHIP CHEESE BALL, 101

HOW TO BUILD A...
CHOCOLATE LOVERS BOARD

ITEMS TO INCLUDE

- Chocolate Chip Cheese Ball
- Salted Caramel Sauce
- Chocolate Ganache
- Malted milk balls
- Pirouette cookies
- Graham crackers
- Red and green apples, sliced
- Dark cherries
- Almonds
- Pretzel rods
- Quadruple Chocolate Chunk Cookies
- Turtle Candies
- Chocolate Truffles
- Chocolate macarons
- Chocolate wafer cookies
- Ghirardelli squares
- White chocolate-covered pretzels
- Chocolate-covered strawberries
- Cannoli

EASY ASSEMBLY

Step 1: Place the cheese ball on the board as well as small bowls of the caramel sauce, ganache and malted milk balls. Stand Pirouette cookies in a mug and add to the platter.

Step 2: Place graham crackers, apple slices, cherries, almonds and pretzel rods near dips and sauces.

Step 3: Leaving room for the strawberries and cannoli, fill in gaps with Quadruple Chocolate Chunk Cookies, Turtle Candies, Chocolate Truffles, macarons, chocolate wafers, Ghirardelli squares and white chocolate-covered pretzels.

Step 4: Set strawberries and cannoli on the board immediately before serving.

TURTLE CANDIES

I am a self-taught candy maker through trial and error. These turtles are a favorite of friends and family.
—Carole Wiese, New Berlin, WI

PREP: 40 MIN. • **COOK:** 20 MIN. + STANDING
MAKES: 4 DOZEN

- 1   lb. pecan halves, toasted
- 1   can (14 oz.) sweetened condensed milk
- ¾   cup light corn syrup
- ½   cup sugar
- ⅓   cup packed brown sugar
- ¼   cup butter, cubed
- 1½ tsp. vanilla extract
- 1   lb. milk chocolate candy coating, chopped
   Flake sea salt, optional

1. On waxed paper-lined baking sheets, arrange pecans in small clusters of 4-5 pecans each.
2. For caramel, in a small saucepan, combine the milk, corn syrup and sugars. Cook and stir over medium heat until a candy thermometer reads 238° (soft-ball stage). Remove from the heat. Stir in butter and vanilla. Working quickly, spoon caramel onto pecan clusters. Let stand until set.
3. In a microwave, melt candy coating; stir until smooth. Spoon over caramel. If desired, top with flake sea salt. Chill for 10 minutes or until set. Store in an airtight container.
Note: We recommend that you test your candy thermometer before each use by bringing water to a boil; the thermometer should read 212°. Adjust your recipe temperature up or down based on your test.
1 turtle: 171 cal., 11g fat (4g sat. fat), 5mg chol., 20mg sod., 19g carb. (15g sugars, 1g fiber), 2g pro.

CHOCOLATE TRUFFLES

You may be tempted to save this recipe for a special occasion since these smooth, creamy chocolates are divine. But with just a few ingredients, they're easy to make anytime you want.
—Darlene Wiese-Appleby, Creston, OH

PREP: 20 MIN. + CHILLING
MAKES: ABOUT 4 DOZEN

- 3   cups semisweet chocolate chips
- 1   can (14 oz.) sweetened condensed milk
- 1   Tbsp. vanilla extract
   Optional coatings: Chocolate sprinkles, Dutch-processed cocoa, espresso powder and cacao nibs

1. In a microwave, melt chocolate chips and milk; stir until smooth. Stir in vanilla. Refrigerate, covered, 2 hours or until firm enough to roll.
2. Shape into 1-in. balls. Roll in coatings as desired.
1 truffle: 77 cal., 4g fat (2g sat. fat), 3mg chol., 12mg sod., 11g carb. (10g sugars, 1g fiber), 1g pro.

WHAT DRINKS CAN I SERVE WITH MY CHOCOLATE BOARD?

When choosing beverages for your chocolate charcuterie board, consider the time of year, the type of gathering and the time of day you'll be hosting.

Coffee is always a smart choice for a day gathering, but you can go with red, port or ice wine in the evening. Try the Chocolate Espresso Martini on page 103 or Chocolate-Caramel Rum Coffee from page 104. You can also serve amaretto or Irish cream, and eggnog is always fun during the holidays.

CHOCOLATE GANACHE

This satiny smooth chocolate treat will bring a touch of elegance to even the simplest dessert. It's so versatile!
—*Taste of Home* Test Kitchen

PREP: 15 MIN. + CHILLING
MAKES: 1¼ CUPS

CHOCOLATE CHIP CHEESE BALL

Your guests are in for a sweet surprise when they try this unusual cheese ball. It tastes just like cookie dough! Rolled in chopped pecans, the chip-studded spread is wonderful on regular or chocolate graham crackers. I especially like it because it can be assembled in a wink.
—Kelly Glascock, Syracuse, MO

PREP: 15 MIN. + CHILLING
MAKES: 16 SERVINGS

- 1   pkg. (8 oz.) cream cheese, softened
- ½   cup butter, softened
- ¼   tsp. vanilla extract
- ¾   cup confectioners' sugar
- 2   Tbsp. brown sugar
- ¾   cup miniature semisweet chocolate chips
- ¾   cup finely chopped pecans
     Graham crackers

1. Beat cream cheese, butter and vanilla until smooth; beat in sugars just until blended. Stir in chocolate chips. Refrigerate, covered, until firm enough to shape, about 2 hours.
2. Shape mixture into a ball. Wrap and refrigerate at least 1 hour.
3. To serve, roll cheese ball in pecans. Serve with graham crackers.
2 Tbsp.: 203 cal., 17g fat (8g sat. fat), 30mg chol., 92mg sod., 14g carb. (12g sugars, 1g fiber), 2g pro.

PLATTER POINTER
Place a square of parchment paper underneath this cheese ball if you're serving it on a board. This prevents a sticky mess on the board while also making it easier for guests to scoop up the cheese without scraping the board directly.

- 1   cup semisweet chocolate chips
- ⅔   cup heavy whipping cream

Place chocolate chips in a small bowl. In a small saucepan, bring cream just to a boil. Pour over chocolate; whisk until smooth.
2 Tbsp.: 135 cal., 11g fat (7g sat. fat), 22mg chol., 8mg sod., 11g carb. (10g sugars, 1g fiber), 1g pro.
White Chocolate Ganache: Substitute 6 oz. chopped white baking chocolate for the chocolate chips. Proceed as directed.

SALTED CARAMEL SAUCE

Rich and delicious, this sauce is the perfect blend of sweet, salty and creamy all in one. I like to make a big batch and refrigerate it for up to 2 weeks.
—Angie Stewart, Memphis, TN

TAKES: 20 MIN. • **MAKES:** 1¼ CUPS

- 1 cup sugar
- 1 cup heavy whipping cream
- 3 Tbsp. butter, cubed
- 1½ tsp. salt
- 1 tsp. almond extract

In a large heavy saucepan, spread the sugar; cook, without stirring, over medium-low heat until it begins to melt. Gently drag melted sugar to center of pan so sugar melts evenly. Cook, without stirring, until melted sugar turns a medium-dark amber, 5-10 minutes. Immediately remove from heat, then slowly stir in cream, butter, salt and almond extract.

2 Tbsp.: 191 cal., 12g fat (8g sat. fat), 36mg chol., 388mg sod., 21g carb. (21g sugars, 0 fiber), 1g pro.

QUADRUPLE CHOCOLATE CHUNK COOKIES

Of all the recipes in my repertoire, my Quadruple Chocolate Chunk Cookies are true winners. But really, when your cookies feature Oreos, candy bars and all the other goodies that go into a sweet treat, you're nearly guaranteed to turn out a winner.
—Jeff King, Duluth, MN

PREP: 25 MIN. • **BAKE:** 10 MIN./BATCH
MAKES: 8 DOZEN

- 1 cup butter, softened
- 1 cup sugar
- 1 cup packed brown sugar
- 2 large eggs, room temperature
- 2 tsp. vanilla extract
- 2½ cups all-purpose flour
- ¾ cup Dutch-processed cocoa
- 1 tsp. baking soda
- ¼ tsp. salt
- 1 cup white baking chips, chopped
- 1 cup semisweet chocolate chips, chopped
- 1 cup chopped Oreo cookies (about 10 cookies)
- 1 Hershey's Cookies 'n' Creme candy bar (1.55 oz.), chopped

1. Preheat oven to 375°. In a large bowl, cream butter, sugar and brown sugar until light and fluffy, 5-7 minutes. Beat in eggs and vanilla. In another bowl, whisk flour, cocoa, baking soda and salt; gradually beat into creamed mixture. Stir in remaining ingredients.
2. Drop by tablespoonfuls 2 in. apart onto greased baking sheets. Bake 6-8 minutes or until set. Cool on pans 1 minute. Remove to wire racks to cool completely. Store in an airtight container.

1 cookie: 79 cal., 4g fat (2g sat. fat), 10mg chol., 44mg sod., 11g carb. (7g sugars, 1g fiber), 1g pro.

CUSTOMIZE YOUR BOARD

Use these recipes to create your own Chocolate Lovers Board.

CHOCOLATE ESPRESSO MARTINI

Liven up happy hour with this coffee-flavored cocktail that's sure to perk up java lovers. A drizzle of chocolate syrup on the inside of the glass adds a stylish flair.
—*Taste of Home* Test Kitchen

TAKES: 5 MIN. • **MAKES:** 1 SERVING

    Ice cubes
2½ oz. chocolate liqueur
 ½ oz. brewed espresso
 ½ oz. vanilla-flavored vodka
    Coarse sugar
 1 tsp. chocolate syrup

1. Fill a mixing glass or tumbler three-fourths full with ice. Add the chocolate liqueur, espresso and vodka; stir until condensation forms on outside of glass.
2. Sprinkle sugar on a plate. Moisten the rim of a chilled cocktail glass with water; hold glass upside down and dip rim into sugar. Drizzle chocolate syrup on the inside of glass. Strain vodka mixture into glass.
1 martini: 342 cal., 0 fat (0 sat. fat), 0 chol., 12mg sod., 45g carb. (37g sugars, 0 fiber), 0 pro.

ULTIMATE DOUBLE CHOCOLATE BROWNIES

We live in the city—but within just a block of our house, we can see cattle grazing in a grassy green pasture. As someone who grew up in the country, I love home-style recipes like these brownies.
—*Carol Prewett, Cheyenne, WY*

PREP: 15 MIN. • **BAKE:** 35 MIN.
MAKES: 3 DOZEN

 ¾ cup baking cocoa
 ½ tsp. baking soda
 ⅔ cup butter, melted, divided
 ½ cup boiling water
 2 cups sugar
 2 large eggs, room temperature
 1 tsp. vanilla extract
1⅓ cups all-purpose flour
 ¼ tsp. salt
 ½ cup coarsely chopped pecans
 2 cups (12 oz.) semisweet chocolate chunks

1. Preheat oven to 350°. In a large bowl, combine cocoa and baking soda. Stir in ⅓ cup melted butter. Add boiling water; stir until well blended. Stir in sugar, eggs, remaining ⅓ cup butter and vanilla. Combine flour and salt; stir into cocoa mixture. Stir in pecans and chocolate chunks.
2. Pour into a greased 13x9-in. baking pan. Bake 35-40 minutes or until brownies begin to pull away from sides of pan. Cool in pan on a wire rack.
1 brownie: 159 cal., 8g fat (4g sat. fat), 21mg chol., 73mg sod., 22g carb. (17g sugars, 1g fiber), 2g pro.

CHOCOLATE ANGEL FOOD CANDY

You might want to hide this candy until Christmas. Also called fairy food or sponge candy, it's crunchy, honeycombed, chocolate-covered and irresistible.
—Geralyn Emmerich, Hubertus, WI

PREP: 20 MIN. • **COOK:** 20 MIN. + COOLING
MAKES: ABOUT 1¼ LBS.

- 1 tsp. butter
- 1 cup sugar
- 1 cup dark corn syrup
- 1 Tbsp. white vinegar
- 1 Tbsp. baking soda
- ½ lb. dark chocolate candy coating, coarsely chopped
- 1 tsp. shortening, divided
- ½ lb. milk chocolate candy coating, coarsely chopped

1. Line a 9-in. square pan with foil and grease foil with butter; set aside. In a large heavy saucepan, combine sugar, corn syrup and vinegar. Cook and stir over medium heat until sugar is dissolved. Bring to a boil. Cook, without stirring, until a candy thermometer reads 300° (hard-crack stage).
2. Remove from heat; stir in baking soda. Immediately pour into prepared pan; do not spread candy. Cool. Using foil, lift candy out of pan. Gently peel off foil; break candy into pieces.
3. In a microwave, melt dark chocolate coating and ½ tsp. shortening; stir until smooth. Dip half the candies in the melted dark chocolate mixture, allowing excess to drip off. Place on waxed paper; let stand until set. Repeat with milk chocolate coating and remaining ½ tsp. shortening and candies. Store in an airtight container.
Note: We recommend that you test your candy thermometer before each use by bringing water to a boil; the thermometer should read 212°.
2 oz.: 413 cal., 14g fat (12g sat. fat), 1mg chol., 431mg sod., 76g carb. (57g sugars, 1g fiber), 1g pro.

CHOCOLATE-CARAMEL RUM COFFEE

This decadent coffee drink can stand alone as a final course or as a complement to any chocolate or caramel dessert. Our family loves it after a special dinner or just for sipping in front of the fireplace.
—Joyce Conway, Westerville, OH

TAKES: 25 MIN. • **MAKES:** 8 SERVINGS

- 2 cans (12 oz. each) evaporated milk
- ¾ cup rum
- ½ cup chocolate syrup
- ½ cup caramel sundae syrup
- ¼ cup packed brown sugar
- 4 cups hot brewed coffee
- 2 Tbsp. coffee liqueur

COFFEE WHIPPED CREAM
- 1 cup heavy whipping cream
- 6 Tbsp. confectioners' sugar
- 2 Tbsp. coffee liqueur
  Instant espresso powder, optional

1. In a large saucepan, combine the milk, rum, syrups and brown sugar. Cook over medium heat until hot (do not boil). Stir in coffee and liqueur.
2. Meanwhile, in a small bowl, beat cream until it begins to thicken. Add the confectioners' sugar; beat until stiff peaks form. Fold in the liqueur until combined.
3. Pour coffee mixture into mugs. Garnish with a dollop of coffee whipped cream and, if desired, espresso powder.
1 cup coffee with ¼ cup coffee whipped cream: 437 cal., 16g fat (11g sat. fat), 68mg chol., 166mg sod., 50g carb. (43g sugars, 0 fiber), 7g pro.

CHOCOLATE-COVERED COFFEE BEANS

Coffee and chocolate come together in this recipe. Enjoy them as a snack or use them to top your favorite mocha desserts.
—*Taste of Home* Test Kitchen

TAKES: 30 MIN. • **MAKES:** 1 CUP

- ⅔ cup semisweet chocolate chips
- 1½ tsp. shortening
- ½ cup coffee beans
  Baking cocoa, optional

In a microwave, melt chocolate chips and shortening; stir until smooth. Dip coffee beans in chocolate; allow excess to drip off. Place on waxed paper; let stand until set, 10-15 minutes. If desired, roll in cocoa. Store in an airtight container.

1 Tbsp.: 39 cal., 2g fat (1g sat. fat), 0 chol., 2mg sod., 5 g carb. (4g sugars, 0 fiber), 0 protein.

> ### PLATTER POINTER
> While these coffee beans are ideal on a chocolate charcuterie board, consider adding them to a coffee or tea service, dessert platter or hot cocoa bar, too.

NUT FRUIT BARK

Here's a sophisticated version of fruit bark. Dark chocolate turns into a rich mocha flavor with the espresso powder. If you're a fan of sweet-salty tidbits, make sure to use the sea salt.
—Thomas Faglon, Somerset, NJ

PREP: 15 MIN. + CHILLING • **MAKES:** 1½ LBS.

- 1 lb. dark chocolate, coarsely chopped
- 1 tsp. instant espresso powder
- ½ cup dried cherries or blueberries
- ½ cup macadamia nuts, chopped
- ½ cup chopped cashews
- ½ tsp. coarse sea salt, optional

1. Line the bottom and sides of a 15x10x1-in. baking pan with parchment; grease the paper and set aside.
2. In a double boiler or metal bowl over hot water, melt chocolate; stir until smooth. Stir in espresso powder and half the cherries and nuts. Spread into the prepared pan; top with remaining cherries and nuts (pan will not be full). Sprinkle with sea salt if desired. Refrigerate 30 minutes or until firm.
3. Break into pieces. Store bark in an airtight container.

1 oz.: 147 cal., 10g fat (5g sat. fat), 1mg chol., 26mg sod., 14g carb. (11g sugars, 2g fiber), 2g pro.

S'mores Board

HOMEMADE HONEY
GRAHAMS, 107

HOW TO BUILD A...
S'MORES BOARD

Get ready for fun when guests gather around the fire and you set out this sweet assortment of s'more fixings.

ITEMS TO INCLUDE

- Nutella
- Peanut butter
- Chocolate chip cookies
- Homemade Honey Grahams
- White chocolate-covered pretzels
- Peanut butter cups
- White chocolate squares
- Marshmallows
- Chocolate bars
- Strawberries, halved
- Oreo cookies
- Miniature marshmallows

EASY ASSEMBLY

Step 1: Spoon Nutella and peanut butter into small bowls and set on opposite ends of board.

Step 2: Line chocolate chip cookies and Homemade Honey Grahams in groupings on board.

Step 3: Add groupings of white chocolate-covered pretzels, peanut butter cups, white chocolate squares, marshmallows, chocolate bars, strawberries and Oreo cookies.

Step 4: Fill in gaps with miniature marshmallows.

Step 5: Add serving utensils.

HOMEMADE HONEY GRAHAMS

The way my boys eat them, I would spend a fortune on honey graham crackers at the grocery store. That's why I decided to make a version that is less processed—and less expensive. These are wonderful, although they don't last long!
—Crystal Jo Bruns, Iliff, CO

PREP: 15 MIN. + CHILLING
BAKE: 10 MIN./BATCH
MAKES: 32 CRACKERS

 1 cup whole wheat flour
 ¾ cup all-purpose flour
 ½ cup toasted wheat germ
 2 Tbsp. dark brown sugar
 1 tsp. baking powder
 1 tsp. ground cinnamon
 ½ tsp. salt
 ½ tsp. baking soda
 6 Tbsp. cold butter, cubed
 ¼ cup honey
 4 Tbsp. ice water

1. In a bowl, whisk first 8 ingredients; cut in butter until crumbly. In another bowl, whisk honey and ice water; gradually add to dry ingredients, tossing with a fork until dough holds together when pressed.
2. Divide dough in half. Shape each into a disk; cover and refrigerate until firm enough to roll, about 30 minutes.
3. Preheat oven to 350°. On a lightly floured surface, roll each portion of dough to an 8-in. square. Using a knife or fluted pastry wheel, cut each into sixteen 2-in. squares. If desired, prick holes with a fork. Place 1 in. apart on parchment-lined baking sheets.
4. Bake until the edges are light brown, 10-12 minutes. Remove from pans to wire racks to cool. Store crackers in an airtight container.
1 cracker: 60 cal., 2g fat (1g sat. fat), 6mg chol., 89mg sod., 9g carb. (3g sugars, 1g fiber), 1g pro. **Diabetic exchanges:** ½ starch, ½ fat.

Cookies & Cocktails Board

CRANBERRY-LIME SANGRIA, 110

CARAMEL WHISKEY COOKIES, 110

HOLIDAY MOCHA SPRITZ, 111

ANISE PIZZELLE, 111

DOUBLE CHOCOLATE MARTINI, 109

HOW TO BUILD A...
COOKIES & COCKTAILS BOARD

Treat your guests to two different kinds of decadence right on the same board.

ITEMS TO INCLUDE
- Double Chocolate Martini
- Cranberry-Lime Sangria
- Anise Pizzelle
- Gumdrops
- Peppermint candies
- Holiday Mocha Spritz
- Caramel Whiskey Cookies
- White chocolate-covered pretzels
- White chocolate squares
- Red and green chocolate candies
- Candy canes
- Ribbon candy

EASY ASSEMBLY
Step 1: If you plan to actually set cocktails on the platter, do so first.

Step 2: Set two groupings of Anise Pizzelle cookies on the board.

Step 3: Fill small bowls with gumdrops and peppermint candies. Set bowls on the platter.

Step 4: Set groupings of Holiday Mocha Spritz and Caramel Whiskey Cookies on the platter.

Step 5: Fill in gaps with pretzels, white chocolate squares and candies.

DOUBLE CHOCOLATE MARTINI

Is it a beverage or a dessert? Don't let its sweet looks fool you—this chocolate martini is potent! And it's so good.
—Deborah Williams, Peoria, AZ

TAKES: 5 MIN. • **MAKES:** 1 SERVING

    Grated chocolate
1 maraschino cherry
    Chocolate syrup, optional
    Ice cubes
2½ oz. half-and-half cream
1½ oz. vodka
1½ oz. chocolate liqueur
1½ oz. creme de cacao

1. Sprinkle grated chocolate onto a plate. Moisten the rim of a martini glass with water; hold glass upside down and dip rim into chocolate. Place maraschino cherry in glass. If desired, garnish glass with chocolate syrup.
2. Fill a tumbler or a mixing glass three-fourths full of ice. Add cream, vodka, chocolate liqueur and creme de cacao; stir until condensation forms on outside of tumbler or mixing glass. Strain into the prepared martini glass; serve immediately.

1 serving: 569 cal., 8g fat (5g sat. fat), 38mg chol., 45mg sod., 51g carb. (46g sugars, 0 fiber), 3g pro.

CARAMEL WHISKEY COOKIES

A bit of yogurt replaces part of the butter in the traditional version of this cookie, but you would never know. I get a lot of requests for these, and I can't make a cookie tray without them.
—Priscilla Yee, Concord, CA

PREP: 30 MIN.
BAKE: 10 MIN./BATCH + COOLING
MAKES: 4 DOZEN

- ½ cup butter, softened
- ½ cup sugar
- ½ cup packed brown sugar
- ¼ cup plain Greek yogurt
- 2 Tbsp. canola oil
- 1 tsp. vanilla extract
- 2½ cups all-purpose flour
- 2 tsp. baking powder
- 1 tsp. baking soda
- ¼ tsp. salt

TOPPING
- 24 caramels
- 1 Tbsp. whiskey
- 3 oz. semisweet chocolate, melted
- ½ tsp. kosher salt, optional

1. Preheat oven to 350°. In a large bowl, beat butter and sugars until crumbly. Beat in yogurt, oil and vanilla. In another bowl, whisk flour, baking powder, baking soda and salt; gradually beat into sugar mixture.
2. Shape into 1-in. balls; place 2 in. apart on ungreased baking sheets. Flatten with the bottom of a glass dipped in flour. Bake cookies until edges are light brown, 7-9 minutes. Cool on pans for 2 minutes. Remove to wire racks to cool completely.
3. In a microwave, melt caramels with whiskey; stir until smooth. Spread over the cookies. Drizzle with chocolate; sprinkle with salt if desired. Let stand until set. Store in an airtight container.
1 cookie: 93 cal., 4g fat (2g sat. fat), 6mg chol., 83mg sod., 14g carb. (9g sugars, 0 fiber), 1g pro.

CRANBERRY-LIME SANGRIA

Tart, light and fruity, this partyworthy sangria is a hit any time of the year.
—Katy Joosten, Little Chute, WI

TAKES: 20 MIN.
MAKES: 13 SERVINGS (ABOUT 2½ QT.)

- 2 cups water
- 1 cup fresh or frozen cranberries, thawed
- 1 bottle (750 ml) white wine, chilled
- ¾ cup frozen limeade concentrate, thawed
- 1 each medium orange, lime and apple, peeled and diced
- 1 bottle (1 liter) citrus soda, chilled

1. In a small saucepan, combine water and cranberries. Cook over medium heat until berries pop, about 5 minutes. Drain and discard the liquid; set the cranberries aside.
2. In a pitcher, combine the wine and limeade concentrate. Stir in the diced fruit and reserved cranberries; add the soda. Serve over ice.
¾ cup: 134 cal., 0 fat (0 sat. fat), 0 chol., 12mg sod., 24g carb. (21g sugars, 1g fiber), 0 pro.

PLATTER POINTER
While this board is ideal for Christmas gatherings, any time is a good time for cookies and cocktails! Alter this idea to fit parties any time of year.

ANISE PIZZELLE

These golden brown pizzelle cookies are lovely and classic, with a crisp texture and a delicate anise flavor. I create them using a pizzelle iron.

—Barbara Colucci, Rockledge, FL

PREP: 15 MIN. • **COOK:** 5 MIN./BATCH
MAKES: ABOUT 2 DOZEN

HOLIDAY MOCHA SPRITZ

When I began to use my spritz press, this was the first flavor combination I tried. It took a few attempts to get the hang of it, but now I'm playing with a new dough and disk every time I make them. I plan on making several batches of spritz cookies throughout the year.

—Shelly Bevington, Hermiston, OR

PREP: 35 MIN. • **BAKE:** 10 MIN./BATCH
MAKES: ABOUT 10 DOZEN

- 1½ cups unsalted butter, softened
- 1 cup sugar
- 1 large egg, room temperature
- 1 Tbsp. instant coffee granules
- 1 tsp. vanilla extract
- 3½ cups all-purpose flour
- ⅓ cup dark baking cocoa or baking cocoa
- 2 tsp. instant espresso powder
- 1 tsp. baking powder
- ½ tsp. salt
- ½ tsp. ground nutmeg
- ⅓ cup orange juice
  Colored nonpareils, optional

1. Preheat oven to 375°. In a large bowl, beat butter and sugar until light and fluffy, 5-7 minutes. Combine egg, instant coffee and vanilla; beat into creamed mixture. In another bowl, whisk the flour, cocoa, espresso powder, baking powder, salt and nutmeg; add to creamed mixture alternately with orange juice, beating well after each addition.
2. Using a cookie press fitted with a disk of your choice, press dough shapes 1 in. apart onto ungreased baking sheets. If desired, sprinkle with nonpareils. Bake 8-10 minutes or until set (do not brown). Remove cookies from pans to wire racks to cool.
1 cookie: 42 cal., 2g fat (1g sat. fat), 8mg chol., 15mg sod., 5g carb. (2g sugars, 0 fiber), 1g pro.

- 3 large eggs, room temperature
- ¾ cup sugar
- ½ cup butter, melted
- 1¾ cups all-purpose flour
- 2 tsp. baking powder
- 1 tsp. aniseed
- ½ tsp. vanilla extract
- ½ tsp. anise extract

1. In a large bowl, beat the eggs, sugar and butter until smooth. Combine flour and baking powder; gradually add to the egg mixture and mix well. Stir in aniseed and extracts.
2. Bake in a preheated pizzelle iron according to manufacturer's directions until golden brown. Carefully remove pizzelle to wire racks to cool. Store in an airtight container.
1 cookie: 76 cal., 3g fat (2g sat. fat), 27mg chol., 52mg sod., 10g carb. (5g sugars, 0 fiber), 1g pro.

CUSTOMIZE YOUR BOARD

Use these recipes to create your own Cookies & Cocktails Board.

JAMAICAN CHOCOLATE COOKIES WITH CARAMEL CREME

I made these for an office party cookie contest—and not a crumb was left on the platter! Sweet potatoes are the secret ingredient. Canned sweet potatoes will work, too, if you're short on time.
—Noelle Myers, Grand Forks, ND

PREP: 45 MIN. + STANDING
BAKE: 10 MIN./BATCH + COOLING
MAKES: ABOUT 2½ DOZEN COOKIES

- 1   pkg. (11½ oz.) semisweet chocolate chunks, divided
- ½   cup butter, softened
- ½   cup confectioners' sugar
- ½   cup mashed sweet potatoes
- 1   tsp. minced fresh gingerroot
- ½   tsp. vanilla extract
- 1¼ cups all-purpose flour
- ¼   cup cornstarch
- 2   Tbsp. baking cocoa
- 1½ tsp. baking powder
- ¼   tsp. baking soda
- ¼   tsp. salt

FILLING

- ⅔   cup whipped cream cheese
- ⅓   cup dulce de leche
- 2   Tbsp. sweetened condensed milk
- ⅛   tsp. ground cinnamon
- ⅛   tsp. ground allspice
- ⅛   tsp. salt

1. Preheat oven to 375°. In a microwave, melt ⅔ cup chocolate chunks; stir until smooth. Cool slightly. In a large bowl, cream together butter and confectioners' sugar until light and fluffy. Beat in sweet potatoes, cooled melted chocolate, ginger and vanilla. In another bowl, whisk flour, cornstarch, baking cocoa, baking powder, baking soda and salt; gradually beat into creamed mixture.

2. Shape dough into ¾-in. balls; place 2½ in. apart on parchment-lined baking sheets. Flatten balls slightly with the bottom of a glass dipped in confectioners' sugar. Bake until edges are firm, 8-10 minutes. Remove from pans to wire racks to cool completely.

3. Meanwhile, mix filling ingredients until smooth. Spread filling on bottoms of half the cookies; cover with the remaining cookies.

4. For chocolate coating, microwave remaining chocolate chunks; stir until smooth. Dip cookies halfway into chocolate or drizzle chocolate over tops of cookies; let stand until set. Store between pieces of waxed paper in an airtight container in the refrigerator.

1 sandwich cookie: 134 cal., 7g fat (5g sat. fat), 12mg chol., 103mg sod., 17g carb. (10g sugars, 1g fiber), 2g pro.

COCONUT-MACADAMIA BISCOTTI

I came up with this biscotti recipe after my husband and I returned from our first trip to Hawaii. Dipping these tropical treats in a good cup of coffee brings us right back to the wonderful memories we made there.
—Shannon Koene, Blacksburg, VA

PREP: 20 MIN. • **BAKE:** 55 MIN. + STANDING
MAKES: ABOUT 2½ DOZEN

- 6 Tbsp. butter, softened
- ¾ cup sugar
- ⅓ cup canola oil
- 3 large eggs, room temperature
- 2 tsp. vanilla extract
- 1 tsp. coconut extract
- 3¼ cups all-purpose flour
- 1¾ tsp. baking powder
- ¼ tsp. salt
- 1 cup sweetened shredded coconut, toasted and finely chopped
- 1 cup macadamia nuts, coarsely chopped
- 2 cups semisweet chocolate chips
- 2 Tbsp. shortening

1. Preheat oven to 350°. In a large bowl, beat butter, sugar and oil until blended. Beat in eggs and extracts. In another bowl, whisk flour, baking powder and salt; gradually beat into creamed mixture. Stir in the coconut and macadamia nuts.
2. Divide dough in half. On parchment-lined baking sheets, shape each half into an 8x3-in. rectangle. Bake until set, about 25 minutes.
3. Place pans on wire racks. When cool enough to handle, transfer the baked rectangles to a cutting board. Using a serrated knife, cut crosswise into ½-in. slices. Return to pans, cut side down.
4. Bake 15-18 minutes on each side or until golden brown. Remove from pans to wire racks to cool completely.

5. In a microwave, melt chocolate chips and shortening; stir until smooth. Dip each cookie halfway into the mixture; allow excess chocolate to drip. Place on waxed paper until set. Store in an airtight container.
1 cookie: 228 cal., 14g fat (6g sat. fat), 25mg chol., 99mg sod., 25g carb. (13g sugars, 2g fiber), 3g pro.

ALMOND ICEBOX COOKIES

With a roll of this cookie dough on hand, I can serve freshly baked cookies in a snap.
—Elizabeth Montgomery, Allston, MA

PREP: 20 MIN. + CHILLING • **BAKE:** 10 MIN.
MAKES: 10 DOZEN

- 1½ cups butter, softened
- 1 cup sugar
- 1 cup packed brown sugar
- 3 large eggs, room temperature
- 4 cups all-purpose flour
- 3 tsp. ground cinnamon
- 1 tsp. baking soda
- ½ cup finely chopped almonds
- 2 pkg. (2½ oz. each) whole unblanched almonds

1. In a large bowl, cream together butter and sugars until light and fluffy, 5-7 minutes. Add eggs, 1 at a time, beating well after each addition. Combine the flour, cinnamon and baking soda; gradually add to the creamed mixture and mix well. Fold in chopped almonds. Shape into two 15-in. rolls; wrap each in waxed paper. Refrigerate for 2 hours or overnight.
2. Unwrap and cut into ¼-in. slices. Place 2 in. apart on ungreased baking sheets; top each with a whole almond. Bake at 375° for 8-10 minutes or until edges begin to brown. Remove to wire racks to cool.
2 cookies: 113 cal., 6g fat (3g sat. fat), 23mg chol., 72mg sod., 14g carb. (7g sugars, 1g fiber), 2g pro.

Meal Boards

Jazz up breakfast, lunch and dinner when you set one of these hearty platters on the table.

Pancake Board

FLUFFY PANCAKES, 118

GINGERBREAD-SPICED SYRUP, 119

MAPLE-GLAZED SAUSAGES, 119

HOW TO BUILD A...
PANCAKE BOARD

Dig in to early morning comfort with this collection of classic breakfast items.

ITEMS TO INCLUDE

- Fluffy Pancakes
- Buffet Scrambled Eggs
- Gingerbread-Spiced Syrup
- Strawberry syrup
- Chocolate chips
- Peanut butter
- Nutella
- Whipped cream
- Butter
- Maple-Glazed Sausages
- Bananas, sliced
- Blueberries
- Raspberries
- Blackberries

EASY ASSEMBLY

Step 1: Fan the pancakes out across the board.

Step 2: Spoon Buffet Scrambled Eggs into a small serving bowl. Pour syrups into small syrup pitchers. Set chocolate chips, peanut butter, Nutella and the whipped cream in small bowls. Put the butter on a butter dish. Set all on board.

Step 3: Set Maple-Glazed Sausages on board in a grouping.

Step 4: Fill in gaps on the board with bananas and berries.

Platter Pointer: If you can't find a board big enough to hold this pancake breakfast, a sheet pan will do just fine.

BUFFET SCRAMBLED EGGS, 119

TIPS FOR MAKING A PANCAKE BOARD

Need more ideas on how to make your pancake-filled brunch board a success?

How do you keep the pancakes warm?

To keep your pancakes, bacon, sausage and other foods warm, place the items on sheet pans and pop them into the oven on the Warm setting. If you don't have this setting, heat the oven to 200°. Pancakes and other hot foods will be fine for 30 minutes or more.

If you only need to keep things hot for a few minutes while the coffee brews, just cover the tray with another platter or a sheet of aluminum foil.

What drinks pair well with a pancake board?

All you need to accompany your board are the breakfast classics: coffee, milk, orange juice and maybe a bottle of bubbly for mimosas. You can add tea or iced coffee. If you're having kids over, consider surprising them with mugs of hot chocolate.

What other pancake toppings can you include?

- Other fresh fruits
- Toasted nuts
- Agave syrup
- Dulce de leche
- Jams, preserves and compotes
- Sour cream or Greek yogurt
- Confectioners' sugar
- Honey
- Cinnamon butter

FLUFFY PANCAKES

I found this delightful pancake recipe among our old family favorites, and I adapted it to make a small amount. It's quick and easy to prepare, but we still consider it a special treat.
—Eugene Presley, Council, VA

TAKES: 15 MIN. • **MAKES:** 8 PANCAKES

1	cup all-purpose flour
1	Tbsp. sugar
2	tsp. baking powder
½	tsp. salt
1	large egg, room temperature
¾	cup 2% milk
¼	cup shortening or butter, melted

1. In a small bowl, combine flour, sugar, baking powder and salt. Combine egg, milk and shortening; stir into dry ingredients just until moistened.

2. Pour batter by ¼ cupfuls onto a greased hot griddle. Flip pancakes when bubbles form on top; cook until the second side is golden brown.

2 pancakes: 274 cal., 15g fat (9g sat. fat), 82mg chol., 664mg sod., 29g carb. (5g sugars, 1g fiber), 6g pro.

Chocolate Chip Pancakes: Stir ½ cup miniature chocolate chips into batter. Proceed as recipe directs.

Maple Pancakes: Omit sugar. Add 1 Tbsp. maple syrup to milk mixture. Proceed as recipe directs.

BUFFET SCRAMBLED EGGS

These are my favorite scrambled eggs. The white sauce, flavored with chicken bouillon, keeps the eggs creamy and moist. It's a tasty twist on a morning mainstain.
—Elsie Beachy, Plain City, OH

TAKES: 20 MIN. • **MAKES:** 8 SERVINGS

- 8 Tbsp. butter, divided
- ¼ cup all-purpose flour
- 2 cups whole milk
- 4 tsp. chicken bouillon granules
- 16 large eggs, lightly beaten
  Optional: Minced fresh parsley, tarragon and chives

1. In a small saucepan, melt 2 Tbsp. butter. Stir in the flour until smooth. Gradually add milk and bouillon. Bring to a boil; cook and stir for 2 minutes or until thickened. Set aside.
2. In a large skillet, melt remaining butter. Add eggs; cook over medium heat until eggs begin to set, stirring occasionally. Stir in white sauce. Cook until the eggs are completely set. If desired, sprinkle with minced parsley, tarragon and chives (or serve herbs on the side).
¾ cup: 304 cal., 24g fat (11g sat. fat), 464mg chol., 692mg sod., 7g carb. (4g sugars, 0 fiber), 15g pro.

GINGERBREAD-SPICED SYRUP

Here's a wonderful treat for the winter months. Stir a tablespoon of this syrup into coffee, tea or cider. Drizzle it over pancakes, hot cereal or yogurt. Or use it as a glaze for roast chicken or chops.
—Darlene Brenden, Salem, OR

PREP: 20 MIN. • **COOK:** 35 MIN. + COOLING
MAKES: 2 CUPS

- 2 cinnamon sticks (3 in.), broken into pieces
- 16 whole cloves
- 3 Tbsp. coarsely chopped fresh gingerroot

- 1 tsp. whole allspice
- 1 tsp. whole peppercorns
- 2 cups sugar
- 2 cups water
- 2 Tbsp. honey
- 1 tsp. ground nutmeg

1. Place the first 5 ingredients on a double thickness of cheesecloth; bring up corners of cloth and tie with string to form a bag.
2. In a large saucepan, combine the sugar, water, honey, nutmeg and spice bag; bring to a boil. Reduce heat; simmer, uncovered, until the syrup reaches desired consistency, 30-45 minutes.
3. Remove from the heat; cool to room temperature. Discard spice bag; transfer syrup to airtight containers. Store in the refrigerator for up to 1 month.
2 Tbsp.: 108 cal., 0 fat (0 sat. fat), 0 chol., 0 sod., 28g carb. (27g sugars, 0 fiber), 0 pro.

MAPLE-GLAZED SAUSAGES

These sausages kissed with sugar and spice are my first choice when I want to round out a morning menu of French toast and fruit compote.
—Trudie Hagen, Roggen, CO

TAKES: 20 MIN. • **MAKES:** 10 SERVINGS

- 2 pkg. (6.4 oz. each) frozen fully cooked breakfast sausage links
- 1 cup maple syrup
- ½ cup packed brown sugar
- 1 tsp. ground cinnamon

In a large skillet, brown sausage links. In a small bowl, combine the syrup, brown sugar and cinnamon; pour over sausages. Bring to a boil. Reduce heat; simmer, uncovered, until sausages are glazed.
2 sausages: 247 cal., 11g fat (3g sat. fat), 20mg chol., 283mg sod., 34g carb. (30g sugars, 0 fiber), 5g pro.

CUSTOMIZE YOUR BOARD

Use these recipes to create your own Pancake Board.

SILVER DOLLAR OAT PANCAKES

I combined two of my grandson Joshua's favorite foods—applesauce and oatmeal—into these wholesome little pancakes. He likes their fun size.

—Margaret Wilson, San Bernardino, CA

TAKES: 25 MIN. • **MAKES:** 4 SERVINGS

- ½ cup all-purpose flour
- ½ cup quick-cooking oats
- 1½ tsp. sugar
- 1 tsp. baking powder
- ½ tsp. baking soda
- ½ tsp. salt
- 1 large egg, room temperature
- ¾ cup buttermilk
- ½ cup cinnamon applesauce
- 2 Tbsp. butter, melted
  Maple syrup or topping of your choice

1. In a large bowl, combine the dry ingredients. In a small bowl, beat the egg, buttermilk, applesauce and butter; stir into dry ingredients just until moistened.

2. Pour batter by 2 tablespoonfuls onto a greased hot griddle; flip when bubbles form on top. Cook until second side is golden brown. Serve with syrup.

5 pancakes: 211 cal., 8g fat (4g sat. fat), 70mg chol., 660mg sod., 29g carb. (10g sugars, 2g fiber), 6g pro. **Diabetic exchanges:** 2 starch, 1½ fat.

SLOW-COOKED CHAI TEA

A friend of my mother's brought chai tea to her house. She told us that in India it is served every day. I had never tried it before. I liked it so much I came up with a recipe to re-create it.

—Patty Crouse, Warren, PA

PREP: 10 MIN. • **COOK:** 3 HOURS
MAKES: 8 SERVINGS

- 6 cups water
- 1 cup sugar
- 1 cup nonfat dry milk powder
- 6 black tea bags
- 1 tsp. ground ginger
- 1 tsp. ground cinnamon
- ½ tsp. pepper
- ½ tsp. ground cardamom
- ½ tsp. ground cloves
- ½ tsp. vanilla extract

Place all ingredients in a 3- or 4-qt. slow cooker. Cook, covered, on high until heated through, 3-4 hours. Discard tea bags. Serve tea warm.

¾ cup: 131 cal., 0 fat (0 sat. fat), 2mg chol., 48mg sod., 30g carb. (30g sugars, 0 fiber), 3g pro.

SPICE IT UP
Cinnamon sticks are a fun addition to this tasty chai tea. You can also dress up individual servings with a dash of ground nutmeg or pumpkin pie spice.

COLD-BREW COFFEE

Cold brewing reduces the acidity of coffee,
which enhances its natural sweetness and
complex flavors. Even those who take hot
coffee with sugar and cream might find
themselves sipping cold brew plain.
—*Taste of Home* Test Kitchen

PREP: 10 MIN. + CHILLING
MAKES: 8 SERVINGS

1   cup coarsely ground
    medium-roast coffee
1   cup hot water (205°)
6   to 7 cups cold water
    Optional: 2% milk or
    half-and-half cream

1. Place the coffee grounds in a clean glass container. Pour hot water over the grounds; let stand 10 minutes. Stir in cold water. Cover and refrigerate 12-24 hours. (The longer the coffee sits, the stronger the flavor.)

2. Strain coffee through a fine-mesh sieve; discard grounds. Strain coffee again through a coffee filter; discard grounds. Serve over ice, with milk or cream if desired. May be stored in the refrigerator for up to 2 weeks.

1 cup: 2 cal., 0 fat (0 sat. fat), 0 chol., 4mg sod., 0 carb. (0 sugars, 0 fiber), 0 pro.

Crepe Board

BUCKWHEAT BRUNCH
CREPES, 123

HOW TO BUILD A...
CREPE BOARD

Easily impress with this upscale board that offers your friends and family the chance to assemble their own crepes.

ITEMS TO INCLUDE
- Buckwheat Brunch Crepes
- Confectioners' sugar
- Pistachios
- Pecans
- Breakfast sausage links, cooked
- Green grapes
- Blackberries
- Strawberries
- Orange slices

EASY ASSEMBLY

Step 1: Prepare the Buckwheat Brunch Crepes as directed. Spoon the cream mixture and berry sauce into small bowls. Spoon confectioners' sugar into another small bowl.

Step 2: Set bowls of cream mixture, berry sauce and confectioners' sugar on your board or serving platter.

Step 3: Gently fold crepes into fourths. Add to board between bowls.

Step 4: Put nuts in separate small bowls and add to board.

Step 5: Fill in gaps with groupings of sausages, grapes, berries and oranges.

Step 6: Add serving utensils.

BUCKWHEAT BRUNCH CREPES

My husband and I enjoy these delicious crepes with berry sauce and cream on Saturday mornings. Sometimes we even eat them for supper with sausages and eggs. Buckwheat crepes are considered a delicacy here.
—Sharon Dyck, Roxton Falls, QC

PREP: 20 MIN. + CHILLING • **COOK:** 15 MIN.
MAKES: 3 SERVINGS

- 5 Tbsp. heavy whipping cream
- ½ cup sour cream
- 2 large eggs, room temperature
- ½ cup 2% milk
- ⅓ cup all-purpose flour
- 3 Tbsp. buckwheat flour or whole wheat flour
- ½ tsp. salt

BERRY SAUCE

- ½ cup sugar
- 1 Tbsp. cornstarch
  Dash salt
- ½ cup water
- ⅓ cup fresh blueberries
- ⅓ cup fresh raspberries
- 4½ tsp. butter, divided
- 1 tsp. lemon juice

1. In a small bowl, beat the whipping cream until stiff peaks form; fold into sour cream. Cover and refrigerate.
2. In a large bowl, whisk eggs and milk. In another bowl, mix flours and salt; add to the egg mixture and mix well. Refrigerate batter, covered, 1 hour.
3. Meanwhile, in a small saucepan, combine sugar, cornstarch and salt; whisk in the water until smooth. Bring to a boil; cook and stir until thickened, 1-2 minutes. Add berries; cook over medium-low heat until berries pop. Stir in 1½ tsp. butter and lemon juice until butter is melted. Set aside and keep warm.
4. Heat 1 tsp. remaining butter in an 8-in. nonstick skillet over medium heat. Stir batter. Fill a ¼-cup measure halfway with batter; pour into center of pan. Quickly lift and tilt pan to coat bottom evenly. Cook until top appears dry; turn crepe over and cook until the bottom is cooked, 15-20 seconds longer. Remove to a wire rack. Repeat with remaining batter, adding butter to the skillet as needed. When cool, stack the crepes between pieces of waxed paper. Serve crepes with berry sauce and cream mixture.

2 crepes with toppings: 516 cal., 27g fat (16g sat. fat), 180mg chol., 577mg sod., 60g carb. (40g sugars, 2g fiber), 10g pro.

CUSTOMIZE YOUR BOARD

Use these recipes to create your own Crepe Board.

CANDIED WALNUTS

You can turn ordinary walnuts into a taste sensation with this simple recipe prepared on the stovetop. With plenty of brown sugar and a hint of pepper, the crunchy candied nuts make a nice addition to any fruit and cheese tray. But they can stand on their own, as well, because they're so munchable!
—*Taste of Home* Test Kitchen

TAKES: 20 MIN. • **MAKES:** 2 CUPS

- 2 **Tbsp. canola oil**
- 2 **Tbsp. balsamic vinegar**
- ⅛ **tsp. pepper**
- 2 **cups walnut halves**
- ½ **cup packed brown sugar**

1. In a large heavy skillet, combine the oil, vinegar and pepper. Cook and stir over medium heat until blended. Add the walnuts and cook over medium heat until nuts are toasted, about 4 minutes.
2. Sprinkle with brown sugar. Cook and stir until sugar is melted, 2-4 minutes. Spread nuts on foil to cool. Store in an airtight container.
2 Tbsp.: 124 cal., 10g fat (1g sat. fat), 0 chol., 3mg sod., 9g carb. (7g sugars, 1g fiber), 2g pro.

AIR-FRYER SAUSAGE BACON BITES

Try surprising your family one Sunday morning by pulling these out of the air fryer as everyone heads to breakfast, and get ready for oohs and aahs. They're equally delicious as a party appetizer.
—Pat Waymire, Yellow Springs, OH

PREP: 20 MIN. + CHILLING
COOK: 15 MIN./BATCH
MAKES: ABOUT 3½ DOZEN

- ¾ **lb. sliced bacon**
- 2 **pkg. (8 oz. each) frozen fully cooked breakfast sausage links, thawed**
- ½ **cup plus 2 Tbsp. packed brown sugar, divided**

1. Cut bacon strips in half widthwise; cut sausage links in half. Wrap a piece of bacon around each piece of sausage. Place ½ cup brown sugar in a shallow bowl; roll bacon-wrapped sausages in the sugar. Secure each with a toothpick. Place in a large bowl. Cover bowl and refrigerate 4 hours or overnight.
2. Preheat air fryer to 325°. Sprinkle wrapped sausages with 1 Tbsp. brown sugar. In batches, arrange sausages in a single layer in greased air fryer. Cook 15-20 minutes or until bacon is crisp, turning once. Sprinkle with remaining 1 Tbsp. brown sugar.
Note: In our testing, we find cook times vary dramatically among brands of air fryers. As a result, we give wider-than-normal ranges on suggested cook times. Begin checking at the first time listed and adjust as needed.
1 piece: 74 cal., 6g fat (2g sat. fat), 9mg chol., 154mg sod., 4g carb. (4g sugars, 0 fiber), 2g pro.

until shrimp turn pink. Return broccoli mixture to skillet and combine. Spoon filling down center of 16 crepes; roll up. Place in an ungreased 15x10x1-in. baking pan. Bake crepes, uncovered, 15-20 minutes or until heated through. Meanwhile, prepare an envelope of bearnaise sauce according to package directions. Serve over crepes. Yield: 8 servings.

Creamy Strawberry Crepes: In a large bowl, add 1 package (8 oz.) softened cream cheese, 1¼ cups confectioners' sugar, 1 Tbsp. lemon juice, 1 tsp. grated lemon peel and ½ tsp. vanilla extract; beat until smooth. Fold in 2 cups sliced fresh strawberries and 2 cups whipped cream. Spoon about ⅓ cup filling down center of 14 crepes; roll up. Garnish with additional berries. Yield: 7 servings.

EXTRA CREPE TOPPERS

Sweet ideas: Jam, marmalade, honey, maple syrup, lemon curd, pie filling, nut butters, cinnamon butter, chocolate chips, whipped cream, hot fudge, caramel sauce, ice cream, shaved chocolate.

Savory ideas: Shredded cheese, grape tomatoes, mixed greens, bacon, prosciutto, salami, ham, mushrooms, pesto, avocado.

BASIC CREPES

This is my favorite simple crepe recipe. It's best to make the batter at least 30 minutes ahead of time so the flour can absorb all the moisture before you start cooking the crepes.
—*Taste of Home* Test Kitchen

PREP: 10 MIN. + CHILLING • **COOK:** 20 MIN.
MAKES: 20 CREPES

- 4 large eggs, room temperature
- 1½ cups 2% milk
- 1 cup all-purpose flour
- 1½ tsp. sugar
- ⅛ tsp. salt
- 8 tsp. butter

1. In a small bowl, whisk eggs and milk. In another bowl, mix flour, sugar and salt; add to egg mixture and mix well. Refrigerate, covered, 1 hour.
2. Melt 1 tsp. butter in an 8-in. nonstick skillet over medium heat. Stir batter.

Fill a ¼-cup measure halfway with batter; pour into center of pan. Quickly lift and tilt pan to coat bottom evenly. Cook until top appears dry; turn crepe over and cook until bottom is cooked, 15-20 seconds longer. Remove to a wire rack. Repeat with remaining batter, adding butter to skillet as needed. When cool, stack crepes between pieces of waxed paper or paper towels.

1 crepe: 61 cal., 3g fat (2g sat. fat), 43mg chol., 50mg sod., 6g carb. (1g sugars, 0 fiber), 3g pro.

Shrimp Crepes: Preheat oven to 350°. In a large skillet, melt 3 Tbsp. butter. Add 4½ cups chopped fresh broccoli, 6 chopped green onions, 2 tsp. minced garlic, ½ tsp. salt, ¼ tsp. pepper and ¼ tsp. Worcestershire sauce; cook until broccoli is crisp-tender, 7-9 minutes. Remove and set aside. In the same skillet, saute 1 lb. peeled and deveined uncooked shrimp in ¼ cup white wine

HARD-BOILED
EGGS, 129

Waffle
Board

FLUFFY
WAFFLES, 128

WAFFLE BOARD

Fresh fruit, yogurt, deli ham and bakery finds make this eye-opening board a snap to put together.

ITEMS TO INCLUDE

- Fluffy Waffles with Cinnamon Cream Syrup
- Hard-Boiled Eggs
- Whipped Cream
- Cinnamon sugar
- Melted butter
- Strawberry yogurt
- Deli ham
- Cheddar cheese slices
- Avocado, sliced
- Yellow and red tomatoes, sliced
- Grape or cherry tomatoes, sliced
- Bacon
- Mini cinnamon rolls or other bite-sized pastries
- Green grapes
- Oranges, sliced
- Blood oranges, sliced
- Strawberries, halved
- Tangerine segments

EASY ASSEMBLY

Step 1: Cut the waffles into quarters and arrange across board. Pour the Cinnamon Cream Syrup into a small syrup pitcher and set on board.

Step 2: Slice the eggs in half and group them together on the board.

Step 3: Fill small bowls and creamers with whipped cream, cinnamon sugar, melted butter, and yogurt. Set on board.

Step 4: Add groupings of ham, cheese, avocado, tomatoes, bacon and mini cinnamon rolls.

Step 5: Fill in gaps with fruit.

Step 6: Add serving utensils.

FLUFFY WAFFLES

A friend shared the recipe for these light and delicious waffles. The cinnamon syrup is a nice change from maple syrup, and it keeps quite well in the fridge.
—Amy Gilles, Ellsworth, WI

PREP: 25 MIN. • **COOK:** 20 MIN.
MAKES: 10 WAFFLES (6½ IN.)
AND 1⅔ CUPS SYRUP

- 2 cups all-purpose flour
- 1 Tbsp. sugar
- 2 tsp. baking powder
- ½ tsp. salt
- 3 large eggs, separated, room temperature
- 2 cups 2% milk
- ¼ cup canola oil

CINNAMON CREAM SYRUP
- 1 cup sugar
- ½ cup light corn syrup
- ¼ cup water
- 1 can (5 oz.) evaporated milk
- 1 tsp. vanilla extract
- ½ tsp. ground cinnamon
  Mixed fresh berries, optional

1. In a bowl, combine the flour, sugar, baking powder and salt. Combine the egg yolks, milk and oil; stir into dry ingredients just until moistened. In a small bowl, beat egg whites until stiff peaks form; fold into batter. Bake in a preheated waffle iron according to manufacturer's directions.
2. For syrup, combine the sugar, corn syrup and water in a saucepan. Bring to a boil over medium heat; cook and stir for 2 minutes or until thickened. Remove from heat; stir in evaporated milk, vanilla and cinnamon.
3. Serve waffles with the syrup and, if desired, fresh berries.

Freeze option: Cool the waffles on wire racks. Freeze between layers of waxed paper in a resealable container. Reheat waffles in a toaster on medium setting. Or, microwave each waffle on high for 30-60 seconds or until heated through.
1 waffle with 2½ Tbsp. syrup: 424 cal., 12g fat (4g sat. fat), 94mg chol., 344mg sod., 71g carb. (41g sugars, 1g fiber), 9g pro.

Ham & Cheese Waffles: Omit sugar and Cinnamon Cream Syrup. Increase flour to 2½ cups. Fold in 1½ cups shredded mozzarella cheese and ½ cup cubed fully cooked ham.
Tropical Waffles: Omit the Cinnamon Cream Syrup. Increase baking powder to 4 tsp. Before adding egg whites, stir in 1 can (8 oz.) well-drained crushed pineapple, ¼ cup flaked coconut and ¼ cup chopped macadamia nuts.
Blueberry Waffles: Increase baking powder to 2½ tsp. Before adding egg whites, fold in 1½ cups fresh or frozen blueberries.
Cinnamon Waffles: Substitute brown sugar for sugar. With flour, stir in ½ tsp. ground cinnamon. With egg yolks, stir in ¾ tsp. vanilla.

HOW TO BUILD A...
CONTINENTAL BREAKFAST BOARD

Rise and shine! A quick breakfast board is perfect when hosting a few overnight guests. Surprise them with this simply eye-opening presentation.

ITEMS TO INCLUDE
- Garlic-Herb Bagel Spread
- Avocado, diced
- Egg bread, sliced
- Bacon, cooked
- Everything bagel seasoning
- Honey
- Tangerine segments
- Green grapes

EASY ASSEMBLY
Step 1: Set Garlic-Herb Bagel Spread in a small serving bowl; add to board.

Step 2: Place avocado in a separate small serving bowl; add to board.

Step 3: Add bread slices to board in 2 groupings.

Step 4: Group slices of bacon in center of board.

Step 5: Set bagel seasoning and honey on opposite ends of board.

Step 6: Fill in gaps with tangerines and grapes. Add serving utensils and a bread knife.

GARLIC-HERB BAGEL SPREAD
This creamy spread is loaded with oregano, basil, garlic and feta, for a flavorful combination that's perfect slathered on a toasted bagel. But don't stop there—try it on sandwiches, too, or as a dip for crunchy breadsticks.
—*Taste of Home* Test Kitchen

TAKES: 10 MIN.
MAKES: 8 SERVINGS (1 CUP)

- 3 oz. cream cheese, softened
- ⅓ cup sour cream
- ¼ cup crumbled feta cheese
- 2 garlic cloves, minced
- ½ tsp. each garlic powder, dried oregano and basil

In a bowl, beat the cream cheese until smooth. Add sour cream, feta cheese, garlic and seasonings; mix well.
2 Tbsp.: 68 cal., 6g fat (4g sat. fat), 15mg chol., 71mg sod., 2g carb. (1g sugars, 0 fiber), 2g pro.

PLATTER POINTER
Before arranging the breakfast items, consider covering your board with parchment paper to protect it from any bacon grease.

CUSTOMIZE YOUR BOARD

Use these recipes to create your own Continental Breakfast Board.

MANGO BELLINI

Simple yet delicious, this Bellini is made with fresh mango puree and your favorite sparkling wine—I usually use Prosecco for mine. You can easily turn this drink into a mocktail by using sparkling water in place of the sparkling wine.
—Ellen Folkman, Crystal Beach, FL

TAKES: 5 MIN. • **MAKES:** 6 SERVINGS

- ¾ cup mango nectar or fresh mango puree, chilled
- 1 bottle (750 ml) champagne or other sparkling wine, chilled

Add 2 Tbsp. mango nectar to each of 6 champagne flutes. Top each with champagne; gently stir to combine.
1 Bellini: 101 cal., 0 fat (0 sat. fat), 0 chol., 1mg sod., 6g carb. (4g sugars, 0 fiber), 0 pro.

PLATTER POINTER
Bellinis are a hit at any brunch gathering, but don't forget to offer orange juice, coffee, milk and mimosas alongside your breakfast board.

HONEY BAGELS

Who has the time to make from-scratch bagels? You do, with this easy recipe! The chewy golden bagels offer a hint of honey and will delight even the pickiest eaters.
—*Taste of Home* Test Kitchen

PREP: 1 HOUR + RISING
BAKE: 20 MIN. • **MAKES:** 1 DOZEN

- 1 Tbsp. active dry yeast
- 1¼ cups warm water (110° to 115°)
- 3 Tbsp. canola oil
- 3 Tbsp. sugar
- 3 Tbsp. plus ¼ cup honey, divided
- 1 tsp. brown sugar
- 1½ tsp. salt
- 1 large egg, room temperature
- 4 to 5 cups bread flour
- 1 Tbsp. dried minced onion
- 1 Tbsp. sesame seeds
- 1 Tbsp. poppy seeds

1. In a large bowl, dissolve yeast in warm water. Add the oil, sugar, 3 Tbsp. honey, brown sugar, salt and egg; mix well. Stir in enough of the flour to form a soft dough.

2. Turn onto a floured surface; knead 8-10 minutes or until a smooth, firm dough forms. Cover dough; let rise for 10 minutes.

3. Punch dough down. Shape into 12 balls. Push a thumb through the center of each ball to form a 1½-in. hole. Stretch and shape the dough to form even rings. Place the rings on a floured surface. Cover and let rise for 10 minutes; flatten bagels slightly.

4. In a large saucepan or Dutch oven, bring 8 cups water and the remaining honey to a boil. Drop the bagels, 1 at a time, into the boiling water. Cook the bagels for 45 seconds; turn and cook 45 seconds longer. Remove bagels with a slotted spoon; drain. Sprinkle with dried minced onion, sesame seeds and poppy seeds.

5. Place bagels 2 in. apart on baking sheets lined with parchment. Bake at 425° for 12 minutes. Flip the bagels and bake until golden brown, about 5 minutes longer.
1 bagel: 265 cal., 5g fat (1g sat. fat), 16mg chol., 303mg sod., 48g carb. (14g sugars, 2g fiber), 7g pro.

BRAIDED EGG BREAD

For Rosh Hashana, loaves of braided bread—commonly called challah—are baked to symbolize continuity. Since I first made this bread some years ago, it has become a much-requested recipe.
—Marlene Jeffery, Holland, MB

PREP: 30 MIN. + RISING
BAKE: 25 MIN.
MAKES: 1 LOAF (16 PIECES)

- 3¼ to 3¾ cups all-purpose flour
- 1 Tbsp. sugar
- 1 pkg. (¼ oz.) active dry yeast
- ¾ tsp. salt
- ¾ cup water
- 3 Tbsp. canola oil
- 2 large eggs, room temperature

TOPPING
- 1 large egg
- 1 tsp. water
- ½ tsp. poppy seeds

1. In a large bowl, combine 2½ cups flour, sugar, yeast and salt. In a small saucepan, heat the water and oil to 120°-130°. Add to dry ingredients along with eggs. Beat on medium speed for 3 minutes. Stir in enough remaining flour to form a soft dough.
2. Turn onto a lightly floured surface; knead 6-8 minutes or until smooth and elastic. Place dough in a greased bowl, turning once to grease top. Cover and let rise in a warm place until doubled, about 1½ hours.
3. Punch dough down. Turn onto a lightly floured surface. Set a third of the dough aside. Divide the remaining dough into 3 pieces. Shape each into a 13-in. rope. Place ropes on a greased baking sheet; braid ropes. Pinch ends to seal and tuck under.
4. Divide reserved dough into 3 equal pieces; shape each into a 14-in. rope. Braid ropes. Center 14-in. braid on top of the shorter braid. Pinch ends to seal and tuck under. Cover and let rise until doubled, about 30 minutes.

5. Preheat oven to 375°. In a small bowl, beat egg and water; brush over dough. Sprinkle with poppy seeds. Bake 25-30 minutes or until golden brown. Cover with foil during the last 15 minutes of baking. Remove from pan to a wire rack to cool.
1 piece: 134 cal., 4g fat (1g sat. fat), 40mg chol., 123mg sod., 20g carb. (1g sugars, 1g fiber), 4g pro.

ORANGE-GLAZED BACON

Just when you thought bacon couldn't get any tastier, we whipped up this version starring the favorite breakfast staple drizzled with sweet orange glaze.
—*Taste of Home* Test Kitchen

PREP: 20 MIN. • **BAKE:** 25 MIN.
MAKES: 8 SERVINGS

- ¾ cup orange juice
- ¼ cup honey
- 1 Tbsp. Dijon mustard
- ¼ tsp. ground ginger
- ⅛ tsp. pepper
- 1 lb. bacon strips

1. Preheat the oven to 350°. In a small saucepan, combine the first 5 ingredients. Bring to a boil; cook until liquid is reduced to ⅓ cup.
2. Place the bacon on a rack in an ungreased 15x10x1-in. baking pan. Bake for 10 minutes; drain.
3. Drizzle half of glaze over the bacon. Bake for 10 minutes. Turn bacon and drizzle with remaining glaze. Bake until golden brown, 5-10 minutes longer. Place bacon on waxed paper until set. Serve warm.
3 glazed bacon strips: 146 cal., 8g fat (3g sat. fat), 21mg chol., 407mg sod., 12g carb. (11g sugars, 0 fiber), 7g pro.

Share-a-Salad Platter

BARBECUE CHICKEN COBB SALAD

I turned barbecue chicken into a major salad with romaine, carrots, sweet peppers and avocados. That's how I got my family to eat more veggies.
—Camille Beckstrand, Layton, UT

PREP: 30 MIN. • **COOK:** 3 HOURS
MAKES: 6 SERVINGS

- 1 bottle (18 oz.) barbecue sauce
- 2 Tbsp. brown sugar
- ½ tsp. garlic powder
- ¼ tsp. paprika
- 1½ lbs. boneless skinless chicken breasts
- 12 cups chopped romaine
- 2 avocados, peeled and chopped
- 3 plum tomatoes, chopped
- 2 small carrots, thinly sliced
- 1 medium sweet red or green pepper, chopped
- 3 hard-boiled large eggs, chopped
- 6 bacon strips, cooked and crumbled
- 1½ cups shredded cheddar cheese
  Salad dressing of your choice

1. In a greased 3-qt. slow cooker, mix barbecue sauce, brown sugar, garlic powder and paprika. Add chicken; turn to coat. Cook, covered, on low for 3-4 hours or until the chicken is tender (a thermometer should read at least 165°).
2. Remove chicken from slow cooker; cut into bite-sized pieces. In a bowl, toss chicken with 1 cup barbecue sauce mixture. Place romaine on a large serving platter; arrange chicken, avocados, vegetables, eggs, bacon and cheese over romaine. Drizzle with dressing.
1 serving: 571 cal., 26g fat (9g sat. fat), 192mg chol., 1314mg sod., 47g carb. (32g sugars, 7g fiber), 39g pro.

CUSTOMIZE YOUR BOARD

Jazz up your salad platter (or weeknight dinner) with one of these easy homemade dressings.

Greek Salad Dressing
In a jar with a tight-fitting lid, combine ½ cup olive oil, ¼ cup red wine vinegar, 2 Tbsp. lemon juice, 2 minced garlic cloves, 1 tsp. Dijon mustard, ½ tsp. salt, ¼ tsp. pepper and ½ tsp. dried oregano; shake well.

Lemon Vinaigrette
In a large bowl, whisk 2 Tbsp. fresh lemon juice, 2 tsp. Dijon mustard, ¼ tsp. salt, and ⅛ tsp. coarsely ground pepper. Slowly add 6 Tbsp. extra virgin olive oil while whisking constantly.

Italian Herb Salad Dressing
Place ¾ cup olive oil, ½ cup red wine vinegar, 1 Tbsp. grated Parmesan or Romano cheese, 1 minced garlic clove, ½ tsp. salt, ½ tsp. sugar, ½ tsp. dried oregano and a pinch of pepper in a jar with a tight-fitting lid; shake well. Refrigerate until serving. Shake dressing again just before serving.

Green Goddess Salad Dressing
Place 1 cup mayonnaise, ½ cup sour cream, ¼ cup chopped green pepper, ¼ cup packed fresh parsley sprigs, 3 anchovy fillets, 2 Tbsp. lemon juice, 2 coarsely chopped green onion tops, 1 peeled garlic clove, ¼ tsp. pepper and ⅛ tsp. Worcestershire sauce in a blender; cover and process until smooth. Transfer to a bowl or jar; cover and store in the refrigerator.

Sandwich Board

SUN-DRIED TOMATO
MAYONNAISE, 140

QUICK & EASY
HONEY MUSTARD, 140

HOW TO BUILD A...
SANDWICH BOARD

Who doesn't love a sammie piled high with flavor? Let your gang build their own with this hearty board. Add whatever sandwich fixings your friends and family like best, and be sure to serve some potato chips on the side!

ITEMS TO INCLUDE

- Pretzel rolls
- Rye bread, sliced
- Dinner rolls
- Sun-Dried Tomato Mayonnaise
- Quick & Easy Honey Mustard
- Pepperoncini, sliced
- Sliced black olives
- Pepper jack, sliced
- Sharp cheddar sliced
- Provolone, sliced
- Colby jack, sliced
- Deli ham, sliced
- Deli roast beef, sliced
- Deli turkey, sliced
- Salami, sliced
- Green leaf lettuce
- Red tomato, sliced
- Yellow tomato, sliced
- Green pepper, sliced into rings
- Red onion, sliced
- Avocado, sliced
- Sliced pickles
- Pickle halves

EASY ASSEMBLY

Step 1: Group together the pretzel rolls, rye bread and dinner rolls at the top of the board.

Step 2: Spoon the Sun-Dried Tomato Mayonnaise, Quick & Easy Honey Mustard, pepperoncini and olives into small servings bowls. Set on the board.

Step 3: Fan the cheese slices onto the board in a grouping. Repeat with deli meats.

Step 4: Set lettuce leaves at bottom of board. Add tomatoes, green pepper and onion.

Step 5: Fill in gaps on board with avocado and pickles.

Step 6: Add serving utensils.

Platter Pointer: It is best to assemble and serve this board quickly. If the board is completed but guests are running late, remove the breads to a storage bag, cover the board and set in the refrigerator until you're ready to serve.

Note: Look for pepperoncini (pickled peppers) in the pickle and olive section of your grocery store.

QUICK & EASY HONEY MUSTARD

This fast, easy mustard with rice vinegar and honey has more flavor than any other honey mustard I have ever tried.
—Sharon Rehm, New Blaine, AR

TAKES: 5 MIN. • **MAKES:** 1 CUP

- ½ cup stone-ground mustard
- ¼ cup honey
- ¼ cup rice vinegar

In a small bowl, whisk all ingredients. Refrigerate until serving.
1 Tbsp.: 28 cal., 1g fat (0 sat. fat), 0 chol., 154mg sod., 6g carb. (5g sugars, 0 fiber), 0 pro.

SUN-DRIED TOMATO MAYONNAISE

I admit it—I'm a mayo fanatic. And I'm always looking for ways to kick it up. This tomato-y sauce is good slathered on burgers or brushed on grilled meats or as a dipping sauce for just about anything.
—Debbie Glasscock, Conway, AR

TAKES: 5 MINUTES • **MAKES:** ABOUT ½ CUP

- ½ cup mayonnaise
- 2 Tbsp. jarred sun-dried tomato pesto

Stir together the mayonnaise and pesto until well blended. Refrigerate until serving.
1 Tbsp.: 96 cal., 10g fat (2g sat. fat), 1mg chol., 109mg sod., 1g carb. (0 sugars, 0 fiber), 0 pro.
Honey BBQ: Substitute 2 Tbsp. honey barbecue sauce for pesto.
Honey-Dijon: Substitute 2 Tbsp. honey and 2 Tbsp. Dijon mustard for pesto.

QUICK & EASY HONEY MUSTARD TIPS

Can I use different types of mustard or vinegar?
When making this honey mustard recipe, you can substitute your favorite brown mustard such as Dijon, spicy brown or Dusseldorf for the stone ground mustard. If substituting the vinegar, reach for one with a more neutral flavor such as apple cider, red wine or champagne vinegar.

What can I add honey mustard to?
In addition to sandwiches, burgers and hot dogs, you can use this mustard on pork chops or salmon. You can toss it with fresh greens for a tasty salad as well.

How long does homemade honey mustard last?
Homemade honey mustard will last for up to 6 weeks in the refrigerator if it's tightly sealed. But before using, let your eyes and nose determine if it's still fresh. Both the aroma and the appearance should be unchanged. If a little liquid has settled on the top, it's OK to stir it back in as long as it still smells fresh and there is no appearance of mold.

CHICKEN TOSTADA CUPS

Years ago, I tried a version of these cups at a restaurant in Santa Fe, and I wanted to make my own spin. Serve them on a platter for perfect party fare, and let guests add their own toppings.
—Marla Clark, Moriarty, NM

PREP: 25 MIN. • **BAKE:** 15 MIN.
MAKES: 6 SERVINGS

- 12 corn tortillas (6 in.), warmed
     Cooking spray
- 2   cups shredded rotisserie chicken
- 1   cup salsa
- 1   can (16 oz.) refried beans
- 1   cup shredded reduced-fat Mexican cheese blend
     Optional toppings: Shredded lettuce, reduced-fat sour cream, chopped cilantro, diced avocado, sliced jalapeno, lime wedges, sliced ripe olives, sliced green onions, sliced radishes, and pico de gallo or additional salsa

1. Preheat oven to 425°. Press warm tortillas into 12 muffin cups coated with cooking spray, pleating sides as needed. Spritz tortillas with additional cooking spray.
2. Bake 5-7 minutes or until lightly browned. Toss chicken with salsa. Layer each cup with beans, chicken mixture and cheese.
3. Bake 9-11 minutes or until heated through. Serve with optional toppings as desired.

2 tostada cups: 338 cal., 11g fat (4g sat. fat), 52mg chol., 629mg sod., 35g carb. (2g sugars, 6g fiber), 25g pro. **Diabetic exchanges:** 3 lean meat, 2 starch, 1 fat.

Tostada Platter

REFRESHING BEER
MARGARITAS, 148

MILD TOMATO
SALSA, 148

HOMEMADE
GUACAMOLE, 150

SEASONED
TACO MEAT, 149

PICO DE
GALLO, 149

SLOW-COOKED
CARNITAS, 151

Taco Tuesday Platter

SOUTHWESTERN
SAUTEED CORN, 151

HOW TO BUILD A...
TACO TUESDAY PLATTER

ITEMS TO INCLUDE
- Seasoned Taco Meat
- Slow-Cooked Carnitas
- Mild Tomato Salsa
- Homemade Guacamole
- Southwestern Sauteed Corn
- Pico de Gallo
- Prepared refried beans
- Sour cream
- Hard taco shells
- Flour or corn tortillas
- Red onion, separated into rings
- Cotija cheese, crumbled
- Sliced black olives
- Shredded red cabbage
- Bibb lettuce leaves
- Jalapeno peppers, sliced
- Shredded cheese
- Sweet red pepper, julienned
- Limes, cut into halves and wedges
- Shredded lettuce
- Radishes, thinly sliced
- Refreshing Beer Margaritas

EASY ASSEMBLY
Step 1: Put the Seasoned Taco Meat and Slow-Cooked Carnitas in medium bowls. Put the Mild Tomato Salsa, Homemade Guacamole, Southwestern Sauteed Corn, Pico de Gallo, refried beans and sour cream in smaller bowls. Place bowls on a rimmed baking pan.

Step 2: Add taco shells and tortillas.

Step 3: Fill in gaps with onion, Cotija, olives, cabbage, Bibb lettuce, jalapenos, shredded cheese, red peppers, limes, shredded lettuce and radishes.

Step 4: Serve taco platter with Refreshing Beer Margaritas.

REFRESHING BEER MARGARITAS

I'm always surprised when people say they didn't know this drink existed. It's an ideal summertime cocktail, and it's easy to double or even triple the recipe.
—Arianne Barnett, Kansas City, MO

TAKES: 5 MIN. • **MAKES:** 6 SERVINGS

      Optional: Lime slices and
      kosher salt
   2 bottles (12 oz. each) beer
   1 can (12 oz.) frozen limeade
      concentrate, thawed
   ¾ cup tequila
   ¼ cup sweet-and-sour mix
      Ice cubes
GARNISH
      Lime slices

1. If desired, garnish rims of glasses. Moisten rims of 6 margarita or cocktail glasses with lime slices. Sprinkle salt on a plate; hold each glass upside down and dip rims into salt. Discard remaining salt.
2. In a pitcher, combine beer, limeade concentrate, tequila and sweet-and-sour mix. Serve over ice in prepared glasses. Garnish with lime slices.
¾ cup: 243 cal., 0 fat (0 sat. fat), 0 chol., 8mg sod., 37g carb. (33g sugars, 0 fiber), 1g pro.

MILD TOMATO SALSA

I got this salsa recipe from my sister, and my children and I have been making it ever since. We pair pint jars of our salsa with packages of tortilla chips for gifts. When my kids give this present to their teachers, they can truly say they helped make it.
—Pamela Lundstrum, Bird Island, MN

PREP: 40 MIN. + SIMMERING
PROCESS: 20 MIN. + COOLING
MAKES: 10 PINTS

 10½ lbs. tomatoes (about 35 medium),
      blanched, peeled and quartered
    4 medium green peppers, chopped
    3 large onions, chopped
    2 cans (12 oz. each) tomato paste
 1¾ cups white vinegar
   ½ cup sugar
    1 medium sweet red pepper,
      chopped
    1 celery rib, chopped
   15 garlic cloves, minced
    4 to 5 jalapeno peppers,
      seeded and chopped
   ¼ cup canning salt
   ¼ to ½ tsp. hot pepper sauce

1. In a stockpot, cook the tomatoes, uncovered, over medium heat for 20 minutes. Drain, reserving 2 cups liquid. Return tomatoes to the pot.
2. Stir in the green peppers, onions, tomato paste, vinegar, sugar, red pepper, celery, garlic, jalapenos, canning salt, hot pepper sauce and reserved tomato liquid. Bring to a boil. Reduce heat and simmer, uncovered, 1 hour, stirring frequently.
3. Ladle hot mixture into 10 hot 1-pint jars, leaving ½-in. headspace. Remove air bubbles and adjust headspace, if necessary, by adding hot mixture. Wipe rims. Center lids on jars; screw on the bands until fingertip tight.
4. Place jars into a canner filled with simmering water, ensuring they are completely covered with water. Bring to a boil; process 20 minutes. Remove jars and cool.
Note: Wear disposable gloves when cutting hot peppers; the oils can burn skin. Avoid touching your face.
2 Tbsp.: 14 cal., 0 fat (0 sat. fat), 0 chol., 182mg sod., 3g carb. (2g sugars, 1g fiber), 0 pro.

SEASONED TACO MEAT

I got this recipe from the restaurant where I work. Everyone in town loves the blend of different seasonings, and now the secret is out for everyone to enjoy!
—Denise Mumm, Dixon, IA

PREP: 10 MIN. • **COOK:** 35 MIN.
MAKES: 6½ CUPS

- 3 lbs. ground beef
- 2 large onions, chopped
- 2 cups water
- 5 Tbsp. chili powder
- 2 tsp. salt
- 1 tsp. ground cumin
- ¾ tsp. garlic powder
- ¼ to ½ tsp. crushed red pepper flakes

In a large cast-iron skillet or Dutch oven, cook the beef and onion over medium heat, crumbling meat, until the meat is no longer pink; drain. Add water and seasonings. Bring to a boil. Reduce heat; simmer, uncovered, until water is evaporated, about 15 minutes.
¼ cup: 113 cal., 7g fat (3g sat. fat), 35mg chol., 277mg sod., 2g carb. (1g sugars, 1g fiber), 10g pro.

PICO DE GALLO

This easy pico de gallo recipe is a classic for good reason. It pairs with just about everything! My tip is to let it chill for an hour or two before serving to help the flavors blend. Also, it's best to serve it the same day that it's made.
—Jeannie Trudell, Del Norte, CO

TAKES: 10 MIN. + CHILLING
MAKES: 8 SERVINGS

- 6 plum tomatoes, chopped
- 1 small onion, finely chopped
- ½ cup chopped fresh cilantro
- 1 to 2 jalapeno peppers, seeded and finely chopped
- 3 Tbsp. lime juice (about 1 lime)
- 1 Tbsp. cilantro stems, finely chopped
- 1 garlic clove, minced
- ¼ tsp. salt

In a medium bowl, combine all the ingredients. Cover and refrigerate for 1-2 hours before serving.
¼ cup: 14 cal., 0 fat (0 sat. fat), 0 chol., 40mg sod., 3g carb. (2g sugars, 1g fiber), 1g pro. **Diabetic exchanges:** free food.

HOMEMADE TACO SEASONING MIX

Skip the store-bought stuff and make this zesty homemade taco seasoning mix yourself. This recipe tastes like purchased mixes, but it is cheaper and has nearly half the sodium. Your heart and wallet will surely thank you.
—*Taste of Home* Test Kitchen

- ¼ cup all-purpose flour
- ¼ cup chili powder
- 3 Tbsp. dried minced onion
- 1 Tbsp. garlic powder
- 2½ tsp. salt
- 2 tsp. dried oregano
- 2 tsp. ground cumin
- 1½ tsp. cayenne pepper
- 1 tsp. ground coriander

Combine all ingredients. Store in an airtight container in a cool, dry place for up to 1 year.

HOMEMADE GUACAMOLE

Nothing is better than freshly made guacamole when you're eating something spicy. This recipe is easy to whip together in a matter of minutes, and it quickly tames anything that's too hot.

—Joan Hallford, North Richland Hills, TX

TAKES: 10 MIN. • **MAKES:** 2 CUPS

- 3 medium ripe avocados, peeled and cubed
- 1 garlic clove, minced
- ¼ to ½ tsp. salt
- 1 small onion, finely chopped
- 1 to 2 Tbsp. lime juice
- 1 Tbsp. minced fresh cilantro
- 2 medium tomatoes, seeded and chopped, optional
- ¼ cup mayonnaise, optional

Mash avocados with garlic and salt. Stir in remaining ingredients, adding tomatoes and mayonnaise if desired. **¼ cup:** 90 cal., 8g fat (1g sat. fat), 0 chol., 78mg sod., 6g carb. (1g sugars, 4g fiber), 1g pro. **Diabetic exchanges:** 1½ fat.

HOW TO MAKE CORN TORTILLAS

Step 1: In a bowl, combine 2 cups masa harina and ½ tsp. salt; stir in 1½ cups hot water. Add additional hot water, 1 Tbsp. at a time, until the dough is firm but moist. Cover and let rest for 1 hour.

Step 2: Divide dough into 12 portions; roll into balls.

Step 3: Gently flatten 1 dough ball between 2 pieces of waxed paper, using a tortilla press or by pressing with the bottom of a large saucepan or skillet.

Step 4: Remove 1 piece of the waxed paper. Transfer tortilla, paper side up, to a preheated skillet over medium-high heat. Carefully remove remaining piece of waxed paper and cook tortilla for 1 minute until slightly dry. Flip and cook 1 minute longer until dry and light brown but still soft.

Step 5: Transfer to a tortilla warmer or wrap in foil.

Step 6: Repeat with remaining dough balls. Serve tortillas on board or in tortilla warmer.

SOUTHWESTERN SAUTEED CORN

My mother-in-law came up with this dish one night for dinner. The lime juice might sound like a wild card, but everyone who tries it asks for more!
—Chandy Ward, Aumsville, OR

TAKES: 20 MIN. • **MAKES:** 5 SERVINGS

1	Tbsp. butter
3⅓	cups fresh corn or 1 pkg. (16 oz.) frozen corn
1	plum tomato, chopped
1	Tbsp. lime juice
½	tsp. salt
½	tsp. ground cumin
⅓	cup minced fresh cilantro

In a large cast-iron or other heavy skillet, heat butter over medium-high heat. Add corn; cook and stir until tender, 3-5 minutes. Reduce heat to medium low; stir in tomato, lime juice, salt and cumin. Cook until heated through, 3-4 minutes. Remove from heat; stir in cilantro.

⅔ cup: 104 cal., 3g fat (2g sat. fat), 6mg chol., 256mg sod., 20g carb. (2g sugars, 2g fiber), 3g pro. **Diabetic exchanges:** 1 starch, ½ fat.

SLOW-COOKED CARNITAS

Simmer succulent pork the slow-cooker way. Sometimes, instead of eating it on tortillas, I put the seasoned meat on top of shredded lettuce for a tasty salad.
—Lisa Glogow, Aliso Viejo, CA

PREP: 20 MIN. • **COOK:** 6 HOURS
MAKES: 12 SERVINGS

1	boneless pork shoulder butt roast (3 to 4 lbs.)
3	garlic cloves, thinly sliced
2	tsp. olive oil
½	tsp. salt
½	tsp. pepper
1	bunch green onions, chopped
1½	cups minced fresh cilantro
1	cup salsa
½	cup chicken broth
½	cup tequila or additional chicken broth
2	cans (4 oz. each) chopped green chiles
12	flour tortillas (8 in.) or corn tortillas (6 in.), warmed

Optional toppings: Fresh cilantro leaves, sliced red onion and chopped tomatoes

1. Cut roast in half; place in a 5-qt. slow cooker. Sprinkle with the garlic, oil, salt and pepper. Add the onions, cilantro, salsa, broth, tequila and chiles. Cover and cook on low for 6-8 hours or until meat is tender.
2. Remove meat; cool slightly. Shred with 2 forks and return to the slow cooker; heat through. Spoon about ⅔ cup meat mixture onto each tortilla; serve with toppings of your choice.

1 carnitas taco: 363 cal., 15g fat (5g sat. fat), 67mg chol., 615mg sod., 28g carb. (1g sugars, 1g fiber), 24g pro.

Seafood Boil Platter

SEAFOOD BOIL PLATTER

Grilled bratwurst and onion add a nice smoky flavor to corn, potatoes and fish for a hearty meal that's always a hit.
—Trisha Kruse, Eagle, ID

PREP: 25 MIN. • **COOK:** 30 MIN.
MAKES: 6 SERVINGS

- 1   pkg. (19 oz.) uncooked bratwurst links
- 1   medium onion, quartered
- 2   bottles (12 oz. each) beer or 3 cups reduced-sodium chicken broth
- ½   cup seafood seasoning
- 5   medium ears sweet corn, cut into 2-in. pieces
- 2   lbs. small red potatoes
- 1   medium lemon, halved
- 1   lb. cod fillet, cut into 1-in. pieces
     Coarsely ground pepper

1. Grill the bratwurst, covered, over medium heat, turning frequently, until meat is no longer pink, 15-20 minutes. Grill the onion, covered, until lightly browned, 3-4 minutes on each side. Cut grilled bratwurst into 2-in. pieces.
2. In a stockpot, combine 2 qt. water, beer and seafood seasoning; add corn, potatoes, lemon, bratwurst and onion. Bring to a boil. Reduce heat; simmer, uncovered, until potatoes are tender, 15-20 minutes. Stir in the cod; cook 4-6 minutes or until fish flakes easily with a fork. Drain; transfer to a large serving bowl. Sprinkle with pepper.
1 serving: 553 cal., 28g fat (9g sat. fat), 95mg chol., 1620mg sod., 46g carb. (8g sugars, 5g fiber), 30g pro.

FRESH FISH
You'll have the catch of the day when you follow this advice.

How to Buy
All fish should have shiny, bright skin and a mild aroma. Select whole fish with clear eyes (not sunken or cloudy) and a firm body that is springy to the touch.

How to Store
Store fish on ice to keep it at its freshest. Place frozen blue ice blocks in a container, then top with wrapped fish. Use within a few days, replacing ice blocks as needed. Wash the ice blocks with hot soapy water before reuse.

How to Prepare
Always follow the recipe's directions when preparing fish, paying particular attention to the cooking time. Most fish fillets are cooked when the fish flakes apart with a fork.

SWEET CORN
Turn to these handy tips the next time summer's buttery best is on the menu.

How to Buy
Always look for green husks and fresh-looking silk. Pull the husk down slightly to check for firm kernels. Inspect the kernels to ensure they don't appear milky, and avoid buying corn that has uneven rows or rows with gaps.

How to Store
Keep corn, with husks intact, in the refrigerator for up to 2 days.

How to Prep
Remove the husk and silk by grabbing both at the end of the stalk and pulling down. Then snap or cut off the stalk.

FLAVORFUL PIZZA
SAUCE, 156

BASIC PIZZA
CRUST, 156

Pizza
Board

HOW TO BUILD A...
PIZZA BOARD

ITEMS TO INCLUDE

- Basic Pizza Crust
- Flavorful Pizza Sauce
- Pineapple, chopped
- Sliced black olives
- Shredded mozzarella
- Pepperoncini
- Deli ham, thinly sliced
- Bacon, cooked and diced
- Red onion, sliced
- Tomatoes, sliced
- Green peppers, julienned
- Mushrooms, sliced
- Sliced pepperoni
- Sausage, cooked and crumbled
- Parmesan wedge
- Crushed red pepper flakes
- Fresh basil

EASY ASSEMBLY

Step 1: Prepare Basic Pizza Crust, dividing dough into multiple crusts for single-serving pizzas and adjusting baking time as needed.

Step 2: Spoon Flavorful Pizza Sauce, pineapple, black olives and mozzarella cheese into small bowls. Scatter the bowls evenly over board along with jar of Pepperoncini.

Step 3: Set the ham and bacon on either side of pineapple.

Step 4: Fill in gaps with onions, tomatoes, green peppers, mushrooms, pepperoni and sausage.

Step 4: Serve board with Parmesan, red pepper flakes and basil.

Note: After pizzas are assembled, bake in a 425° oven for 10-15 minutes.

Platter Pointers

- Keep things simple by using packaged individual pizza crusts instead of making your own.
- Try to keep classic pizza fixings together. We set the ham, pineapple and bacon together so guests instantly understood they could make a Hawaiian pizza. Do the same with the veggies for a meatless pie.
- Using sliced tomatoes instead of chopped helps give the eye a place to rest since many of the items on the board are small.
- Try to balance out sliced items such as the onion and green pepper with round foods like the pepperoni and tomato slices.
- Don't forget to add a cheese grater to the wedge of Parmesan.

FLAVORFUL PIZZA SAUCE

I could never find the right pizza sauce recipe for me. So I experimented with my own version until I got it just right. I think you'll enjoy it!
—Cheryl Williams, Evington, VA

TAKES: 15 MIN. • **MAKES:** ABOUT 2½ CUPS

- 2 cans (8 oz. each) tomato sauce
- 1 can (12 oz.) tomato paste
- 4 tsp. Worcestershire sauce
- 1 Tbsp. dried parsley flakes
- 1 Tbsp. Italian seasoning
- 1½ tsp. garlic powder
- 1 tsp. sugar
- 1 tsp. dried basil
- 1 tsp. dried oregano
- ¾ tsp. salt
- ¼ tsp. pepper

In a large bowl, combine all of the ingredients. Spread desired amount over a pizza crust or transfer to a storage container. Refrigerate, covered, up to 1 week or keep sauce frozen for up to 6 months.

2 Tbsp.: 24 cal., 0 fat (0 sat. fat), 0 chol., 217mg sod., 5g carb. (3g sugars, 1g fiber), 1g pro.

BASIC PIZZA CRUST

I like to double this recipe and keep one baked crust in the freezer for a quick snack or meal later.
—Beverly Anderson, Sinclairville, NY

PREP: 10 MIN. + RESTING • **BAKE:** 25 MIN.
MAKES: 1 PIZZA CRUST (6 SLICES)

- 1 pkg. (¼ oz.) active dry yeast
- 1 cup warm water (110° to 115°)
- 2 Tbsp. canola oil
- 1 tsp. sugar
- ¼ tsp. salt
- 2½ to 2¾ cups all-purpose flour
  Cornmeal
  Pizza toppings of your choice

1. In a large bowl, dissolve yeast in warm water. Add the oil, sugar, salt and 1½ cups flour. Beat until smooth. Stir in enough remaining flour to form a firm dough. Turn onto a floured surface; cover and let rest for 10 minutes.

2. Roll into a 13-in. circle. Grease a 12-in. pizza pan and sprinkle with cornmeal. Transfer dough to prepared pan, building up edges slightly. Do not let rise. Bake at 425° until browned, 12-15 minutes. Add toppings; bake 10-15 minutes longer.

1 piece: 236 cal., 5g fat (1g sat. fat), 0 chol., 100mg sod., 41g carb. (2g sugars, 2g fiber), 6g pro.

5 TIPS FOR PIZZA-CRUST PERFECTION

Making your own pizza crust is way easier than you might think. Just keep these secrets in mind.

- Make sure to use the type of yeast called for in the pizza crust recipe.
- Use a thermometer to check the temperature of the water. If it's too cool, it won't activate the yeast; if too hot, it may kill the yeast.
- Don't use too much flour. Start with the minimum amount and add more only until the dough reaches the consistency indicated in the method.
- Use only enough flour on your work surface to keep the dough from sticking when you're kneading it.
- Continue kneading until the dough is no longer sticky, has a smooth, satiny texture and springs back when pressed with your fingers.

CUSTOMIZE YOUR BOARD

GARLIC & CHEESE FLATBREAD

Unless you plan to make two, don't count on leftovers. As an appetizer or side, this cheesy flat bread will be devoured in less time than it takes to bake. And that's not very long!
—Suzanne Zick, Maiden, NC

TAKES: 25 MIN. • **MAKES:** 12 SERVINGS

- 1 tube (11 oz.) refrigerated thin pizza crust
- 2 Tbsp. butter, melted
- 1 Tbsp. minced fresh basil
- 4 garlic cloves, minced
- ¾ cup shredded cheddar cheese
- ½ cup grated Romano cheese
- ¼ cup grated Parmesan cheese

1. Unroll dough into a greased 15x10x1-in. baking pan; flatten dough to a 13x9-in. rectangle and build up edges slightly.
2. Drizzle with butter. Sprinkle with basil, garlic and cheeses.

3. Bake at 425° until crisp, roughly 11-14 minutes. Cut into squares; serve flatbread warm.
1 piece: 146 cal., 8g fat (4g sat. fat), 19mg chol., 317mg sod., 13g carb. (1g sugars, 0 fiber), 6g pro.

ZESTY PIZZA SAUCE

Besides using this as a pizza sauce, I also use it as an all-purpose pasta sauce. I like to freeze it in small portions and defrost it as needed.
—Beth Dauenhauer, Pueblo, CO

PREP: 25 MIN. • **COOK:** 70 MIN.
MAKES: 4 CUPS

- 1 small green pepper, chopped
- ⅓ cup chopped onion
- ¼ cup finely chopped carrot
- 2 garlic cloves, minced
- 1½ tsp. olive oil
- 1 can (28 oz.) whole tomatoes, undrained
- 1 can (15 oz.) tomato sauce
- ¾ cup brewed coffee
- ⅓ cup tomato paste
- 1½ tsp. Worcestershire sauce
- ¾ tsp. paprika
- ¼ tsp. salt
- ⅛ tsp. each dried basil, marjoram, oregano and thyme
- ⅛ tsp. fennel seed, crushed
- ⅛ tsp. pepper

1. In a large nonstick saucepan, saute the green pepper, onion, carrot and garlic in oil until tender. Stir in the remaining ingredients. Bring to a boil. Reduce heat; simmer, uncovered, for 1 hour or until sauce reaches desired thickness, stirring occasionally.
2. Cool slightly. In a food processor, process sauce in batches until blended. Spread desired amount over a pizza crust, or cool and then refrigerate or freeze. Sauce may be frozen for up to 3 months.
¼ cup: 30 cal., 1g fat (0 sat. fat), 0 chol., 243mg sod., 5g carb., (3g sugars, 2g fiber), 1g pro.

ITALIAN SEASONING

Who needs salt when you can give pizzas, breads, pasta, spaghetti sauce and other dishes an Italian flair with this distinctive dried herb blend?
—*Taste of Home* Test Kitchen

TAKES: 5 MIN. • **MAKES:** 7 TBSP.

- 3 Tbsp. each dried basil, oregano and parsley flakes
- 1 Tbsp. garlic powder
- 1 tsp. dried thyme
- 1 tsp. dried rosemary, crushed
- ¼ tsp. pepper
- ¼ tsp. crushed red pepper flakes

Place all ingredients, in batches if necessary, in a spice grinder or small bowl. Grind or crush with the back of a spoon until mixture becomes a coarse powder. Store in an airtight container for up to 6 months.
¼ tsp.: 1 cal., 1g fat (0 sat. fat), 0 chol., 1mg sod., 1g carb. (0 sugars, 1g fiber), 1g pro.

Holiday Boards

From Easter brunches to Christmas buffets, these platters make parties merry and bright.

Valentine's Day Platter

FLUFFY STRAWBERRY
FRUIT DIP, 162

MARBLED
MERINGUE
HEARTS, 161

KETTLE
CORN, 162

HOW TO BUILD A...
VALENTINE'S DAY PLATTER

Surprise your sweetie with a platter of vivacious delights. Featuring homemade treats and store-bought sweets, it's both easy and impressive.

ITEMS TO INCLUDE
- Fluffy Strawberry Fruit Dip
- Heart-shaped cookies
- Dragonfruit, sliced and quartered
- Strawberries, hulled, halved and cut to resemble hearts
- Blueberries
- Grapes
- Wheel of Brie
- Raspberries
- Cranberry Cheese
- Heart-shaped crackers
- Kettle Corn
- Conversation hearts
- Marbled Meringue Hearts
- Heart-shaped chocolates
- Chocolate-covered pretzels
- Gummy hearts
- Hershey Kisses

EASY ASSEMBLY

Step 1: Spoon Fluffy Strawberry Dip into a small bowl and set on board.

Step 2: Set the heart-shaped cookies and fruit around the dip.

Step 3: Set Brie on board. Top with raspberries. Set cranberry cheese and crackers near Brie.

Step 4: Place the Kettle Corn and conversation hearts in small serving bowls; add to board.

Step 5: Set Marbled Meringue Hearts in groupings on the board.

Step 6: Fill in any gaps on the board with remaining items.

MARBLED MERINGUE HEARTS

Pretty pastel cookies are a fun way to brighten any special occasion. Replace the vanilla with a different extract for a change of flavor.
—Laurie Herr, Westford, VT

PREP: 25 MIN. • **BAKE:** 20 MIN. + COOLING
MAKES: ABOUT 2 DOZEN

- 3 **large egg whites**
- ½ **tsp. vanilla extract**
- ¼ **tsp. cream of tartar**
- ¾ **cup sugar**
  Red food coloring

1. Place egg whites in a large bowl; let stand at room temperature for 30 minutes. Line baking sheets with parchment.
2. Preheat oven to 200°. Add vanilla and cream of tartar to egg whites; beat on medium speed until soft peaks form. Gradually beat in sugar, 1 Tbsp. at a time, on high until stiff peaks form.

Remove ¼ cup and tint pink. Lightly swirl pink mixture into the remaining meringue. Fill pastry bag with the meringue. Pipe 2-in. heart shapes 2 in. apart onto prepared baking sheets.
3. Bake until set and dry, about 20 minutes. Turn oven off; leave meringues in oven until oven has completely cooled. Store hearts in an airtight container.

1 meringue: 27 cal., 0 fat (0 sat. fat), 0 chol., 7mg sod., 6g carb. (6g sugars, 0 fiber), 0 pro.

PLATTER POINTER
Chocolates wrapped in foil make quick, easy additions to boards. The shiny wrappers add a bit of flair, and the small size fills in gaps nicely.

FLUFFY STRAWBERRY FRUIT DIP

Our family enjoys fruit of all kinds, so this fluffy dip is one of our favorites.
—Virginia Krites, Cridersville, OH

TAKES: 5 MIN. • **MAKES:** 4 CUPS

- 1 carton (8 oz.) spreadable strawberry cream cheese
- 2 Tbsp. strawberry preserves
- 1 carton (8 oz.) frozen whipped topping, thawed
- 1 jar (7 oz.) marshmallow creme
  Assorted fresh fruit

In a bowl, beat cream cheese and preserves until blended. Fold in whipped topping and marshmallow creme. Cover and refrigerate until serving. Serve with fruit.

2 Tbsp.: 66 cal., 3g fat (3g sat. fat), 6mg chol., 27mg sod., 9g carb. (7g sugars, 0 fiber), 0 pro.

KETTLE CORN

If one of the reasons you go to fairs is to satisfy your craving for popcorn, you'll get the same wonderful salty-sweet taste at home with my kettle corn recipe. Now you can indulge whenever the mood strikes.
—Jenn Martin, Sebago, ME

TAKES: 15 MIN. • **MAKES:** 3 QT.

- ½ cup popcorn kernels
- ¼ cup sugar
- 3 Tbsp. canola oil
- 2 to 3 Tbsp. butter, melted
- ½ tsp. salt

1. In a Dutch oven over medium heat, cook popcorn, sugar and oil until oil begins to sizzle. Cover and shake until popcorn stops popping, 3-4 minutes.
2. Transfer to a large bowl. Drizzle with butter. Add salt; toss to coat.

1 cup: 91 cal., 6g fat (1g sat. fat), 5mg chol., 114mg sod., 11g carb. (4g sugars, 1g fiber), 1g pro.

TAKE YOUR PLATTER TO A NEW LEVEL

It's easy to amp up your Valentine game when you add even more to your platter.

What else can I put on a Valentine's Day platter?
Think about all the Valentine's Day candies you can put on a dessert board like this! Start with pink and red M&Ms, Ferrero Rocher truffles, red licorice, chocolate roses, or even red, pink and white candy corn. If you have time to go the homemade route, whip up a batch of fudge or conversation cupcakes, or upgrade the popcorn by drizzling it with melted colored white chocolate. Consider making treats you can adorn with red, white and pink sprinkles, like sugar cookies or chocolate-covered pretzel rods. If you want to add a few savory options to your Valentine's Day charcuterie-style board, use cookie cutters to cut hearts out of tea sandwiches or slices of cheese or meat (and don't forget salami roses!). You can even cut a heart shape from a wheel of cheese and fill it with red jam.

What drinks can I serve with a Valentine's Day platter?
Stay on theme by pouring sparkling wine, rosé or sangria. If you're looking for something bubbly without booze, go for sparkling ciders, grape juices or water with a few raspberries tossed into the glass. If you can never get enough chocolate, serve your Valentine's Day charcuterie board with creamy hot cocoa—or serve it alongside a hot chocolate board!

CUSTOMIZE YOUR BOARD

PALMIERS

It takes just two ingredients to make these impressive but easy-to-do French pastries, which are often called palm leaves. You'll be hooked after one bite.
—*Taste of Home* Test Kitchen

PREP: 20 MIN. + FREEZING
BAKE: 10 MIN. • **MAKES:** 2 DOZEN

- 1   cup sugar, divided
- 1   sheet frozen puff pastry, thawed

1. Preheat oven to 425°. Sprinkle a surface with ¼ cup sugar; unfold puff pastry sheet on surface. Sprinkle with 2 Tbsp. sugar. Roll into a 14x10-in. rectangle. Sprinkle with ½ cup sugar to within ½ in. of edges. Lightly press into pastry.

2. With a knife, very lightly score a line crosswise across the middle of the pastry. Starting at a short side, roll up jelly-roll style, stopping at the score mark in the middle. Starting at the other side, roll up pastry jelly-roll style to the score mark. Freeze until firm, 20-30 minutes. Cut into ⅜-in. slices.

3. Place cut side up 2 in. apart on parchment-lined baking sheets; sprinkle lightly with 1 Tbsp. sugar. Bake for 8 minutes. Turn pastries over and sprinkle with final 1 Tbsp. sugar. Bake until golden brown and glazed, about 3 minutes longer. Remove to wire racks to cool completely. Store in airtight containers.

1 pastry: 83 cal., 3g fat (1g sat. fat), 0mg chol., 34mg sod., 14g carb. (8g sugars, 1g fiber), 1g pro.

SUGARED DOUGHNUT HOLES

These tasty, tender doughnut bites are easy to make. Serve them warm in a small paper bag, as is done at the fair, or tucked in a small gift box wrapped with ribbon as a party favor. No matter how they arrive, they make any day special.
—Judy Jungwirth, Athol, SD

TAKES: 20 MIN. • **MAKES:** ABOUT 3 DOZEN

- 1½ cups all-purpose flour
- ⅓   cup sugar
- 2   tsp. baking powder
- ½   tsp. salt
- ½   tsp. ground nutmeg
- 1   large egg, room temperature
- ½   cup 2% milk
- 2   Tbsp. butter, melted
      Oil for deep-fat frying
      Confectioners' sugar

1. In a large bowl, combine the flour, sugar, baking powder, salt and nutmeg. In a small bowl, combine the egg, milk and butter. Add to dry ingredients and mix well.

2. In an electric skillet or deep-fat fryer, heat oil to 375°. Drop dough by heaping teaspoonfuls, 5 or 6 at a time, into oil. Fry until browned, 1-2 minutes, turning once. Drain on paper towels. Roll warm doughnut holes in confectioners' sugar.

1 doughnut hole: 47 cal., 2g fat (1g sat. fat), 7mg chol., 68mg sod., 6g carb. (2g sugars, 0 fiber), 1g pro.

Rainbow Snack Platter

EASY ASSEMBLY
Arrange multicolored snacks—
including raw vegetables, cheese
cubes and crackers—in a rainbow
pattern on a serving tray. Put a
small bowl of honey-mustard
salad dressing or hummus at the
end of the rainbow for dipping.

HOMEMADE HONEY-MUSTARD DRESSING

This creamy dressing is a tangy way to top off a green salad tossed with grapes or grapefruit segments. Or, use it as a dip for pretzels or veggies. Dijon mustard provides the lively flavor.
—Carol Severson, Shelton, WA

TAKES: 15 MIN. • **MAKES:** 2 CUPS

- ⅓ cup honey
- ¼ cup Dijon mustard
- ¼ cup white wine vinegar
- 2 Tbsp. lemon juice
- 1 garlic clove, minced
- 1 cup vegetable oil

In a blender, combine the first 5 ingredients. While processing, gradually add oil in a steady stream until smooth and creamy. Store dressing in the refrigerator.
2 Tbsp.: 148 cal., 14g fat (2g sat. fat), 0 chol., 95mg sod., 7g carb. (6g sugars, 0 fiber), 0 pro.

CUSTOMIZE YOUR BOARD

MARSHMALLOW FRUIT DIP

You can whip up this sweet and creamy dip in just 10 minutes. I like to serve it in a bowl surrounded by fresh-picked strawberries at spring brunches or luncheons.
—Cindy Steffen, Cedarburg, WI

TAKES: 10 MIN.
MAKES: 5 CUPS (40 SERVINGS)

- 1 pkg. (8 oz.) cream cheese, softened
- ¾ cup cherry yogurt
- 1 carton (8 oz.) frozen whipped topping, thawed
- 1 jar (7 oz.) marshmallow creme
  Assorted fresh fruit

In a large bowl, beat cream cheese and yogurt until blended. Fold in whipped topping and marshmallow creme. Serve with fruit arranged as desired.
2 Tbsp.: 56 cal., 3g fat (2g sat. fat), 7mg chol., 24mg sod., 6g carb. (5g sugars, 0 fiber), 1g pro.

PLATTER POINTER
Rainbow-themed boards are a low-fuss choice for anyone new to charcuterie. You can even have the kids assemble them. Simply group together foods of similar colors for an oh-so easy yet very impressive presentation.

Easter Candy Board

PINWHEEL
MINTS, 167

HOW TO BUILD AN...
EASTER CANDY BOARD

Let the Easter Bunny surprise your guests this year with a sensational assortment of candies, mints and other nibbles.

ITEMS TO INCLUDE
- Yellow Easter grass
- Pinwheel Mints
- Light blue M&Ms
- FunFetti Jelly Beans
- Milk chocolate bunny
- Easter grass bubble gum
- Whoppers Robin Eggs
- Easter bunny Peeps
- Yellow chick Peeps
- Shimmer Pastel Almond Blend
- Bunny grahams honey-baked snacks
- Hershey Kisses, pink foiled
- Foil-wrapped chocolate carrots
- Speckled fruit jelly beans
- Foil-wrapped Chocolate Eggs

EASY ASSEMBLY

Step 1: Line a rimmed tray with yellow Easter grass.

Step 2: Add two groupings of Pinwheel Mints to tray.

Step 3: Set two Easter-themed cookie cutters in tray; fill with blue M&Ms and Funfetti Jelly Beans. Add chocolate bunny to tray.

Step 4: Shape bubble gum into a nest. Fill with Whoppers; set in the tray.

Step 5: Add two groupings of bunny and chick Peeps to the tray.

Step 6: Fill in gaps with groupings of remaining items.

PINWHEEL MINTS

Both my grandmother and my mom used to make these eye-catching confections as a replacement for ordinary mints. When I offer them at parties, guests tell me the mints are wonderful, and then ask how I create the pretty swirl pattern.
—Marilou Roth, Milford, NE

PREP: 45 MIN. + CHILLING
MAKES: ABOUT 3 DOZEN

- 1 pkg. (8 oz.) cream cheese, softened
- ½ to 1 tsp. mint extract
- 7½ to 8½ cups confectioners' sugar
  Red and green food coloring
  Additional confectioners' sugar

1. In a large bowl, beat cream cheese and extract until smooth. Gradually beat in as much of the confectioners' sugar as possible.
2. Turn onto a work surface dusted with confectioners' sugar; knead in the remaining confectioners' sugar until smooth and sugar is absorbed (mixture will be stiff). Divide mixture in half. Using food coloring, tint 1 portion pink and the other portion light green, kneading until blended.
3. Divide each portion in half; shape each half into a 10-in. log to make 2 pink logs and 2 green logs. Place 1 log on a 12-in. piece of waxed paper lightly dusted with confectioners' sugar. Flatten log slightly; cover with a second piece of waxed paper. Roll out candy mixture into a 12-in. x 5-in. rectangle. Repeat with remaining logs.
4. Remove the top sheet of waxed paper from 1 pink and 1 green rectangle. Place 1 rectangle over the other. Roll up jelly-roll style, starting with a long side. Wrap in waxed paper; twist ends. Repeat with remaining rectangles. Chill overnight.
5. To serve, cut candy into ½-in. slices. Store in an airtight container in the refrigerator for up to 1 week.
2 pieces : 239 cal., 4g fat (3g sat. fat), 14mg chol., 38mg sod., 50g carb. (47g sugars, 0 fiber), 1g pro.

CUSTOMIZE YOUR BOARD

Use these recipes to create your own Easter Candy Board.

BUNNY TAILS

My granddaughters and I came up with this clever and easy treat for Easter.
—Kelly Ciepluch, Kenosha, WI

TAKES: 20 MIN. • **MAKES:** ABOUT 4 DOZEN

- 1 cup white baking chips, melted
- 1 cup sweetened shredded coconut

Drop melted chocolate by teaspoonfuls onto waxed paper or parchment. Sprinkle each generously with sweetened flaked coconut, and let stand until dry.

1 piece: 29 cal., 2g fat (1g sat. fat), 1mg chol., 8mg sod., 3g carb. (3g sugars, 0 fiber), 0 pro.

TEST KITCHEN TIP

When melting chocolate in a microwave or double boiler, be sure to watch it carefully. Overcooked or seized chocolate can be very difficult to return to liquid form. In fact, you're often better off simply starting over rather than trying to reverse the damage.

EASTER SUGAR COOKIES

Cream cheese contributes to the rich taste of these melt-in-your-mouth cookies. They have such a nice flavor, you can skip the frosting and sprinkle them with colored sugar for a change.
—Julie Brunette, Green Bay, WI

PREP: 15 MIN. + CHILLING
BAKE: 10 MIN./BATCH
MAKES: 4 DOZEN

- 1 cup butter, softened
- 3 oz. cream cheese, softened
- 1 cup sugar
- 1 large egg yolk, room temperature
- ½ tsp. vanilla extract
- ¼ tsp. almond extract
- 2¼ cups all-purpose flour
- ½ tsp. salt
- ¼ tsp. baking soda
- Tinted frosting or colored sugar

1. In a bowl, cream butter, cream cheese and sugar. Beat in egg yolk and extracts. Combine the flour, salt and baking soda; gradually add to the creamed mixture. Cover and refrigerate 3 hours or until dough is easy to handle.

2. Preheat oven to 375°. On a lightly floured surface, roll out dough to ⅛-in. thickness. Cut with 2½-in. cookie cutters dipped in flour. Place 1 in. apart on ungreased baking sheets. Bake until the edges begin to brown, 8-10 minutes. Cool for 2 minutes before removing from pans to wire racks. Decorate as desired.

1 cookie: 79 cal., 5g fat (3g sat. fat), 16mg chol., 67mg sod., 9g carb. (4g sugars, 0 fiber), 1g pro.

MARSHMALLOW EASTER EGGS

I've been making this wonderful Easter candy for years. These eggs are a big hit with everyone who loves marshmallows.
—Betty Claycomb, Alverton, PA

PREP: 45 MIN. + STANDING • **COOK:** 15 MIN.
MAKES: 3 DOZEN

- 25 cups all-purpose flour (about 8 lbs.)
- 1 large egg
- 2 Tbsp. unflavored gelatin
- ½ cup cold water
- 2 cups sugar
- 1 cup light corn syrup, divided
- ¾ cup hot water
- 2 tsp. vanilla extract
- 1 lb. dark chocolate candy coating, melted
  Candy coating disks, multiple colors, melted

1. Spread 7 cups all-purpose flour in each of three 13x9-in. pans and 4 cups flour in a 9-in. square pan. Carefully wash the egg in a mild bleach solution (1 tsp. chlorine bleach to 1 qt. warm water); dry. Press washed egg halfway into the flour to form an impression. Repeat 35 times, 2 in. apart; set aside.
2. In a small bowl, sprinkle the gelatin over cold water. In a large saucepan, combine the sugar, ½ cup corn syrup and hot water. Bring to a boil over medium heat, stirring constantly, until a candy thermometer reads 238° (softball stage). Remove from the heat; stir in the remaining ½ cup corn syrup.
3. Pour into a large bowl. Add the reserved gelatin, 1 Tbsp. at a time, beating on high speed until candy is thick and has cooled to lukewarm, about 10 minutes. Beat in vanilla.
4. Spoon lukewarm gelatin mixture into egg depressions; dust with flour. Let stand for 3-4 hours or until set.
5. Brush excess flour off marshmallow eggs. Dip each in chocolate candy coating. Place flat side down on waxed paper. Let stand until set. Drizzle candy coating over eggs.
1 piece: 147 cal., 4g fat (4g sat. fat), 0 chol., 7mg sod., 28g carb. (28g sugars, 0 fiber), 1g pro.

BIRD'S NEST TREATS

I make this recipe in the spring when the birds are starting to build their own nests. They are so easy to make, and they disappear just as fast.
—Pam Painter, Poseyville, IN

PREP: 25 MIN. • **COOK:** 15 MIN.
MAKES: 1 DOZEN

- ¼ cup butter, cubed
- 4½ cups miniature marshmallows
- ¼ cup creamy peanut butter
- ¼ cup semisweet chocolate chips
- 4 cups chow mein noodles
- 1 cup jelly beans or candy eggs

1. In a large saucepan over medium heat, melt butter and marshmallows until smooth, stirring occasionally. Add the peanut butter and chocolate chips; heat and stir for 2 minutes or until smooth. Remove from heat; stir in chow mein noodles until well coated.
2. Divide into 12 mounds on a waxed paper-lined baking sheet. Using your fingers, shape each into a nest; press an indentation in the center of each nest. Fill each nest with 3 or 4 jelly beans or candy eggs. Cool.
1 treat: 296 cal., 12g fat (4g sat. fat), 10mg chol., 149mg sod., 46g carb. (27g sugars, 1g fiber), 3g pro.

LEMON-GARLIC HUMMUS
Whipping up this smooth and creamy bean dip requires just five ingredients.
—Kris Capener, Ogden, UT

TAKES: 10 MIN. • **MAKES:** 1½ CUPS

- ¾ cup olive oil
- 2 cups canned garbanzo beans or chickpeas, rinsed and drained
- 3 Tbsp. lemon juice
- 2 tsp. minced garlic
- ½ tsp. salt
  Pita wedges, cucumber, carrots, watermelon radishes, snow peas and sweet red pepper

In a food processor, combine the oil, beans, lemon juice, garlic and salt; cover and process until smooth. Transfer to a small bowl. Serve with pita wedges and vegetables.
¼ cup: 324 cal., 29g fat (3g sat. fat), 0 chol., 309mg sod., 14g carb. (2g sugars, 3g fiber), 3g pro.

Light & Lively Spring Board

Mom's Day Platter

WHIPPED FETA DIP

The base of this whipped feta dip is a great blank canvas for different flavors.
—Dawn Parker, Surrey, BC

TAKES: 10 MIN. • **MAKES:** 1⅓ CUPS

- **8** oz. feta cheese
- **½** cup plain Greek yogurt
- **1** tsp. Greek seasoning
- **1** garlic clove, chopped
- **¾** tsp. grated lemon zest
- **1** Tbsp. extra virgin olive oil
  Fresh mint
  Pita wedges and various raw vegetables for dipping

Place first 5 ingredients in a food processor; process until smooth. Spoon into serving dish; drizzle with olive oil and sprinkle with mint. Serve with pita wedges and vegetables.

2 Tbsp.: 85 cal., 7g fat (4g sat. fat), 23mg chol., 311mg sod., 2g carb. (1g sugars, 0 fiber), 4g pro.

Patriotic Platter

HONEY-LIME
YOGURT DIP, 173

HOW TO BUILD A...
PATRIOTIC PLATTER

It's easy to fill a board with red, white and blue snacks that are sure to please. Consider this simple idea or give a nod to Old Glory with your own platter!

ITEMS TO INCLUDE

- Honey-Lime Yogurt Dip
- Blue M&M's
- Blackberries
- Figs, halved
- Red grapes
- Grape licorice
- Blueberries
- Chocolate candies with red, white and blue nonpareils or sprinkles
- Blueberry yogurt pretzels
- White cheddar
- Cranberry Stilton
- Star-shaped crackers
- Blue cheese
- Strawberries
- Watermelon, sliced
- Raspberries
- Strawberry licorice
- Maraschino cherries
- Wrapped mini peanut butter cups

EASY ASSEMBLY

Step 1: Visually divide your tray or board into thirds horizontally.

Step 2: Pour Honey-Lime Yogurt Dip into a serving bowl and set it in the middle of the tray.

Step 3: Fill in bottom third of tray with like groupings of M&M's, blackberries, figs, red grapes, grape licorice, blueberries, chocolates and pretzels.

Step 4: Working around the bowl of dip, fill center of board with like groupings of cheddar, cranberry Stilton, crackers and blue cheese.

Step 5: Fill top third of tray with strawberries, watermelon and raspberries.

Step 6: Fill in any gaps with strawberry licorice, cherries and mini peanut butter cups.

HONEY-LIME YOGURT DIP

When it comes to this tangy fruit dip, I don't mind my kids playing with their food. We like to dip strawberries, but friends have reported happy results with bananas, pears and other fruits.
—Shelly Bevington, Hermiston, OR

TAKES: 5 MIN. • **MAKES:** 2 CUPS

  2 **cups plain yogurt**
  ¼ **cup honey**
  2 **Tbsp. lime juice**
  ½ **tsp. grated lime zest**
     Assorted fresh fruit

Whisk the yogurt, honey, lime juice and lime zest in a small bowl. Refrigerate until serving. Serve with fruit.
¼ cup: 70 cal., 2g fat (1g sat. fat), 8mg chol., 29mg sod., 12g carb. (12g sugars, 0 fiber), 2g pro.

Fireworks Watching Tray

WATERMELON & BLACKBERRY SANGRIA, 175

SUMMER FRESH PASTA SALAD, 176

CHOCOLATE-COVERED STRAWBERRY SNACK MIX, 176

HOW TO BUILD A...
FIREWORKS WATCHING TRAY

Consider this casual combo for your Independence Day party as well as summer picnics, barbecues and other warm-weather parties. All of the items travel well and can be easily packed as individual servings.

ITEMS TO INCLUDE
- Chocolate-Covered Strawberry Snack Mix
- Summer Fresh Pasta Salad
- Watermelon & Blackberry Sangria

EASY ASSEMBLY
Step 1: Set the Chocolate-Covered Strawberry Snack Mix in a large serving bowl, and place on tray.

Step 2: Set Summer Fresh Pasta Salad into individual serving bowls. Set all on tray.

Step 3: Add drinking straws, napkins and serving utensils to tray (or see the Handy Utensil Holder idea on page 176).

Step 4: Serve tray with Watermelon & Blackberry Sangria.

Platter Pointer: Add bowls of berries, fresh mint or basil, and sliced limes and peaches to your tray so guests can garnish their glasses of sangria.

WATERMELON & BLACKBERRY SANGRIA
This recipe is deliciously pink! Living in the zinfandel wine country of Northern California's Gold Country, I often use our local fare in my recipes. I like to garnish this drink with sprigs of mint or basil for personal flair. It's perfect for entertaining. Try the peach version, too!
—Carolyn Kumpe, El Dorado, CA

PREP: 5 MIN. + CHILLING
MAKES: 8 SERVINGS

- 1   bottle (750 ml) white zinfandel or rose wine, chilled
- ¼   cup watermelon schnapps liqueur
- 1½ cups cubed seedless watermelon (½-in. cubes)
- 1   medium lime, thinly sliced
- ½   to 1 cup fresh blackberries, halved
- 1   can (12 oz.) lemon-lime soda, chilled
     Ice cubes
     Fresh basil or mint leaves

In a large pitcher, stir together wine and schnapps; add watermelon, lime and blackberries. Chill at least 2 hours. Just before serving, stir in soda. Serve over ice. Garnish with basil or mint.
¾ cup: 119 cal., 0 fat (0 sat. fat), 0 chol., 10mg sod., 12g carb. (8g sugars, 1g fiber), 0 pro.
Peach and Raspberry: Substitute peach schnapps or raspberry liquor for the melon liquor, and use fresh peaches and raspberries instead of the watermelon and blackberries.

SUMMER FRESH PASTA SALAD

I made this fast and easy salad for dinner while preparing lunch. We love to enjoy the fresh fruits and veggies in season. I served this salad with almond crackers and sharp cheddar slices. So tasty!
—Cathy Orban, Chandler, AZ

PREP: 20 MIN. + CHILLING
MAKES: 12 SERVINGS

- 4 cups uncooked campanelle or spiral pasta
- 2 medium carrots, finely chopped
- 2 medium peaches, chopped
- 1 pouch (11 oz.) light tuna in water
- ½ cup sliced celery
- ½ cup julienned cucumber
- ½ cup julienned zucchini
- ½ cup fresh broccoli florets, chopped
- ½ cup grated red cabbage
- ½ tsp. salt
- ½ tsp. pepper
- 2 cups Caesar salad dressing

Cook pasta according to package directions for al dente. Drain; rinse with cold water and drain well. Transfer to a large bowl. Add carrots, peaches, tuna, celery, cucumber, zucchini, broccoli, cabbage, salt and pepper. Drizzle with dressing; toss to coat. Refrigerate, covered, at least 3 hours before serving.

¾ cup: 357 cal., 23g fat (4g sat. fat), 25mg chol., 651mg sod., 26g carb. (5g sugars, 2g fiber), 10g pro.

CHOCOLATE-COVERED STRAWBERRY SNACK MIX

I love chocolate-covered strawberries, but it's a treat you want to make only on special occasions. With a little experimenting, I've captured the same incredible flavor in a snack I can take anywhere. Everyone is always amazed when I pull these out at a picnic or tailgate, or on a car trip.
—TerryAnn Moore, Vineland, NJ

PREP: 15 MIN. + STANDING • **MAKES:** 2 QT.

- 6 cups Rice Chex
- 2 cups Chocolate Chex
- 1 cup semisweet chocolate chips
- ½ cup seedless strawberry jam
- 3 Tbsp. butter
- 1 tsp. almond extract
- 2 cups ground almonds
- 1 cup white baking chips
  Sprinkles, optional

1. In a large bowl, combine the cereals. In a microwave, melt the chocolate chips, jam and butter; stir until smooth. Add the extract. Pour over the cereal mixture and toss to coat. Sprinkle with almonds; toss to coat.

2. Immediately spread onto waxed paper. In a microwave, melt white chips; stir until smooth. Drizzle over the cereal mixture. If desired, add sprinkles. Let stand until set. Break into pieces. Store snack mix in an airtight container.

¾ cup: 443 cal., 24g fat (9g sat. fat), 11mg chol., 231mg sod., 55g carb. (33g sugars, 3g fiber), 7g pro.

HANDY UTENSIL HOLDER
Turn a basket into a convenient carrier that corrals napkins and utensils when you're on the go. Pop in a mini flag for a little bit of extra flair.

CUSTOMIZE YOUR BOARD

PATRIOTIC COOKIES & CREAM CUPCAKES

Bring on the red, white and blue with these creative cupcakes, perfect for the Fourth of July, Memorial Day or any favorite occasion. With some delicious and colorful frosting and a careful arrangement, your sweet display will be a patriotic nod to our great American flag.
—Rebecca Wetherbee, Marion, OH

PREP: 40 MIN. • **BAKE:** 20 MIN. + COOLING
MAKES: 2 DOZEN

- ½ cup butter, softened
- 1⅔ cups sugar
- 3 large egg whites, room temperature
- 2 tsp. vanilla extract
- 2¼ cups all-purpose flour
- 3 tsp. baking powder
- ½ tsp. salt
- 1 cup 2% milk
- 1 cup Oreo cookie crumbs

FROSTING

- ¾ cup butter, softened
- 6 cups confectioners' sugar
- ½ tsp. clear or regular vanilla extract
- 3 to 4 Tbsp. 2% milk
  Blue and red paste food coloring
  Star sprinkles

1. Preheat oven to 350°. Line 24 muffin cups with paper or foil liners.
2. In a large bowl, cream butter and sugar until crumbly. Add 1 egg white at a time, beating well after each addition. Beat in vanilla. In another bowl, whisk flour, baking powder and salt; add to creamed mixture alternately with milk, beating well after each addition. Fold in cookie crumbs.
3. Fill prepared cups two-thirds full. Bake 20-24 minutes or until a toothpick inserted in center comes out clean. Cool in pans 10 minutes before removing cupcakes to wire racks to cool completely.
4. In a large bowl, combine butter, confectioners' sugar and vanilla; beat until smooth. Add enough milk to make a stiff frosting. Remove 1 cup frosting to a small bowl; tint with blue food coloring. Divide remaining frosting in half; tint 1 portion red and leave the remaining portion plain.
5. Cut a small hole in the tip of a pastry bag; insert a #1M star pastry tip. Fill bag with plain frosting; pipe over 9 cupcakes. With red frosting, pipe 9 more cupcakes. Pipe remaining cupcakes blue; top with sprinkles. Arrange cupcakes on a large platter, forming a flag.

1 cupcake: 338 cal., 11g fat (7g sat. fat), 26mg chol., 230mg sod., 58g carb. (46g sugars, 1g fiber), 2g pro.

WATERMELON CUPS

This lovely appetizer is almost too pretty to eat! Sweet watermelon cubes hold a refreshing topping that showcases cucumber, red onion and fresh herbs.
—*Taste of Home* Test Kitchen

TAKES: 25 MIN. • **MAKES:** 16 APPETIZERS

- 16 seedless watermelon cubes (1 in.)
- ⅓ cup finely chopped cucumber
- 5 tsp. finely chopped red onion
- 2 tsp. minced fresh mint
- 2 tsp. minced fresh cilantro
- ½ to 1 tsp. lime juice

1. Using a small melon baller or measuring spoon, scoop out the center of each watermelon cube, leaving a ¼-in. shell (save flesh for another use).
2. In a small bowl, combine the remaining ingredients; spoon into watermelon cubes.

1 piece: 7 cal., 0 fat (0 sat. fat), 0 chol., 1mg sod., 2g carb. (2g sugars, 0 fiber), 0 pro.

Halloween Treat Board

PEANUT BUTTER
POPCORN BALLS, 179

HOW TO BUILD A...
HALLOWEEN TREAT BOARD

The boo-board is more treats than tricks! It comes together easily with mini popcorn balls and the colorful candies kids of all ages love!

ITEMS TO INCLUDE
- Black jelly beans
- Black Licorice Cats
- Black Licorice Bites
- Eyeball gumballs
- Peanut Butter Popcorn Balls
- Pumpkin Halloween Peeps
- Cheez-It® Original Snack Crackers
- Fall Gummy Worms
- Oreos
- Hershey Kisses (Purple Foiled)
- Mellocreme pumpkins
- Orange M&Ms
- Candy corn
- Cheddar cheese balls
- Gummy peach rings
- Gummy teeth

EASY ASSEMBLY

Step 1: On a round board create left eye with jelly beans, right eye with Licorice Cats and mouth with Licorice Bites. Use gumballs for eyeballs.

Step 2: Prepare Peanut Butter Popcorn Balls, leaving out sticks. Line balls on a curve along right side of board.

Step 3: Line Peeps on curve along left side of the board. Complete pumpkin outline with crackers and Gummy Worms. Add Oreos at top for stem.

Step 4: Fill in with remaining items as seen in photo. Add additional Oreo for the nose.

PEANUT BUTTER POPCORN BALLS

Friends and family are always happy to see these popcorn balls. I love making them just as much as eating them!
—Betty Claycomb, Alverton, PA

PREP: 20 MIN. + STANDING
MAKES: 10 SERVINGS

- 5   cups popped popcorn
- 1   cup dry roasted peanuts
- ½   cup sugar
- ½   cup light corn syrup
- ½   cup chunky peanut butter
- ½   tsp. vanilla extract
- 10   lollipop sticks

1. Place popcorn and peanuts in a large bowl. In a large heavy saucepan over medium heat, bring sugar and corn syrup to a rolling boil, stirring occasionally. Remove from the heat; stir in the peanut butter and vanilla. Quickly pour over popcorn mixture and mix well.

2. When cool enough to handle, quickly shape into ten 2½-in. balls; insert a lollipop stick into each ball. Let stand at room temperature until firm; wrap each until ready to serve.

1 popcorn ball: 281 cal., 16g fat (2g sat. fat), 0 chol., 228mg sod., 32g carb. (25g sugars, 3g fiber), 7g pro.

CUSTOMIZE YOUR BOARD

Use these recipes to create your own Halloween Treat Board.

WITCHES' BREW

Stir up some Halloween beverages that are as bewitching as the rest of your menu. For a nonalcoholic version, just omit the vodka—then the kids can have some, too!
—*Taste of Home* Test Kitchen

PREP: 20 MIN. + CHILLING
MAKES: 6 SERVINGS

- 1 **cup sugar**
- 1 **cup water**
- 8 **medium kiwifruit, peeled and quartered**
- ½ **cup fresh mint leaves**
- 1 **cup vodka, optional**
- 1 **liter ginger ale, chilled**
  Ice cubes

1. In a small saucepan, bring sugar and water to a boil. Cook and stir until sugar is dissolved; set aside to cool.
2. Place the kiwi, mint and sugar syrup in a blender; cover and process until blended. Pour into a large pitcher; stir in vodka if desired. Refrigerate mixture until chilled.
3. Just before serving, stir in the ginger ale. Serve over ice.

1 cup: 253 cal., 1g fat (0 sat. fat), 0 chol., 17mg sod., 64g carb. (57g sugars, 4g fiber), 1g pro.

SPICED CHOCOLATE TRUFFLES

I make truffles for gift-giving and family events. Someone once asked me to add pumpkin spice—now my recipe has become legendary.
—Gerry Cofta, Milwaukee, WI

PREP: 45 MIN. + CHILLING • **COOK:** 5 MIN.
MAKES: ABOUT 2 DOZEN

- 12 **oz. milk chocolate baking bars, divided**
- ½ **cup heavy whipping cream**
- 2 **Tbsp. canned pumpkin**
- ¼ **tsp. ground cinnamon**
- ¼ **tsp. ground ginger**
- ¼ **tsp. ground nutmeg**
  Dash ground cloves
  Baking cocoa
  Candy eyeballs, optional

1. Finely chop 10 oz. chocolate; place in a bowl. In a small heavy saucepan, combine cream, pumpkin and spices; heat just to a boil. Pour over the chocolate; let stand 5 minutes.

2. Stir with a whisk until smooth. Cool to room temperature. Refrigerate, covered, at least 4 hours.
3. Finely grate remaining chocolate; place in a small microwave-safe bowl. With hands dusted lightly with baking cocoa, shape the chocolate mixture into 1-in. balls; roll in grated chocolate. (Mixture will be soft and truffles may flatten slightly upon standing.)
4. If desired, melt unused grated chocolate in a microwave and use to attach eyeballs. Store in an airtight container in the refrigerator.

Note: This recipe was tested with Ghirardelli Milk Chocolate Baking Bars; results may vary if you choose to use a different product.

1 truffle: 89 cal., 6g fat (4g sat. fat), 10mg chol., 7mg sod., 9g carb. (8g sugars, 0 fiber), 1g pro.

WITCHES' FINGERS

You don't need a cauldron to conjure these frightening fingers. They're a sweet-and-salty treat that is spooky easy to make.
—Beth Tomkiw, Milwaukee, WI

TAKES: 20 MIN. • **MAKES:** 1 DOZEN

1½ cups vibrant green candy coating disks
6 pretzel rods, broken in half
6 jelly beans, cut in half lengthwise

In a microwave, melt candy coating; stir until smooth. Dip broken end of pretzel rods in coating; allow excess to drip off. Place on waxed paper; press a jelly bean half onto dipped end of each pretzel to resemble a fingernail. Let stand until almost set. Using a toothpick, make lines on each pretzel to resemble knuckles.

1 pretzel half: 155 cal., 7g fat (7g sat. fat), 1mg chol., 131mg sod., 21g carb. (18g sugars, 0 fiber), 1g pro.

WITCHES' BROOMS

Set these edible mini brooms on a boo-tiful platter for a spellbinding treat. The only ingredients you need are pretzel rods and licorice.
—*Taste of Home* Test Kitchen

TAKES: 30 MIN. • **MAKES:** 6 BROOMS

6 pieces green shoestring licorice
6 pretzel rods
6 pieces black shoestring licorice

Cut 1 green shoestring licorice into 1-in. lengths. Arrange around end of 1 pretzel rod to form broom bristles; tightly wrap bristles with 1 black shoestring licorice, tucking in end to secure. Repeat with remaining ingredients for additional brooms.

1 broom: 106 cal., 0 fat (0 sat. fat), 0 chol., 142mg sod., 24g carb. (10g sugars, 0 fiber), 1g pro.

MIDNIGHT COCKTAILS

This variation on a mojito uses blackberry spreadable fruit, which gives it a deep purple color and a bit of sweetness in every sip.
—*Taste of Home* Test Kitchen

PREP: 15 MIN. + CHILLING
MAKES: 2 SERVINGS

⅓ cup seedless blackberry spreadable fruit
2 Tbsp. water
¼ cup fresh mint leaves
3 Tbsp. lime juice
⅓ cup rum or brandy
1 cup club soda
GARNISH
Mint sprigs

1. In a small saucepan, combine spreadable fruit and water. Cook and stir over medium heat until smooth; transfer to a small bowl. Refrigerate until chilled.
2. In a small pitcher, muddle the mint leaves and lime juice. Add blackberry syrup and rum. Divide between 2 cocktail glasses. Stir in club soda; garnish with mint sprigs.

¾ cup: 203 cal., 0 fat (0 sat. fat), 0 chol., 29mg sod., 30g carb. (22g sugars, 1g fiber), 0 pro.

PLATTER POINTER

Spiced Chocolate Truffles, Witches' Fingers and Witches' Brooms all make great additions to Halloween boards and snack platters. Feel free to get creative, too, with goldfish crackers, orange segments, clementines, dried apricots, circus peanuts, cubes of homemade fudge, bite-size brownies or sugar cookies.

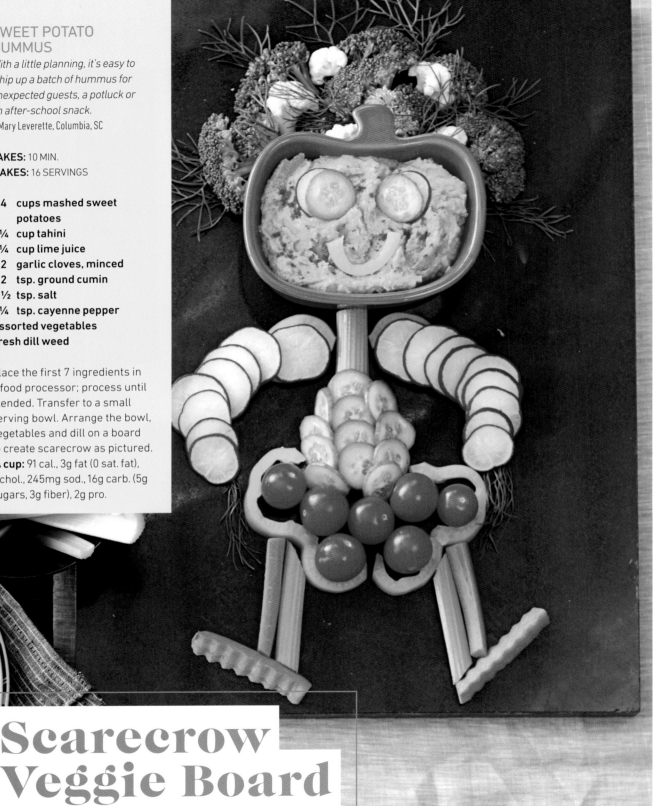

SWEET POTATO HUMMUS

With a little planning, it's easy to whip up a batch of hummus for unexpected guests, a potluck or an after-school snack.
—Mary Leverette, Columbia, SC

TAKES: 10 MIN.
MAKES: 16 SERVINGS

- 4 cups mashed sweet potatoes
- ¼ cup tahini
- ¼ cup lime juice
- 2 garlic cloves, minced
- 2 tsp. ground cumin
- 1½ tsp. salt
- ¼ tsp. cayenne pepper
- **Assorted vegetables**
- **Fresh dill weed**

Place the first 7 ingredients in a food processor; process until blended. Transfer to a small serving bowl. Arrange the bowl, vegetables and dill on a board to create scarecrow as pictured.
¼ cup: 91 cal., 3g fat (0 sat. fat), 0 chol., 245mg sod., 16g carb. (5g sugars, 3g fiber), 2g pro.

Scarecrow Veggie Board

Harvesttime Appetizer

PUMPKIN CHEESE BALL

Perfect for fall parties, this cheese ball is shaped to reflect its secret ingredient A touch of pumpkin lends harvest color and extra nutrition.
—Linnea Rein, Topeka, KS

PREP: 20 MIN. + CHILLING
MAKES: 3 CUPS

- 1 pkg. (8 oz.) cream cheese, softened
- ½ cup canned pumpkin
- 1 can (8 oz.) crushed pineapple, well drained
- 2 cups shredded sharp cheddar cheese
- 1 pkg. (2½ oz.) dried beef, finely chopped
- 1 Tbsp. finely chopped onion
- 1 green pepper
  Crackers and sliced apples

In a bowl, beat cream cheese, pumpkin and pineapple. Stir in cheddar cheese, beef and onion. Shape into a ball; wrap in plastic. Wrap cheese ball in 4 pieces of string or 4 rubber bands, creating indentions to resemble a pumpkin. Chill 1 hour. Carefully unwrap cheese ball and set it on a platter. Remove stem from the green pepper; add to cheese ball to serve as a pumpkin stem. Slice remaining pepper. Arrange crackers, apples and sliced pepper on platter; serve.

2 Tbsp.: 85 cal., 6g fat (4g sat. fat), 21mg chol., 174mg sod., 3g carb. (2g sugars, 0 fiber), 4g pro.

Thanksgiving Board

CINNAMON
PRALINE
NUTS, 186

HIGHBUSH
CRANBERRY
JAM, 186

BLUE

HOW TO BUILD A...
THANKSGIVING BOARD

Gather with loved ones for a heartwarming day of family and friendship...and feasting!

ITEMS TO INCLUDE

- Brie
- Highbush Cranberry Jam
- Cinnamon Praline Nuts
- Mixed olives
- Apples, halved
- Pomegranates, halved
- Pears
- Hot uncured capocollo, sliced
- Petite dill pickles
- Merlot BellaVitano cheese wedge
- Colby cheese, cubed
- Blue cheese wedge
- Green beans, blanched
- Maple sandwich cookies
- Dried apricots
- Red grapes
- Fresh sage, rosemary and thyme sprigs
- Miniature pumpkins, optional

EASY ASSEMBLY

Step 1: Use a small leaf-shaped cookie cutter to create a cutout on top of Brie. Scoop out a small amount of Brie from the cutout (save for another use). Fill cutout with Highbush Cranberry Jam. Set Brie on board with jar of Highbush Cranberry Jam.

Step 2: Put Cinnamon Praline Nuts and mixed olives in individual bowls. Space bowls apart on board.

Step 3: Set the apples, pomegranates and pears on board in like groupings.

Step 4: Roll up capocollo slices; set on board.

Step 5: Add a grouping of pickles to the board. Add remaining cheeses to board.

Step 6: Group green beans together, stand on the board by sticking between other items.

Step 7: Add groupings of cookies, apricots and grapes to board.

Step 8: Fill in gaps with sprigs of herbs and, if desired, pumpkins.

Platter Pointer: Artificial miniature pumpkins are a great addition to this tray if fresh miniature pumpkins are not available.

CINNAMON PRALINE NUTS

Take these crunchy bites anywhere! Serve them at your holiday party, wrap up a batch for your favorite hostess or sneak some for a midnight snack.
—Amy Miller, Holstein, IA

PREP: 10 MIN. • **BAKE:** 20 MIN. + COOLING
MAKES: 3 CUPS

- ½ cup packed brown sugar
- ⅓ cup heavy whipping cream
- 1 tsp. ground cinnamon
- ½ tsp. grated orange zest
- ¼ tsp. ground nutmeg
- 2 cups pecan halves
- 1 cup walnut halves

1. Preheat the oven to 350°. In a large bowl, mix the first 5 ingredients until blended. Add the pecans and walnuts; toss to coat.
2. Transfer to a greased baking sheet. Bake 20-25 minutes or until toasted, stirring twice. Cool completely. Store in an airtight container.
¼ cup: 227 cal., 20g fat (3g sat. fat), 8mg chol., 5mg sod., 13g carb. (10g sugars, 2g fiber), 3g pro.

HIGHBUSH CRANBERRY JAM

Although not true cranberries, highbush cranberries also have tart red fruits that can be used in cooking. This is a lovely spread with mouthwatering tangy flavor.
—Evelyn Gebhardt, Kasilof, AK

PREP: 15 MIN.
COOK: 50 MIN.+ CHILLING
MAKES: 4 CUPS

- 7½ cups highbush cranberries
- ¾ cup water
- 2 cups sugar
- 1 Tbsp. grated orange zest
- 2 Tbsp. orange juice
- ¾ tsp. ground allspice
- ½ tsp. ground cinnamon
- ¼ tsp. ground nutmeg

1. In a large covered kettle, simmer cranberries and water 20-25 minutes, stirring occasionally. Press berries through a strainer; discard the skins. Strain mixture through a double layer of cheesecloth (juice will drip through; discard or set aside for another use).
2. Measure 6 cups of the pulp that remains in the cheesecloth and place in kettle. Add remaining ingredients. Simmer, uncovered, 30-40 minutes, stirring frequently. Pour the jam into containers; cool slightly. Cover and refrigerate until cold. Store in the refrigerator up to 1 week or freeze for up to 12 months.
2 Tbsp.: 80 cal., 0 fat (0 sat. fat), 0 chol., 1mg sod., 21g carb. (19g sugars, 1g fiber), 0 pro.

CUSTOMIZE YOUR BOARD

Use these recipes to create your own Thanksgiving Board.

CHERRY-BRANDY BAKED BRIE

No one will ever believe this impressive appetizer is so simple to make. For a twist, substitute dried cranberries or apricots for the cherries and apple juice for the brandy.
—Kevin Phebus, Katy, TX

TAKES: 20 MIN. • **MAKES:** 8 SERVINGS

- 1 round (8 oz.) Brie cheese
- ½ cup dried cherries
- ½ cup chopped walnuts
- ¼ cup packed brown sugar
- ¼ cup brandy or unsweetened apple juice
  French bread baguette, sliced and toasted, or assorted crackers

1. Preheat oven to 350°. Place cheese in a 9-in. pie plate. Combine cherries, walnuts, brown sugar and brandy; spoon over cheese.
2. Bake 15-20 minutes or until cheese is softened. Serve with baguette slices.
1 serving: 210 cal., 13g fat (5g sat. fat), 28mg chol., 182mg sod., 14g carb. (12g sugars, 1g fiber), 7g pro.

CRANBERRY BRIE PINWHEELS

People may wonder when you found the time to make these crisp and flaky pinwheels—but you can whip them up in a snap. The filling is bursting with savory goodness and a touch of sweetness.
—Marcia Kintz, South Bend, IN

PREP: 20 MIN. • **BAKE:** 15 MIN.
MAKES: 1 DOZEN

- 1 sheet frozen puff pastry, thawed
- 2 Tbsp. Dijon mustard
- 2 Tbsp. honey
- 1 cup finely chopped fresh spinach
- ½ cup finely chopped Brie cheese
- ½ cup finely chopped walnuts
- ¼ cup dried cranberries, finely chopped

1. Unfold pastry. Combine mustard and honey; spread over pastry. Layer with spinach, Brie, walnuts and cranberries. Roll up jelly-roll style. Cut the roll into 12 slices. Place cut side down on an ungreased baking sheet.
2. Bake at 400° until golden brown, 15-20 minutes.
Freeze option: Freeze the cooled pinwheels in a freezer container. To use, reheat on a parchment-lined baking sheet in a preheated 400° oven until crisp and heated through.
1 pinwheel: 173 cal., 10g fat (3g sat. fat), 6mg chol., 167mg sod., 18g carb. (5g sugars, 2g fiber), 4g pro.

SMASHED OLIVES

My best friend and I came up with this recipe to celebrate the wonderful flavors of Spain. When you're finished with the olives, you can use the flavored olive oil to marinate chicken or shrimp.
—Tiffani Warner, Fort Leavenworth, KS

PREP: 20 MIN. + MARINATING
MAKES: 2 CUPS

2	cups mixed pitted olives
¾	to 1 cup olive oil
½	small navel orange, cut in half
½	medium onion, cut into wedges
3	to 4 fresh rosemary sprigs
6	to 8 fresh thyme sprigs
5	garlic cloves, peeled
2	bay leaves
1	Tbsp. gin, optional

1. In a large bowl, gently mash olives to break the skins. Add next 7 ingredients and, if desired, gin. Toss to coat; cover and refrigerate for up to 24 hours.
2. To serve, drain olives, reserving oil for another use; discard bay leaves.
¼ cup: 162 cal., 16g fat (2g sat. fat), 0 chol., 555mg sod., 5g carb. (1g sugars, 1g fiber), 1g pro.

MARINATED MOZZARELLA

Cheese is irresistible on its own, but with a light marinade of herbs and spicy red pepper flakes, it's out of this world. Try bocconcini (small round balls of fresh semisoft mozzarella) in place of cubed mozzarella if you'd like a different shape.
—Peggy Cairo, Kenosha, WI

PREP: 15 MIN. + MARINATING
MAKES: 10 SERVINGS

⅓	cup olive oil
1	Tbsp. chopped oil-packed sun-dried tomatoes
1	Tbsp. minced fresh parsley
1	tsp. crushed red pepper flakes
1	tsp. dried basil
1	tsp. minced chives
¼	tsp. garlic powder
1	lb. cubed part-skim mozzarella cheese

In a large bowl, combine the first 7 ingredients; add cheese cubes. Stir to coat. Cover; refrigerate at least 30 minutes.
¼ cup: 203 cal., 16g fat (7g sat. fat), 24mg chol., 242mg sod., 2g carb. (0 sugars, 0 fiber), 12g pro.

WHICH WINE IS BEST?

It can be hard to decide which wine pairs best with your charcuterie creations. Consider these wine and cheese pairings the next time you create a board.

- Brie — Sauvignon blanc
- Cheddar — Cabernet sauvignon
- Gorgonzola — Sweet riesling
- Pecorino Romano — Chardonnay
- Chevre — Rosé

PUMPKIN JUICE

My family loves Harry Potter, so I decided to come up with a recipe for pumpkin juice! My kids tried it and thought it was delicious. I love it because it's healthy and very easy to make.

—Geraldine Saucier, Albuquerque, NM

TAKES: 5 MIN.
MAKES: 14 SERVINGS

- 1   can (15 oz.) pumpkin
- ⅓   cup apricot spreadable fruit
- ¼   cup packed brown sugar
- 1   tsp. pumpkin pie spice
- 1   bottle (64 oz.) apple cider or unsweetened apple juice

Place the pumpkin, spreadable fruit, brown sugar and pie spice in a blender; cover and process until the mixture is blended. Transfer to a pitcher; stir in apple cider until combined. Serve hot or chilled.

¾ cup: 110 cal., 0 fat (0 sat. fat), 0 chol., 17mg sod., 27g carb. (23g sugars, 1g fiber), 0 pro.

BRIE PUFF PASTRY

My husband was in the Air Force, so we have entertained guests all over the United States. I acquired this comforting recipe while we were in California. It's one of my favorite special appetizers.

—Sandra Twait, Tampa, FL

PREP: 15 MIN. • **BAKE:** 20 MIN. + STANDING
MAKES: 10 SERVINGS

- 1   round (13.2 oz.) Brie cheese
- ½   cup crumbled blue cheese
- 1   sheet frozen puff pastry, thawed
- ¼   cup apricot jam
- ½   cup slivered almonds, toasted
- 1   large egg, lightly beaten
     Assorted crackers

1. Preheat oven to 400°. Cut Brie horizontally in half. Sprinkle bottom half with blue cheese; replace top.

2. On a lightly floured surface, roll the pastry into a 14-in. square. Trim corners to make a circle. Spoon jam onto center of pastry; sprinkle with almonds. Top with Brie.

3. Lightly brush edges of pastry with beaten egg. Fold pastry over cheese, pinching edges to seal; trim excess pastry as desired.

4. Transfer to an ungreased baking sheet, seam side down. Brush pastry with beaten egg. Bake until golden brown, 20-25 minutes.

5. Immediately remove from pan to a serving plate; let stand 45 minutes before serving. Serve with crackers.

Note: To toast nuts, bake in a shallow pan in a 350° oven 5-10 minutes (or cook in a skillet over low heat until lightly browned, stirring occasionally).

1 serving: 328 cal., 22g fat (10g sat. fat), 64mg chol., 424mg sod., 20g carb. (3g sugars, 2g fiber), 13g pro.

FLUFFY CARAMEL APPLE DIP

This sweet, smooth dip is a crowd-pleaser.
Kids of all ages will "gobble" it up!
—*Taste of Home* Test Kitchen

TAKES: 30 MIN. • **MAKES:** 2 CUPS

- 1 pkg. (8 oz.) cream cheese, softened
- ½ cup packed brown sugar
- ¼ cup caramel ice cream topping
- 1 tsp. vanilla extract
- 1 cup marshmallow creme

Red and green apple slices
Pretzel sticks

In a bowl, beat cream cheese, brown sugar, caramel topping and vanilla until smooth; fold in the marshmallow creme. Spoon into a small bowl and set on platter. Fan apple slices around bowl. Use apple seeds for eyes and pretzel sticks for claws as pictured.

2 Tbsp.: 110 cal., 5g fat (3g sat. fat), 14mg chol., 69mg sod., 15g carb. (14g sugars, 0 fiber), 1g pro.

Kids-Table Treat

Gobble, Gobble Platter

TWO-BEAN HUMMUS

My children love this easy hummus and even like to help me make it! .You can also serve the hummus in a bread bowl with the vegetable platter.
—Kelly Andreas, Eau Claire, WI

TAKES: 15 MIN. • **MAKES:** 2 CUPS

- 1 **can (15 oz.) garbanzo beans or chickpeas, rinsed and drained**
- 1 **can (15 oz.) cannellini beans, rinsed and drained**
- ¼ **cup olive oil**
- 2 **Tbsp. lemon juice**
- 2 **garlic cloves, minced**
- ¼ **tsp. salt**
- 1 **small cucumber**
- 2 **whole cloves**
- 1 **carrot**
- 1 **sweet red pepper**
  Assorted fresh vegetables

1. Process the first 6 ingredients in a food processor until smooth. Transfer to a small serving bowl.
2. Cut off end of cucumber for the head; insert cloves for eyes and place in hummus. Cut carrot and pepper pieces for beak and wattle; attach with hummus. Cut carrot to resemble claws; set at bottom of serving bowl. Arrange assorted vegetables as seen in the photo.

¼ cup hummus: 152 cal., 8g fat (1g sat. fat), 0 chol., 209mg sod., 16g carb. (1g sugars, 4g fiber), 4g pro.
Diabetic exchanges: 1½ fat, 1 starch.

Charcuter-Tree

CINNAMON
STARS, 194

HOLIDAY MERINGUE
MINIATURES, 193

SLOW-COOKER
CANDIED NUTS, 194

HOMEMADE
GUMDROPS, 195

CHOCOLATE-DIPPED
PHYLLO STICKS, 195

HOW TO BUILD A...
CHARCUTER-TREE

Holidays shine just a little bit brighter with this incredible presentation.

ITEMS TO INCLUDE
- Cinnamon Stars
- Chocolate-Dipped Phyllo Sticks
- Holiday Meringue Miniatures
- Strawberries, halved
- Castelvetrano olives
- Salami, thinly sliced
- Gouda
- Star-shaped pretzels
- Goat cheese log rolled in fresh herbs, sliced
- Slow-Cooker Candied Nuts
- Green grapes
- Snowflake-shaped crackers
- Dried apricots
- Brie
- Blackberries
- Homemade Gumdrops
- Cheddar and mozzarella slices
- Fresh rosemary sprigs

EASILY ASSEMBLY

Step 1: Draw the outline of a Christmas tree onto parchment paper. Cut out the pattern and set on board or platter (or the surface on which you plan to serve the charcuter-tree).

Step 2: Set one Cinnamon Star at top of tree and Chocolate-Dipped Phyllo Sticks at bottom for trunk.

Step 3: Starting at the top of the tree, arrange items in groupings as shown at left.

Step 4: Add cheese slices for points of tree and rosemary sprigs for needles.

Step 5: Add picks and cheese knives.

HOLIDAY MERINGUE MINIATURES

My kids love these light, melt-in-your-mouth cookies and have fun making them. These festive treats were always on our Christmas cookie plate when I was a kid, and now the tradition continues.
—Susan Marshall, Colorado Springs, CO

PREP: 20 MIN. • **BAKE:** 1 HOUR + COOLING
MAKES: ABOUT 7 DOZEN

> 2 **large egg whites, room temperature**
> ½ **tsp. white vinegar**
>   **Dash salt**
> ½ **tsp. almond extract**
> ½ **tsp. vanilla extract**
> ½ **cup sugar**
>   **Red gel food coloring**

1. Preheat oven to 225°. Beat egg whites with vinegar and salt on medium speed until foamy and doubled in volume. Beat in extracts. Gradually add sugar, 1 Tbsp. at a time, beating on high after each addition until sugar is dissolved. Continue beating until stiff glossy peaks form, about 10 minutes.

2. Insert a ½-in. round tip into a pastry bag. Paint 5 stripes of red food coloring inside length of pastry bag. Transfer meringue to pastry bag; pipe striped dollops of meringue 1 in. apart onto parchment-lined baking sheets.

3. Bake until set and dry, about 1 hour. Turn off oven (do not open oven door); leave meringues in oven for 1 hour. Remove from oven; cool completely on baking sheets. Remove meringues from paper; store in airtight container at room temperature.

1 meringue: 5 cal., 0 fat (0 sat. fat), 0 chol., 19mg sod., 1g carb. (1g sugars, 0 fiber), 0 pro. **Diabetic exchanges:** 1 free food.

PLATTER POINTER
Add even more holiday flair to your charcuter-tree by baking batches of the meringues using red and green gel food coloring.

SLOW-COOKER CANDIED NUTS

I like giving spiced nuts as holiday gifts. This slow-cooker recipe with ginger and cinnamon is so good, you just might use it all year long.
—Yvonne Starlin, Westmoreland, TN

PREP: 10 MIN.
COOK: 2 HOURS + COOLING
MAKES: 4 CUPS

½ cup butter, melted
½ cup confectioners' sugar
1½ tsp. ground cinnamon
¼ tsp. ground ginger
¼ tsp. ground allspice
1½ cups pecan halves
1½ cups walnut halves
1 cup unblanched almonds

1. In a greased 3-qt. slow cooker, mix butter, confectioners' sugar and the spices. Add nuts; toss to coat. Cook, covered, on low 2-3 hours or until nuts are crisp, stirring once.
2. Transfer nuts to waxed paper to cool completely. Store nuts in an airtight container.
⅓ cup: 327 cal., 31g fat (7g sat. fat), 20mg chol., 64mg sod., 11g carb. (6g sugars, 3g fiber), 6g pro.

CINNAMON STARS

These cookies are such a hit with my family. They always disappear fast!
—Flo Burtnett, Gage, OK

PREP: 25 MIN. + CHILLING
BAKE: 10 MIN. + COOLING
MAKES: 2½ DOZEN SANDWICH COOKIES

2 cups all-purpose flour
1 cup sugar
1 tsp. ground cinnamon
¾ tsp. baking powder
¼ tsp. salt
½ cup cold butter, cubed
1 large egg, room temperature, lightly beaten
¼ cup 2% milk
GLAZE/FILLING
2 cups confectioners' sugar
½ tsp. vanilla extract
2 to 3 Tbsp. 2% milk
  Colored sugar, optional
⅔ cup raspberry, strawberry or apricot jam

1. In a medium bowl, combine flour, sugar, cinnamon, baking powder and salt. Cut in butter until crumbly. Combine egg and milk; add to flour mixture and stir just until moistened. Cover and chill at least 1 hour.
2. On a lightly floured surface, roll dough to ⅛-in. thickness. Cut with a 3-in. cookie cutter dipped in flour. Place on ungreased baking sheets. Bake at 375° for 7-9 minutes or until edges are lightly brown. Remove to a wire rack; cool completely.
3. For glaze, combine confectioners' sugar, vanilla and enough milk to achieve a spreading consistency. Spread glaze on half the cookies; sprinkle with colored sugar if desired. Let stand until set. Place 1 tsp. jam on each unglazed cookie; top with a glazed cookie.
1 sandwich cookie: 137 cal., 3g fat (2g sat. fat), 15mg chol., 60mg sod., 26g carb. (19g sugars, 0g fiber), 1g pro.

HOMEMADE GUMDROPS

Your friends and family will remember these chewy, fruity candies long after they've licked the last bit of sugar off their fingers! Homemade gumdrops are a great gift any time of year.
—Christin Holt, Kingsburg, CA

PREP: 20 MIN. + STANDING
COOK: 10 MIN. + CHILLING
MAKES: ABOUT 1¾ LBS.

- 2½ cups sugar, divided
- 1⅓ cups applesauce
- 2 pkg. (3 oz. each) red or green gelatin
- 2 envelopes unflavored gelatin
- 1 tsp. lemon juice

1. In a large saucepan, combine 2 cups sugar, the applesauce, red or green gelatin, unflavored gelatin and lemon juice; let stand for 1 minute. Bring the mixture to a boil over medium heat, stirring constantly. Boil for 1 minute. Immediately pour into a cold 11x7-in. baking dish coated with cooking spray. Refrigerate for 3 hours or until firm.
2. With a spatula, loosen gelatin from sides of pan. To remove, invert onto waxed paper. Using kitchen scissors or small sharp cookie cutters dipped in hot water, cut into 1-in. squares or shapes of your choice.
3. Place gumdrops on waxed paper. Dry at room temperature for 8 hours or until slightly sticky. Roll in remaining sugar. Store in an airtight container.
1 gumdrop: 35 cal., 0 fat (0 sat. fat), 0 chol., 3mg sod., 9g carb. (8g sugars, 0 fiber), 0 pro.

CHOCOLATE-DIPPED PHYLLO STICKS

Looking for something light and special to bake up for the holidays? Try these crunchy treats—they are great with coffee or alongside sorbet and sherbet.
—Peggy Woodward, Shullsburg, WI

PREP: 30 MIN. • **BAKE:** 5 MIN.
MAKES: 20 PHYLLO STICKS

- 4 sheets phyllo dough (14x9-in. size)
- 2 Tbsp. butter, melted
- 1 Tbsp. sugar
- ¼ tsp. ground cinnamon Cooking spray
- 2 oz. semisweet chocolate, finely chopped
- ½ tsp. shortening
- ½ oz. white baking chocolate, melted

1. Preheat oven to 425°. Place 1 sheet of the phyllo dough on a work surface; brush with melted butter. Cover with a second sheet of phyllo; brush with butter. (Keep remaining phyllo dough covered with a damp towel to prevent it from drying out.) Cut stacked phyllo sheets lengthwise in half. Cut each half crosswise into 5 rectangles (each 4½x2¾ in.). Tightly roll up rectangles jelly-roll style, starting with long side.
2. Mix sugar and cinnamon. Lightly coat rolled sticks with cooking spray; sprinkle with half the sugar mixture. Place on an ungreased baking sheet. Bake until the phyllo sticks are lightly browned, 3-5 minutes. Gently remove to a wire rack to cool. Repeat with remaining ingredients.
3. In a microwave, melt semisweet chocolate and shortening; stir until smooth. Dip 1 end of each phyllo stick into chocolate; allow excess to drip off. Place on waxed paper; let stand until set. Drizzle with white chocolate.
1 phyllo stick: 42 cal., 3g fat (2g sat. fat), 3mg chol., 19mg sod., 3g carb. (2g sugars, 0 fiber), 0 pro.

Christmas Open House Board

WILD PLUM JELLY, 198

CANDIED PECANS, 199

GENTLEMAN'S WHISKEY BACON JAM, 199

BACON, CHEDDAR & SWISS CHEESE BALL, 198

HOW TO BUILD A...
CHRISTMAS OPEN HOUSE BOARD

Comfort and joy abound with this festive assortment of classic bites.

ITEMS TO INCLUDE
- Whole cloves
- 2 oranges
- Kumquats, halved
- Pomegranate, quartered
- Bacon Cheddar & Swiss Cheese Ball
- Wild Plum Jelly
- Mixed nuts
- Candied Pecans
- Gentleman's Bacon Whiskey Jam
- Provolone, sliced
- Comte cheese
- Manchego cheese
- Brie cheese
- Prosciutto, thinly sliced
- Aged salami, sliced
- Summer sausage, sliced
- Assorted crackers
- Rosemary sprigs
- Red currants

EASY ASSEMBLY

Step 1: Poke whole cloves into an orange. Slice the remaining orange; quarter 1 slice. In a corner of the board, group the clove-studded orange with the orange slices and quarters, kumquats and pomegranate.

Step 2: Set a Bacon, Cheddar & Swiss Cheese Ball on board. Spoon Wild Plum Jelly, mixed nuts, Candied Pecans and Gentleman's Whiskey Bacon Jam into small bowls. Scatter bowls throughout the board.

Step 3: Using snowflake-shaped cookie cutters, cut shapes from provolone. Group on board.

Step 4: Set the Comte, Manchego and Brie cheeses on the board.

Step 5: Fold prosciutto slices into thirds; add to board in a grouping. Shingle salami and sausage slices on board in like groupings.

Step 6: Fill in any gaps on the board with crackers. Add rosemary sprigs and red currants.

Step 7: Add a cheese cutter and serving utensils.

Platter pointers: When adding bowls to a board, select bowls of different colors, shapes and sizes. The bowls will guide the eye around the board, making the presentation that much more attractive. Similarly, placing like-shaped items near each other is visually appealing. That's why we set the round crackers next to the wheel of Brie and the round slices of meat on this particular board.

BACON, CHEDDAR & SWISS CHEESE BALL

When it's time for a party, everyone will request this ultimate cheese ball. It works as a spreadable dip and also makes a fabulous hostess gift.
—Sue Franklin, Lake St. Louis, MO

PREP TIME: 20 MIN. + CHILLING
MAKES: 2 CHEESE BALLS (4 CUPS EACH)

- 1 pkg. (8 oz.) cream cheese, softened
- ½ cup sour cream
- 2 cups shredded Swiss cheese
- 2 cups shredded sharp cheddar cheese
- 1 cup crumbled cooked bacon (about 12 strips), divided
- ½ cup chopped pecans, toasted, divided
- ½ cup finely chopped onion
- 1 jar (2 oz.) diced pimientos, drained
- 2 Tbsp. sweet pickle relish
- ¼ tsp. salt
- ¼ tsp. pepper
- ¼ cup minced fresh parsley
- 1 Tbsp. poppy seeds
  Assorted crackers

1. In a large bowl, beat cream cheese and sour cream until smooth. Stir in the shredded cheeses, ½ cup bacon, ¼ cup pecans, onion, pimientos, pickle relish, salt and pepper. Refrigerate, covered, at least 1 hour.
2. In a small bowl, mix the parsley, poppy seeds and remaining bacon and pecans. Spread half the parsley mixture on a large plate. Shape half the cheese mixture into a ball; roll in parsley mixture to coat evenly. Cover. Repeat with remaining ingredients to make another cheese ball. Refrigerate at least 1 hour. Serve with crackers.
2 Tbsp.: 116 cal., 10g fat (5g sat. fat), 22mg chol., 194mg sod., 2g carb. (1g sugars, 0 fiber), 6g pro.

WILD PLUM JELLY

I've had this wild plum jelly recipe for ages. Each year when the plums are ripe, I'll fill my pail and make this jelly. It's so good!
—Ludell Heuser, Mount Horeb, WI

PREP: 55 MIN. • **PROCESS:** 5 MIN.
MAKES: ABOUT 8 HALF-PINTS

- 5 lbs. wild plums, halved and pitted
- 4 cups water
- 1 pkg. (1¾ oz.) powdered fruit pectin
- 7½ cups sugar

1. In a stockpot, simmer the plums and the water until plums are tender, about 30 minutes. Line a strainer with 4 layers of cheesecloth and place over a bowl. Place plum mixture in strainer; cover with edges of cheesecloth. Let stand until liquid in bowl measures 5½ cups, about 30 minutes.
2. Return the liquid to the pan. Add the pectin; stir and bring to a boil. Add sugar; bring to a full rolling boil. Boil for 1 minute, stirring constantly.
3. Remove from the heat; skim off any foam. Carefully ladle hot mixture into hot sterilized half-pint jars, leaving ¼ in. of headspace. Remove any air bubbles; wipe rims and put on lids. Process the jars for 5 minutes in a boiling-water canner.
Note: The processing time listed is for altitudes of 1,000 feet or less. Add 1 minute to the processing time for each 1,000 feet of additional altitude.
2 Tbsp.: 108 cal., 0 fat (0 sat. fat), 0 chol., 0 sod., 28g carb. (27g sugars, 1g fiber), 0 pro.

PLATTER POINTER
Fruit and berry jams, jellies and compotes are colorful, no-fuss additions to any charcuterie board. You can also consider adding chutney, fig spread or even cranberry sauce.

GENTLEMAN'S WHISKEY BACON JAM

You can slather this smoky jam on pretty much anything. It lasts only a week in the fridge, so I like to freeze small amounts for a quick snack with crackers.
—Colleen Delawder, Herndon, VA

PREP: 15 MIN. • **COOK:** 30 MIN.
MAKES: 3 CUPS

- 1½ lbs. thick-sliced bacon strips, finely chopped
- 8 shallots, finely chopped
- 1 large sweet onion, finely chopped
- 2 garlic cloves, minced
- 1 tsp. chili powder
- ½ tsp. paprika
- ¼ tsp. kosher salt
- ¼ tsp. pepper
- ½ cup whiskey
- ½ cup maple syrup
- ¼ cup balsamic vinegar
- ½ cup packed brown sugar
  Assorted crackers

1. In a large skillet, cook bacon over medium heat until crisp. Drain on paper towels. Discard all but 2 Tbsp. drippings. Add shallots and onion to the drippings; cook over medium heat until caramelized, stirring occasionally.
2. Stir in garlic; cook 30 seconds. Add seasonings. Remove from heat; stir in whiskey and maple syrup. Increase heat to high; bring to a boil and cook for 3 minutes, stirring constantly. Add vinegar and brown sugar; cook another 3 minutes, continuing to stir constantly.
3. Crumble cooked bacon and add to skillet. Reduce heat to low; cook for 12 minutes, stirring every few minutes. Allow jam to cool slightly. Pulse half the jam in a food processor until smooth; stir puree into remaining jam. Serve with assorted crackers.
2 Tbsp.: 112 cal., 8g fat (3g sat. fat), 10mg chol., 118mg sod., 7g carb. (5g sugars, 0 fiber), 2g pro.

CANDIED PECANS

I like to pack these crispy pecans in jars, tied with pretty ribbon, as gifts for family and friends. My granddaughter gave some to a doctor at the hospital where she works, and he said they were too good to be true!
—Opal Turner, Hughes Springs, TX

PREP: 25 MIN. • **BAKE:** 30 MIN.
MAKES: ABOUT 1 LB.

- 2¾ cups pecan halves
- 2 Tbsp. butter, softened, divided
- 1 cup sugar
- ½ cup water
- ½ tsp. salt
- ½ tsp. ground cinnamon
- 1 tsp. vanilla extract

1. Place pecans in a shallow baking pan in a 250° oven for 10 minutes or until warmed. Grease a 15x10x1-in. baking pan with 1 Tbsp. butter; set pan aside.
2. Grease the sides of a large heavy saucepan with remaining butter; add sugar, water, salt and cinnamon. Bring mixture to a boil, stirring constantly to dissolve sugar. Cover; cook 2 minutes to dissolve any sugar crystals that may form on the sides of pan.
3. Cook, without stirring, until a candy thermometer reads 236° (soft-ball stage). Remove from the heat; add vanilla. Stir in warm pecans until evenly coated.
4. Spread onto prepared baking pan. Bake at 250° for 30 minutes, stirring every 10 minutes. Spread on a baking sheet lined with waxed paper to cool.
Note: We recommend that you test your candy thermometer before each use by bringing water to a boil; the thermometer should read 212°. Adjust your recipe temperature up or down based on your test.
2 oz.: 380 cal., 30g fat (4g sat. fat), 8mg chol., 177mg sod., 30g carb. (26g sugars, 4g fiber), 3g pro.

CUSTOMIZE YOUR BOARD

Use these recipes to create your own Christmas Open House Board.

SNOW PEA HOLIDAY WREATH

Santa himself might stop to sample this pretty-as-a-picture finger food! Crunchy green pea pods and juicy red tomatoes add a natural, fresh and festive holiday note to my buffet table.
—Carol Schneck, Lodi, CA

TAKES: 25 MIN. • **MAKES:** 20 SERVINGS

- ½ **lb. fresh snow peas, strings removed**
- 3 **oz. cream cheese, softened**
- ¼ **tsp. garlic powder**
- ¼ **tsp. seasoned salt**
- 2 **cups grape tomatoes**

1. In a large saucepan, bring 6 cups water to a boil. Add snow peas; cook, uncovered, just until crisp-tender and bright green, 1-2 minutes. Drain and immediately drop into ice water. Drain and pat dry.
2. In a small bowl, combine the cream cheese, garlic powder and seasoned salt. Place bowl in the center of a serving platter. Arrange snow peas and tomatoes around the bowl.
1 serving: 23 cal., 2g fat (1g sat. fat), 5mg chol., 33mg sod., 2g carb. (1g sugars, 0 fiber), 1g pro.

MULLED WINE

This mulled wine is soothing and satisfying with a delightful blend of spices warmed to perfection. Refrigerating the wine mixture overnight allows the flavors to blend, so don't omit this essential step.
—*Taste of Home* Test Kitchen

PREP: 15 MIN. • **COOK:** 30 MIN. + CHILLING
MAKES: 5 SERVINGS

- 1 **bottle (750 ml) fruity red wine**
- 1 **cup brandy**
- 1 **cup sugar**
- 1 **medium orange, sliced**
- 1 **medium lemon, sliced**
- ⅛ **tsp. ground nutmeg**
- 2 **cinnamon sticks (3 in.)**
- ½ **tsp. whole allspice**
- ½ **tsp. aniseed**
- ½ **tsp. whole peppercorns**
- 3 **whole cloves**
  Optional garnishes: Orange slices and star anise

1. In a large saucepan, combine first 6 ingredients. Place remaining spices on a double thickness of cheesecloth. Gather corners of the cloth to enclose the spices; tie securely with string. Place in pan.
2. Bring to a boil, stirring occasionally. Reduce heat; simmer gently, covered, 20 minutes. Transfer to a covered container; cool slightly. Refrigerate, covered, overnight.
3. Strain wine mixture into a large saucepan, discarding fruit and spice bag; reheat. Serve warm. Garnish, if desired, with orange slices, star anise or additional cinnamon sticks.
¾ cup: 379 cal., 0 fat (0 sat. fat), 0 chol., 10mg sod., 46g carb. (41g sugars, 0 fiber), 0 pro.

TOM & JERRY

It just wouldn't be Christmas without sipping a warm Tom & Jerry drink. I was surprised to find out that not everyone knows about this beverage treat. One sip and I'm sure you'll be hooked. It's like a warm version of eggnog, only better.
—James Schend, Pleasant Prairie, WI

TAKES: 25 MIN. • **MAKES:** 10 SERVINGS

- 6 large pasteurized eggs, separated
- 2 cups sugar
- 2 Tbsp. brandy or rum
- 1 Tbsp. vanilla extract
- 2 tsp. pumpkin pie spice
- ½ tsp. bitters (preferably Angostura)
- ½ tsp. cream of tartar, optional

EACH SERVING

- ¾ cup boiling water or hot 2% milk
- 1 oz. brandy
- 1 oz. rum
  Freshly grated nutmeg, optional

1. In a large bowl, beat the egg yolks until thin and loose, about 1 minute. Gradually beat in the sugar, brandy, vanilla, pumpkin pie spice and bitters; beat until thick and frothy, 3-5 minutes.
2. In another large bowl, using clean beaters, beat the egg whites and, if desired, cream of tartar on high speed just until stiff but not dry. Fold a fourth of the egg whites into the yolk mixture until no white streaks remain. Fold in remaining egg whites until combined. Refrigerate, covered, until serving.
3. For each serving, place ¾ cup mixture into a large mug. Add boiling water, brandy and rum; stir until blended. If desired, top with freshly grated nutmeg.

1 Tom & Jerry: 340 cal., 3g fat (1g sat. fat), 112mg chol., 44mg sod., 41g carb. (41g sugars, 0 fiber), 4g pro.

CHEESE CRISPIES

For years I've taken these crispy, crunchy snacks to work. They get high marks from everybody in the teachers lounge.
—Eileen Ball, Cornelius, NC

PREP: 20 MIN. + CHILLING
BAKE: 15 MIN./BATCH
MAKES: 4 DOZEN

- 1 cup unsalted butter, softened
- 2½ cups shredded extra-sharp cheddar cheese
- 2 cups all-purpose flour
- ¾ tsp. salt
- ½ tsp. cayenne pepper
- 2½ cups Rice Krispies
  Pecan halves, optional

1. In a medium bowl, beat the butter and cheese until blended. In another bowl, whisk flour, salt and cayenne; gradually beat into cheese mixture. Stir in the Rice Krispies. If necessary, turn onto a lightly floured surface and knead 4-6 times, forming a stiff dough.
2. Divide dough in half; shape each half into a 7-in.-long log. Wrap logs and refrigerate 1 hour or overnight.
3. Preheat oven to 350°. Unwrap logs; cut dough crosswise into ¼-in. slices. Place 1 in. apart on parchment-lined baking sheets. If desired, top each slice with a pecan half. Bake until edges are golden brown, 14-16 minutes. Remove from pans to wire racks to cool.

To make ahead: Dough can be made 2 days in advance.

Freeze option: Freeze wrapped logs in an airtight container. To use, unwrap frozen logs and cut into slices. Bake as directed.

1 cracker: 87 cal., 6g fat (4g sat. fat), 17mg chol., 92mg sod., 6g carb. (0 sugars, 0 fiber), 2g pro.

Santa's Treat Box

TOOTSIE ROLL
FUDGE, 204

MARBLED ALMOND
ROCA, 204

ROLY-POLY
SANTAS, 203

HOW TO BUILD...
SANTA'S TREAT BOX

Take your cookie exchange to a new level! Grab a decorative box or a small tray with raised edges and fill it with an assortment of cookies and candies sure to appease the man in red.

ITEMS TO INCLUDE
- Peppermint candies
- Tootsie Roll Fudge
- Marbled Almond Roca
- Roly-Poly Santas

EASY ASSEMBLY

Step 1: Set 2 groupings of peppermint candies in opposite corners of the box or tray.

Step 2: Fill gaps with alternating groupings of Tootsie Roll Fudge and Marbled Almond Roca.

Step 3: Place Roly-Poly Santas over the peppermint candies.

Platter Pointer: Use cupcake liners, jumbo muffin liners, parchment paper or coffee filters to separate items within your treat box.

ROLY-POLY SANTAS

Tuck these fanciful Santa cookies onto every gift cookie tray you make. They're guaranteed to be a hit.
—Andrew Syer, Oak Ridge, MO

PREP: 1 HOUR • **BAKE:** 15 MIN. + COOLING
MAKES: 1 DOZEN

- 1 cup butter, softened
- ½ cup sugar
- 1 Tbsp. 2% milk
- 1 tsp. vanilla extract
- 2¼ cups all-purpose flour
  Red paste food coloring

ICING
- ½ cup shortening
- ½ tsp. vanilla extract
- 2⅓ cups confectioners' sugar, divided
- 3 Tbsp. 2% milk, divided

ASSEMBLY
  Sanding sugar, sugar pearls and Red Hots

1. Preheat oven to 325°. In a large bowl, cream butter and sugar until light and fluffy, 5-7 minutes. Add milk and vanilla; mix well. Add flour and mix well. Remove 1⅔ cups dough and tint it red. Shape the white dough into balls, making twelve ¾-in. balls, forty-eight ½-in. balls and twelve ¼-in. balls. Shape red dough into balls, making twelve 1¼-in. balls and sixty ½-in. balls.

2. Divide the 1¼-in. red balls between 2 ungreased baking sheets, spacing the balls evenly; these will be the Santa bodies. Attach ¾-in. white balls for heads. Attach ½-in. red balls for arms and legs. Attach ½-in. white balls to the ends of the arms and legs for hands and feet. Lightly press together.

3. Shape the remaining ½-in. red balls into hats; attach to heads. Attach ¼-in. white balls to tips of hats.

4. Bake 12-15 minutes or until cookies are set. Cool for 10 minutes; carefully remove from the pans to wire racks (cookies will be fragile).

5. For icing, combine the shortening and vanilla in a small bowl; mix well. Gradually add 1⅓ cups confectioners' sugar; add 1 Tbsp. milk. Gradually add remaining sugar and milk.

6. Pipe thin bands of icing on hats, on cuffs at hands and feet, and down the front and along the bottom of jackets. While icing is still wet, sprinkle sanding sugar over icing on hat brims and cuffs at hands and feet. Pipe swirls of icing for beards and on tips of hats. Place a Red Hot or red sugar pearl for each nose, black sugar pearls for eyes, and silver sugar pearls for buttons.

1 cookie: 422 cal., 24g fat (12g sat. fat), 41mg chol., 124mg sod., 50g carb. (32g sugars, 1g fiber), 3g pro.

MARBLED ALMOND ROCA

My easy recipe is an old favorite that we keep in steady use from mid-November until the new year. Homemade gifts are still a Christmas tradition at our house.
—Niki-Jeanne Rooke, Pollockville, AB

PREP: 25 MIN. + COOLING • **BAKE:** 15 MIN.
MAKES: 1½ LBS.

- ½ cup slivered almonds
- 1 cup butter, cubed
- 1 cup sugar
- 3 Tbsp. boiling water
- 2 Tbsp. light corn syrup
- ½ cup semisweet chocolate chips
- ½ cup white baking chips

1. Sprinkle almonds on a greased 15x10x1-in. baking pan. Bake at 300° for 15 minutes or until toasted and golden brown; remove from the oven and set aside.
2. In a saucepan over low heat, cook butter and sugar for 5 minutes. Add boiling water and corn syrup. Bring to a boil over medium heat; cook, stirring occasionally, until a candy thermometer reads 300° (hard-crack stage). Quickly pour over almonds. Sprinkle chips on top; let stand for 1-2 minutes or until melted. Spread and swirl chocolate over candy. Cool completely; break into pieces.

2 oz.: 306 cal., 22g fat (12g sat. fat), 42mg chol., 166mg sod., 29g carb. (22g sugars, 1g fiber), 2g pro.

TOOTSIE ROLL FUDGE

When my husband came home with 50 pounds of Tootsie Rolls he had bought at a discount store, I had to figure out a way to use them—so I came up with this recipe. A red or green M&M's candy atop each piece makes this fudge extra jolly.
—Carolyn McDill, Ohatchee, AL

PREP: 30 MIN. + COOLING
MAKES: ABOUT 2 LBS.

- 1 tsp. plus 2 Tbsp. butter, divided
- 2 cups Tootsie Roll Midgees
- 2 Tbsp. peanut butter
- 3¾ cups confectioners' sugar
- 2 Tbsp. 2% milk
- 1 tsp. vanilla extract
- 1 cup chopped pecans
- ⅓ cup green and red M&M's

1. Line a 9-in. square pan with foil. Grease the foil with 1 tsp. butter; set aside. In a heavy saucepan, melt the Tootsie Rolls, peanut butter and the remaining 2 Tbsp. butter over low heat, stirring constantly. Gradually stir in the confectioners' sugar, milk and vanilla (mixture will be very thick). Fold in the chopped pecans.
2. Spread mixture into prepared pan. Using a sharp knife, score the surface into 1-in. squares. Press an M&M's candy into the center of each square. Let cool. Using foil, remove fudge from pan; cut into squares. Store in an airtight container.

1 piece: 67 cal., 3g fat (2g sat. fat), 1mg chol., 11mg sod., 10g carb. (9g sugars, 0 fiber), 0 pro.

CUSTOMIZE YOUR BOARD

HOW TO ASSEMBLE THE PERFECT COOKIE PLATE

A holiday celebration wouldn't be complete without a beautiful display of cookies. These easy tips will have you arranging a cookie tray like a pro in no time!

1. Choose Your Serving Tray: The first step is choosing the container for the cookies you're serving. Box, tray or platter, the size is the first consideration. Too large, and the cookies will appear underwhelming. Too small, and you'll have an unwieldy mess. If you have space, use several trays—it's easier for guests to help themselves if they're not crowding around a single dish. Simple colors will make your cookies the star of the show.

2. Include a Variety of Cookies: Variety is key to creating a tempting cookie tray—but you don't need to make every cookie in your recipe collection, or it will be overwhelming. Stick with 5-7 varieties to keep things interesting. Include a few nostalgic, surefire classics as well as some distinctive and unusual new recipes.

3. Keep Textures and Flavors Together: To keep your cookies at their best, be sure to organize similar types together. Varieties that are strongly flavored, such as mint or molasses cookies, can transfer their flavors to milder sugar cookies. Soft cookies can transfer moisture to crisper cookies, affecting their texture. Consider adding some Christmas candies between different types of cookies to make a decorative (and tasty) border.

GOOEY CARAMEL-TOPPED GINGERSNAPS

Making these cookies is therapeutic for me. They are quite popular at fundraisers. You can create variations by changing the cookie base, varying the nuts or using different kind of sprinkles.
—Deirdre Cox, Kansas City, MO

PREP: 30 MIN. + CHILLING
MAKES: 3½ DOZEN

- 42 gingersnap cookies
- 1 pkg. (14 oz.) caramels
- 2 Tbsp. 2% milk or heavy whipping cream
- 1 cup chopped honey-roasted peanuts
- 12 oz. white or dark chocolate candy coating, melted
  Sprinkles or finely chopped honey-roasted peanuts

1. Arrange cookies in a single layer on waxed paper-lined baking sheets. In a microwave, melt caramels with milk; stir until smooth. Stir in the chopped peanuts. Spoon about 1 tsp. caramel mixture over each cookie; refrigerate until set.

2. Dip each cookie halfway into candy coating; allow excess to drip off. Return to baking sheet. Top with sprinkles or finely chopped peanuts. Refrigerate until set.

1 cookie: 128 cal., 5g fat (3g sat. fat), 1mg chol., 70mg sod., 19g carb. (14g sugars, 0 fiber), 2g pro.

Recipe Index